Inside the Wallabies

Other books by Greg Growden

The Wallabies World Cup (1991) with Spiro Zavos and Simon Poidevin
A Wayward Genius: The Fleetwood Smith story (1991)
With the Wallabies (1995)
Gold Mud and Guts: The incredible Tom Richards story (2001)
The Snowy Baker Story (2003)
Rugby Union for Dummies (2003)
My Sporting Hero (2004)
It's Not Just a Bloody Game: Timeless Rugby Union stories (2007)
Jack Fingleton: The man who stood up to Bradman (2008)

Inside the Wallabies

The real story
the players, the politics, the games from 1908 to today

Greg Growden

greg growden.

ALLEN&UNWIN

First published in Australia in 2010

Allen & Unwin
83 Alexander Street
Crows Nest NSW 2065
Australia
Phone: (61 2) 8425 0100
Fax: (61 2) 9906 2218
Email: info@allenandunwin.com
Web: www.allenandunwin.com

Cataloguing-in-Publication details are available
from the National Library of Australia
www.librariesaustralia.nla.gov.au

ISBN 978 1 74175 970 9

Set in 11/16 pt Palatino Light Pro by Bookhouse, Sydney
Printed and bound in Australia by Griffin Press

10 9 8 7 6 5 4 3 2 1

FSC © Mixed Sources
Product group from well-managed forests, and other controlled sources
www.fsc.org Cert no. SGS-COC-005088
© 1996 Forest Stewardship Council

The paper in this book is FSC certified. FSC promotes environmentally responsible, socially beneficial and economically viable management of the world's forests.

CONTENTS

Courtesy Steve Christo

INTRODUCTION

'Stick around . . . Something's brewing,' said Mark Ella, the first time I met him. I had just informed him that I was covering my first Test match, and that didn't put him at ease. Nonetheless, he looked after me. He saved me. I did stick around.

I'd just babbled a 600-word match report for the *Sun-Herald* on the Australia–Scotland Second Test down the phone to a similarly confused copytaker. There was no time to congratulate myself on getting the score, and hopefully all the names, right before I had to sprint to the Wallaby dressing room to get quotes, reaction and news from the players, coaches and officials. For a novice who knew nothing and no one, I just hoped someone would give me a helping hand.

Even though his team had just won by 24 points on that July afternoon in 1982, a massive margin for a national side more attuned to defeat, the Australian coach Bob Dwyer looked somewhat frazzled. Players huddled in groups made sure they were not overheard, especially by someone like me who they had never seen before. It was clear something was going on.

Then in walked Mark Ella. Following a wave of anger from Queensland after the Wallabies' first Test loss to Scotland in Brisbane when the Ella twins had been selected ahead of Brisbane's finest—Paul

McLean and Roger Gould—the No. 10 had been dropped for this Sydney Test. He weaved his way through the dressing room to congratulate McLean.

Hovering at the back of the rooms, hoping that someone, indeed anyone, would talk to me, I introduced myself. Ella was courteous and generous about McLean before uttering his warning that something bigger was going on. It soon became clear just what that was when nine of the victorious Wallabies announced they had made themselves unavailable for the upcoming tour of New Zealand. Was it a rebellion? Were they out to get Dwyer? Were they out to get the Australian Rugby Union? And what had I walked into? It was certainly an odd, even intimidating initiation to the world of the Wallabies.

Three decades on, six World Cup campaigns, a never-ending merry-go-round of tours and Test matches, I continue to witness the unexpected whenever I cross into Wallaby-land. And despite having hovered around the Wallabies for almost thirty years like a dizzy moth observing the rampant egos, the tension, the heroism, the politics and the stupidity of this beast that often bites, I continue to be impressed by the many good people the Wallabies attract, like Mark Ella, and the teams' ability to so often excel at the most unexpected times.

The Wallabies have been the great over-achievers of Australian sport, overcoming a lack of funds, a shortage of players, sometimes dreadful political infighting and often overwhelming competition from national teams with far greater resources, to remain either No. 1 or close to the best in the world. And so much of that success has come from the intense pride that comes with being a Wallaby.

The Wallaby jersey itself is a powerful talisman. Some have been buried in it, others have hidden theirs away under the bed, at the back of cupboards, even in bank vaults, protecting the unwashed, crumpled and often moth eaten garment as if it were a rare jewel.

It has been sky blue, maroon, emerald green, dark green, gold, even white with green hoops. It has also boasted blue and maroon horizontal stripes. Just before the Second World War the forwards used its heavily embossed coat of arms to rub into the faces of opponents at the bottom of rucks and mauls when they discovered it had the same effect on the male complexion as coarse sandpaper. It has also been an embarrassing abomination, especially during the mid 1990s when it resembled a cheap pair of pyjamas. It is something many thousands of Australians treat as an important national symbol, proudly wearing it to games and when travelling overseas. But as a symbol of pride and respect it has sometimes blinded us to what was really happening behind team doors.

From the outside, the Wallabies have often appeared a powerful, well-tuned machine. Those who have been allowed a closer look, however, have sometimes been left wondering how they actually ever managed to get onto the field with haphazard and amateur preparation and organisation, or how they could have lost despite everything going their way.

For all of this unpredictablity, for all the success and all the failures, the history of the Wallabies is so vibrant that it is hard not to be inspired. From their rough, tough beginning to becoming an integral part of the Australian identity, theirs is a story of innocence, hardship, courage, commitment and great humour.

I have been lucky enough to have travelled with the Wallabies since 1982, and to have been witness to many of their triumphs and disasters all over the world. I have been as intrigued by the past as much as the present, relishing the team's history and its great unpredictable and often hilarious characters. It is the rich textures and colours of this team that I hope to share with you.

This is not a book that relies on dry Test scorelines, or who scored which try in what minute. It is about trying to explain how and why the Wallabies have achieved so much. It is about their tight brotherhood which sees David Brockhoff—more than fifty years after he played for Australia and almost forty years after coaching it—head to Sydney Airport every time the Australian team departs for foreign shores to wish them well. He's also there when they return to make certain there is at least one friendly face to greet them. He unselfishly does that for past and present Wallabies.

The over-rated British and Irish Lions winger Austin Healey once said of Australia: 'The female and children are fine and seem to be perfectly normal human beings, but what are we going to do with this thing called the Australian male?' The Wallabies ranks from 1908 to the present day have boasted every variation of that thing called the Australian male—mostly the good, the honest and the inspiring. These teams of buoyant characters have guaranteed that those like me who have been lucky enough to follow, observe and chronicle them are never bored. Maybe it's because there is always 'something brewing'.

1

ONCE WERE RABBITS

Herbert 'Paddy' Moran was mesmerised by Italian dictator Benito Mussolini. He was fascinated with medicine and the written word, but late in life admitted that he could not find peace. He was also the first captain of a strange, disparate bunch who called themselves the Wallabies.

Moran set the tone for what was to come. From day one, the Wallabies became a haven for odd bods, the free spirited, the hungry and not so hungry, and those who pursued sport for its simple ideals. Moran described his players as: 'A curious people, these Australians, with their rude virtues and glaring faults. Cocksure yet shy, hyper-critical yet childlike in their belief in what a newspaper says. Humorous, but quick to resent anything unfair, hating the shirker terribly. Their one test is virility.'

One hundred years on nothing much has changed. The Wallabies of the twenty-first century are like the twentieth century brand—the team continues to attract and encourage the eccentric, the outlandish, the cocksure, the shy, the childlike and most certainly the virile. The brand is green and gold, but their real colours are many. Who else but those on the fringes would be attracted to a somewhat silly game whose origins lie in the dubious story of an English schoolboy called William Webb Ellis picking up the ball and running with it to create a new football code.

The 1988 Wallabies trained on the same paddock where Webb Ellis was supposed to have created havoc in the middle of a football match. A plaque at the ground read: 'This stone commemorates the exploit of William Webb Ellis who, with a fine disregard for the rules of football as played in his time, first took the ball in his arms and ran with it, thus originating the distinctive feature of the Rugby game. A.D. 1823.'

Unlike the Webb Ellis fairytale, the origins of the Wallabies are far better defined. The facts are there, even if some of them are decidedly odd.

•

The Wallabies were born in 1908 when the Australian rugby team, which had been participating in Test football for almost a decade, decided to embark on its first extensive tour of Great Britain. A name of note was required for the inaugural northern hemisphere adventure. Vigorous, emotional debate followed, not surprising given the name had to satisfy a most diverse group of sportsmen. There was a pastoralist from Wellington, a Sydney clerk, a Newcastle surgeon, a university layabout, a Queensland station owner, a humble miner, a train driver, a Condobolin bank clerk, a 'gentleman of leisure', a rough-as-guts waterfront warehousemen, a Glebe butcher, a public servant, a clay potter, an insurance broker, a grazier, a cattle salesman and an inner city plumber who tried to con the Fleet Street press into believing he was the owner of 'a large station in Woolloomooloo'. They boasted such nicknames as 'Big Dog', 'Giraffe', 'Emu', 'Banger', 'Bull', 'Daisy McIntyre', 'Bowser', 'Monkey', 'Boneta', 'Parky' and 'Possum'.

Giving the captaincy to Paddy Moran was an odd choice. He described himself as a 'miserable, stooped, boring, introspective sort of fellow'. Of Irish Roman Catholic background, he wasn't a standout player—until then, he had not even been considered for Australian Test selection. He didn't seem suited to this game for ruffians, appearing too pale, too sickly. As one British pressman later wrote: 'Surely that delicate-looking man does not play Rugby football?'

But clearly those selecting the side wanted someone with intellect and good sense to keep the ratbags in the touring party in line and to provide the right message in the Mother Country. An upright, correct, standoffish leader was required. Here was the moment when Australia could show that the colonials were civilised, and who better to do that than a bespectacled figure who looked like he was a Cambridge don.

Moran's more assertive teammates wanted to find a distinctive team name that would give them an identity during a mind-bogglingly long itinerary that would see them crisscross Great Britain and play a never-ending schedule of thirty-one matches, including internationals against England and Wales. Eight days before the team left, during a farewell dinner at the Sydney Town Hall, the subject of what they should actually call themselves was first broached. The name 'Rabbits' was suggested, and was apparently popular, but the more cautious among the team recommended they not make a rash decision and instead put it to the vote on arrival in England.

The suggestion of 'Rabbits' nevertheless prompted spirited conversation by the rural members of the team who were already overwhelmed by the pomp and ceremony of the function. In one meandering speech, the Honourable C.W. Oakes MLA babbled on about his old friend the Australian captain, but couldn't remember the skipper's name. Turning to his offsider, he mumbled into the microphone: 'Now, what's his name again?', the words echoing around the Town Hall.

'What's his name' later attempted to blame the English press for trying to force the dreaded 'Rabbits' tag on the team. 'When we arrived at Plymouth a pack of journalists fell upon us,' Moran wrote in his autobiography *Viewless Winds*. 'They were very anxious to give us some distinctive name, but their first suggestion of "Rabbits" we indignantly rejected. It really was going a little too far to palm off on us the name of a pest their ancestors had foisted on our country!

Ultimately we became the "Wallabies", although we wore for emblem on our jerseys not the figure of this marsupial but the floral design of a waratah.'

Moran's telling is not exactly correct. The Rabbits remained the name of choice for some players, with the *Manchester Weekly Times* even going so far as reporting that the Australians had been officially christened the 'Rabbits' at the Sydney Town Hall dinner. Postcards of the Australian team were even issued in England showing the name 'The Rabbits'. On the day of the team's arrival in England F.B. Wilson wrote in the *Daily Mirror* that the Australians 'have been already called the Rabbits, but that won't do. They do not like it, and naturally so, for a rabbit in Australia is not only vermin, it's a curse and no death is too bad for it.'

As agreed before they left Sydney, shortly after the team arrived in England, Moran organised a vote among the players. Suggestions included the Kangaroos, the Kookaburras, the Waratahs, the Wallaroos, even the Convicts. The Wallabies won by a couple of votes. Officials in Australia agreed to the name with the proviso that it would only be used when Australian teams were touring other countries. At home when playing Tests the team would continue to be called Australia. That edict stood until the 1980s. It was lucky the team wasn't called the Snakes, in honour of its first team mascot.

These days the Wallabies carry around a stuffed toy kangaroo, Wally. As team mascot, Wally must be placed on the halfway line facing the way the team is running. Tradition has it that the youngest player in the team has the job of looking after the mascot, which includes never leaving it alone. It is an onerous task, especially as a prime objective of the more easily bored members of the team is to pinch Wally. Some novice players have used this to their advantage, including eighteen-year-old James O'Connor who said just before the 2008 Wallaby northern hemisphere tour that Wally would help him 'pick up' women in France because they apparently are attracted to men carrying stuffed toys.

The 1908 tourists took the significance of the mascot to an extreme when the team's comedian Bob Craig snuck a carpet snake called Bertie into his luggage, believing Bertie's appearance at grounds would strike fear into the English opposition. After forty-two days at sea, the team's first problem was how to sneak Bertie into England without being sighted by English officials. The big, swarthy Queensland forward Tom Richards agreed to sling Bertie inside his singlet and tie him loosely around his stomach. He would stick the snake's head inside a sock, and its tail down the front of his pants. A large overcoat would hide any bulge. Even though Richards grew exceedingly uncomfortable when Bertie started to wriggle during the official speeches, the plan worked. Richards later found a wooden box and hid the snake in a bunch of waratahs that had earlier been sent by the New South Wales Rugby Union.

Sadly Bertie did not last long. He died before the first match. Several British newspapers ran photographs of a limp Bertie. Craig blamed the local fare for Bertie's death, explaining that England was 'an exceedingly poor country, considering that my esteemed snake Bertie died after taking the risk of eating an English mouse for his first meal here. He had survived such ordeals as bushfires, droughts and starvation. To a great extent no doubt, if it had been his good fortune to survive until the advent of the Llannelly versus Australian match, it would have benefited him greatly, as the wild and cannibalistic conditions that prevail there would no doubt have revived him.'

It was because of such boisterous and larrikin behaviour that rugby made its mark in Australia, becoming the country's main winter sport and convincing those in authority that it deserved national representative prominence.

•

Rugby in a proper form had been played in Australia—although primarily New South Wales—for well over fifty years before the Wallabies showed off the national colours overseas. The game, brought across from England by those who had taken the long trip to the new colony, was immediately recognised as a brutal affair. Its primary aim, as described in *Tom Brown's Schooldays,* was to 'try the muscle of the men's bodies, and the endurance of their hearts, to make them rejoice in their strength'. It also involved trying to knock each other's head off.

Even if rugby was the domain of the aristocratic amateur, with a history steeped in the English public school system, in the rough and tumble outpost of Sydney it appealed to the wild men of the colony. The laws of the game encouraged a mixture of flair and fight, artistry and aggression.

Not even calls in the New South Wales Parliament in the 1860s to have the game outlawed could quell the beast. It only inflamed passions. But there was deep concern that if Australia became serious about rugby, it would court disaster if it ever played New Zealand at it. New Zealand had embraced rugby as its lifeblood, prompting the *Sydney Morning Herald* to editorialise in 1884: 'Rugby isn't our game . . . we'll always court defeat if we play the New Zealanders.' To soften the pain of that possibility, there was even a push for the rugby colonies of New Zealand, New South Wales, Queensland and Victoria to amalgamate as a single union. The success of the 1905 All Blacks ended that, and instead Australia had to go it alone.

Rugby kept its footing in the colony, even if sometimes slipping and sliding, and a club competition was formed. Australia made its first appearance on the international stage in 1899 when it played a touring British side over a four Test series (winning the first game, and losing the next three).

Sydney rugby was not a place for shirkers. When Australia's first Test captain Frank 'Banger' Row, who led the team onto the field against the British Isles at the Sydney Cricket Ground, took his father to watch his first rugby match, he was surprised when he left at half-time. When Banger returned home he asked his father why. Banger Senior replied: 'Never seen such a lot of ruffians.'

Wild play and unruly spectators were so common at the grade games that the New South Wales Inspector General of Police agreed to provide plainclothes constables at most grounds. One player was attacked by a spectator swinging a two-metre paling. On the field it was not unusual for players to be knocked out cold in back play, often with a gutless king hit. At one game, a referee who had been heckled by players and spectators produced a pistol out of the pocket of his shorts, waved it above his head and threatened to use it if he suffered any more abuse. Forwards would fill their pockets with pepper and fling it in the eyes of their opponents as soon as a scrum was set.

It was just as fierce on the other side of the field markings. Club officials kept the rabble on the sideline off the field by hitting them with small pieces of sapling that doubled as canes. Not surprisingly, *The Bulletin* described rugby at that time as 'the undertaker's friend'.

Judiciary hearings were also dangerous affairs. Police escorts were often required to get the rugby counsellors safely through the angry crowds waiting for hours outside the meeting room to hear a verdict.

For introspective coves like Paddy Moran, the experience was horrible. He described the grade competition as a 'form of local warfare'. 'When you sank on the ball to stop a dribbling rush, half-a-dozen feet rattled on you like heavy knocks at a door which would not open. Sometimes in a distant suburb when you fell out of bounds the local partisans affectionately trod on you. Both sides, indeed, were accorded the status of belligerents.'

Moran recalled how front-row forwards would grow beards before games and 'thus armed at all points would rub their faces against the newly shaven cheeks of their opposite numbers . . . Sometimes they added onions to their luncheon diet, so what with the sour smell of unwashed jerseys, that had been lying all the week in a locker, and the heavy odour of men's sweaty bodies, the atmosphere of the scrums was pungent.'

Among the rogues was one of Australia's original forwards, Jim O'Donnell. Some years before playing for Australia in 1899 he had travelled with a touring New Zealand team but opted against returning home with them, instead hiding away in Sydney—for good reason, as just before leaving New Zealand he had been arrested in Invercargill as a con man. O'Donnell fled before the case went to court.

Others were handed Test jerseys for just being in the right place at the right time. Queenslander Jack Fihelly found himself in the 1907 Test against New Zealand in Brisbane primarily to avoid the expense of bringing too many better credentialled New South Wales players up from Sydney. Earlier that year, Fihelly ran on as a replacement during a New Zealand–Queensland match after a Queensland forward broke his ankle in the opening minutes. There wasn't enough time to properly kit him out, so he took to the field in his civvies—grey trousers and white business shirt. At the first break of play his teammates formed a ring to enable Fihelly to get his jersey, shorts and boots on.

One of the most notorious players of that time was Blair Swannell. This English-born forward, who had toured Australia twice with British Isles teams before settling in Sydney at the turn of the century, had the unenviable reputation of being the ugliest man to ever play the game. His face was like a battered prune. Swannell's personal hygiene was also an area of serious concern. His prized possession was a once-white pair of football breeches that he wore in every match and refused to wash. An incessant bore who boasted about his military conquests, including fighting among the insurrectionists in the Republic of Uruguay, Swannell would arrive on game day wearing a filthy cream sweater bearing on it the badges and dates of all the countries he had represented.

And on the field, he was an absolute mongrel.

Moran, like many others, clearly had no time for Swannell, describing him as a 'bad influence in Sydney football and also incidentally a greatly over-estimated player. His conception of Rugby was one of trained violence. In appearance, he was extremely ugly, but he could talk his face away in half an hour. He was popular with the fair sex; men, generally, disliked him.' This did not stop him being selected as one of Australia's early representative players.

Swannell was renowned for kicking defenceless players, and belting those looking the other way. During one New South Wales–Queensland match, he was sent off for an action he did not commit. His team knew that the referee had dismissed the wrong man, but no one came forward on Swannell's behalf at the inquiry. He was suspended for a month. Similarly in an Australia–New Zealand match, no one came to his defence when he was kicked in the face by an All Black and it was thought that several of the Australian players later congratulated their opponents for putting in the slipper.

By the time of the first Wallaby tour, Swannell's playing days were over. He was now putting the boot in elsewhere, castigating his one-time colleagues in print. As the first Wallabies took off for Tilbury in 1908, Swannell confidently expected them to be embarrassed. He thought the Australian backs lacked 'devil, initiative, or whatever you like to call it'. The Australian forwards 'cannot wheel and seemingly won't learn'. They wouldn't do as well as the All Blacks or Springboks because of their 'lack of knowledge' and 'lack of use of many of the finer points of the game'.

Swannell did not endear himself to the first Wallabies, prompting some of them to say some years later when he was killed at Gallipoli on 25 April 1915 that because of his domineering English manner he was probably shot by one of his own soldiers. The real story was that as a 1st Battalion Major Swannell led a charge towards the Turks, forcing them to retreat higher up in the cliffs and into a safer trench. His company found itself being shot at from the front and the right flank. While kneeling to show his troops how to take proper aim at the Turks, Swannell was fatally shot in the forehead.

•

In 1908, years before Swannell's heroic death, the antics of the Australians alerted the Home Unions that the Wallabies could easily be a mob of uncivilised thugs. The British press, aware of what had happened in Australia's first decade of Test football, in particular the nasty matches during the 1904 British Isles tour of the colony, thought the Wallabies were cheats. They were also accused of being a bunch of drunks, having been sighted at a race meeting imbibing before one match. Their amateur status was also questioned after they had been presented with a purse of sovereigns by fans before leaving Australia.

And when several games turned violent, the Wallabies became the ultimate enemy. The British press dubbed the 'ill-educated' Wallabies 'the foulest set of players imaginable'. The *Morning Post* even declared that they were 'disturbing Imperial relations'.

It didn't help that during one of the early matches of the tour, against the miners from the Welsh town of Neath, one of the locals was knocked unconscious in the opening minutes. The Australian players claimed that they had been bitten. Despite both teams being guilty of reckless kicking and stray punches, the Wallabies had to return to their hotel that night under police guard.

Then at Llannelly, another grim Welsh town, the game degenerated into a head kicking affair after the local referee lost all control. As Wallaby star forward Tom Richards wrote: 'I never imagined that men could stand up and kick so viciously at each other. I saw one of our men give a Welshman an unmerciful kick. The referee blew his whistle and asked him why he had kicked the man, to which he replied: "He kicked one of our fellows just now."'

But all this was tame compared to when the fearless back-row forward Syd Middleton became the first Australian representative player to be sent from the field, in a game against Oxford. Middleton was the ultimate sportsman. Apart from his rugby skills, he was a quality rower, swimmer and boxer, but according to his skipper was 'irritable and hot-headed'. He was not one to be provoked, as his Oxford opponent G.D. Roberts discovered when he called Middleton 'a convict'. Middleton let fly with a right uppercut, hitting Roberts flush on the nose. He crashed to the turf and Middleton was pointed to the pavilion by A.O. Jones, one-time England Test cricketer.

The London press went ballistic. The *Daily Chronicle* said the incident was typical of the 'unfair and unsportsmanlike methods of the Colonials'. Others described it as 'disgraceful'. Middleton was suspended for five matches and, according to Moran, he paid dearly for that 'indiscretion'. 'It pursued him for thirty years. It followed him to the war and still pops up,' Moran wrote in 1939.

The Wallabies' angst continued shortly after when hooker Tom Griffin was sent off against Swansea for slapping his opponent with an open hand.

The Wallabies were sympathetic towards Middleton and Griffin but were wary about another teammate, Albert 'Son' Burge, a flighty forward who had joined the tour as a replacement after his brother Peter had been sidelined with a broken leg. They even tried to stop him being brought into the squad because they believed he was a reckless and often dirty player, which proved to be the case when he disgracefully kicked the Welsh captain Bill Trew in the head during the Cardiff international.

This disdain turned into a chorus of 'told you so's' when Burge became the third Australian player on tour to be sent off after he kicked opposing forward J.P. Westacott when he was on the ground and well away from the ball. Burge was booed all the way off the ground and did not receive a consoling word from his teammates as he headed to the pavilion.

The Welsh press seized on the incident. One scribe with the pen name 'Old Stager' went for the jugular: 'This is the third man among the Australians to have disgraced the Commonwealth by failing to control his temper in the heat of the play.' He argued that Burge's kick 'might easily not only have maimed, but have killed the man'. Westacott could have been 'crippled for life'.

•

The Wallabies have been involved in some bizarre fixtures, but none more so than when at the 1908 London Olympic Games they became the first and only Australian team to win Olympic Gold.

France, England and Germany were the only countries to compete when rugby was introduced to the Olympics in Paris in 1900. Rugby didn't make an appearance at the 1904 games in St Louis, and the 1908 event was also close to being cancelled. Eventually two teams—Cornwall, chosen by the English Rugby Union to represent the United Kingdom, and the Wallabies—agreed to participate.

The Olympic Gold Medal pursuit involved just one match, the final, played at Shepherd's Bush. On one side of the ground was a 100-yard long cement swimming bath with a long line of netting to catch flying balls and stray players. Large mattresses were spread along the rim of the bath to protect players who accidentally fell into the pool. Men with long poles and small nets were there to fish for the ball when it went over the top of the netting, into touch or into the swimming pool.

In the words of one English newspaper the game itself was virtually a farce. Australia scored seven tries to win 32–3 over a second-rate opposition. This victory did not greatly excite the Australians. Several players, including the match-winning forward Tom Richards, did not even bother to attend the Olympic medal and certificate presentation.

Moran did not play in the final because of a dislocated shoulder, but he did douse down yet another controversy. During the second half, a Cornwall official complained that the Wallabies were using running spikes. A seething Moran insisted on an examination of the boots of all the players as they came off the field at full time, nominating an English doctor to carry out the task. The doctor confirmed that the Wallabies were not wearing illegal footwear, but that the boots of the Cornish players were even more suspect.

One hundred years on the 2008 Wallabies decided to mark the Olympic triumph with a Wembley mid-week match, and it was a similarly ridiculous affair. Unlike a traditional exhibition match against a Barbarians side, this one turned into a cantankerous game with each team wanting to kill the other. To make matters worse, two Wallaby props—Matt Dunning and Sekope Kepu—suffered serious injuries because the Wembley surface was not up to standard. At least the boots could not be blamed this time.

Even if the 1908 Wallabies finished with the enviable record of twenty-five wins from their thirty-one matches, including defeating England in London, there remained great animosity towards their northern hemisphere hosts. They were particularly unimpressed that they had to do a ridiculous pre-match war dance. Moran refused to 'lead the wretched caricature of a native corroboree'. He was disgusted the team had been 'asked to remind British people of the miserable remnants of a race which they had dispossessed and we had maltreated or neglected . . . We were officially expected to leap up in the air and make foolish gestures which somebody thought Australian natives might have used in similar circumstances, and we were also given meaningless words which we were to utter savagely during this pantomime. None of the men liked it.'

The Wallabies were also infuriated that the British treated them as second-class citizens, and that they were targeted by the English press. This prompted one player, Ward Prentice, to go public and complain that 'practically all the newspapers were dead set against the Wallabies . . . we got no praise'.

'Under the carping criticism, and beneath the magnification of minor incidents, their [the Wallabies'] British patriotism wilted,' Moran wrote. 'Most of them developed a dislike for everything English . . . The significance of it all can be seen from what happened six years later. When the war broke out those thirty-one men were still in the flower of their physical vigour, yet only seven took part in the war. There is surely food for reflection in all this.'

Those few Wallabies who did serve in the First World War did make their mark, however. Tom Richards was awarded a Military Cross on the Western Front for outstanding courage under German fire; William 'Twit' Tasker was killed near the end of the war; and Syd Middleton, the man sent off at Oxford, won a DSO. Harold George was among the many to die at Gallipoli. But for most of those who returned home seven and a half months after originally farewelling Sydney, the tour only heightened their own national pride and made them sceptical of everything British. 'We all felt a sentimental attachment to the land of our fathers, but none thought of himself as anything but Australians,' Moran wrote.

But back in Australia, the harsh environment proved too much for some. Richards was wracked with tuberculosis and died of complications from the gas he inhaled on the Western Front. Bob Craig, the tour comedian and snake owner, became a hotel keeper. Hit hard by the Depression, to avoid crippling debt he hung himself and was found, in the words of Moran, 'swinging like trinkets from a Christmas tree'. At around the same time Queensland's first Australian captain Bob McCowan, who had led the team in 1899, was sentenced to fourteen years for misappropriating £15,000 from a trust fund. He had backed Phar Lap to win the 1929 Melbourne Cup but it came in third and he lost thousands. Once a notable in the world of Brisbane law, he ended up cleaning hotel bars.

At the end of the Wallabies tour Moran left for Edinburgh to pursue his medical studies before returning to Sydney to set up practice in a tough suburb. He took over from a 'drunken Glasgow doctor' and catered for 'the diseases, injuries and deformities of chiefly a working-class population'.

At the outbreak of the Great War Moran headed back to London, where he was made a lieutenant in the RAMC, serving in Gallipoli until he contracted amoebic dysentery. Following the war he was celebrated as a physician, being the first doctor to use radium to treat cancer. After retiring from medical practice in 1935 he wrote two memorable biographies, *Viewless Winds* (1939) and *In My Fashion* (1946), a fictionalised biography *Beyond the Hills Lies China,* plus a pamphlet on the war in Abyssinia, *Letters from Rome*. Published in 1936, *Letters from Rome* detailed his fascination with Mussolini and his brief that while Australians did not appreciate his achievements and believed he was a 'somewhat melodramatic dictator', the Italian leader had instead transformed a 'broken and disillusioned' country and had 'rallied the people and provided them with the means of sustenance and the vitamins of self-respect'.

During his three years living in Rome in the 1930s Moran had four audiences with Mussolini, but eventually realised the dictator was a 'cunning showman' and a megalomaniac and that his 'career shows all the weakness of a man debased by power'. Moran became similarly 'disillusioned' with Rome and kept wandering around Europe trying to fight his own demons, which included disdain towards many in his own profession and deep conflicting concerns and confusions about Ireland and Australia.

As he was such a complex, sometimes tortured character it is not surprising that his written works were passionate and intense. They were also at times angry and venomous—in particular his comments on those occasions when he encountered homosexuality among the British troops during the Second World War. He wrote about the subject at length in both of his autobiographies, which for the times was particularly radical considering it was almost a taboo subject.

Moran first encountered homosexual behaviour while playing rugby in Sydney when one well-known Australian forward and later soldier—whose identity Moran refused to reveal in *Viewless Winds*—was sent to gaol after being 'arrested for soliciting boys in the street'. Homosexuality clearly disturbed him, and he was surprised in 1935 when he was involved in an enquiry during which two policemen gave evidence that their vice squad had over two years arrested 150 men for homosexual offences from one lavatory in Sydney's Hyde Park.

Moran died in Cambridge in 1945 from cancer—the disease he was for some time so immersed in finding a cure for. In his final weeks he fantasised about being a star cricketer, winning crucial international matches but refusing to recognise the spectators on the way back to the pavilion because he 'despised' the ignorant and know nothing crowd.

The Wallabies could not have had as their first captain a more fascinating, complicated, intense, self-critical and bewildering character. As one of Moran's sons, Patrick, observed: 'I did not understand him at all . . . yet I appreciated him.'

But Paddy Moran was not unique in the Wallaby ranks. Within a few years, Moran had countless non-conformist Wallaby colleagues. For so many of these wild, eccentric characters who have brought life and vibrancy to the Wallaby brand, Moran was their patron saint.

2

WILD MEN AND WEIRDOS

Over the decades Australian rugby has delighted in its image of being a privileged, essentially private school venture attracting the better elements in society. It was not for the riff raff, but for the pure bloods, the privileged—those not smeared by the greed of professionalism, who instead thrived in being amateur and playing for the sake of the game. A great deal of what those who controlled the game espoused was codswallop, and on many occasions their blinkered, outdated vision came close to derailing the game.

Rugby was hardly elitist. Instead, in Australia it inevitably became a game for everyone. Cricket had a strong Protestant base, prompting near paranoia among the Catholics that they were unfairly overlooked at both the representative and official levels, as evidenced by the New South Wales Cricket Association not employing a Roman Catholic until the 1970s. Rugby was not so sectarian. From its early days it attracted the working class, with the first Wallabies including its fair share from the impoverished parts of New South Wales and Queensland, and over the years state schools have produced more than twenty Australian captains. So much for rugby being a game just for the upper classes.

However, rugby was bound not to be the game of the Australian working man, especially as the game's leaders treated its players so shabbily. Inevitably the inability of those in the privileged classes, who held high ranks in rugby officialdom, to deal with the lower classes led to a dramatic division within the game. A split similar to that which occurred in England with the establishment of a breakaway rugby league competition was inevitable.

From the turn of the century representative players realised that while they got nothing, those running the game were filling their pockets. The players had to pay for the privilege to run onto the field, while the rugby administrators raked in the profits from major representative matches. The imbalance was glaring. As one New South Wales player remarked after a trip to Brisbane to play Queensland in 1903: 'There seemed to be as many officials as players on the trip. The [New South Wales] officials ate oysters and drank whiskey on the train, but the players didn't get any.' Then at their Brisbane hotel, while the officials clearly enjoyed an expensive lunch the players were put on an 'iron ration' diet because their manager thought they were getting too fat and complacent. He didn't want to provide them with any unnecessary luxuries even though many of the players were broke, having left their jobs to play for nothing. And if a player was seriously injured they faced a dreadful plight, as the Rugby Union was reticent to provide compensation if they were then unable to work.

Not surprisingly, the lure of being paid well to play rugby league was irresistible. Rugby's biggest name, Dally Messenger, was signed up in 1907 before the Wallaby tour, and after the first team's return from Great Britain the game was suddenly under threat of collapse when many of its leading names abandoned union for league. League officials offered enormous sums to entice fourteen of the Wallabies into playing a three-Test series against the Kangaroos. Secret meetings were held in inner Sydney hotels, and soon the Wallabies were queuing up to sign.

Chris McKivat, an introvert away from football but a loud mouth on the field where he was the most accomplished halfback and five-eighth, was the star signing. He was paid £200, or the equivalent of two years' ordinary salary. Other players received between £100 and £150. Aghast that so many of its finest had so easily been enticed the Rugby Union banned them for life, and there was huge concern about whether rugby would survive. Crowds immediately slumped. Sydney football fans were far more interested in the new league extravaganza, which had all the best players.

Yet amidst the gloom of 1910, and despite luring only half the crowds the national rugby league team was attracting, Australia was able to defeat New Zealand for the first time. An added delight was keeping those supposedly unbeatable All Blacks scoreless at the Sydney Cricket Ground.

This win provided the excuse for rugby officialdom to ignore the doomsayers and to believe, despite the endless sniping, that the two fighting football codes could actually co-exist. They were even encouraged to organise further Wallaby tours, including one to the United States in 1912. This trip set the tone for countless Australian team tours in future decades.

The 1912 side, which included a core of 1908 tourists, was determined to have a good time. Unlike the domineering Captain James McMahon, manager of the 1908 team, the manager of the 1912 team, Dr Otto Bohrsmann, was a gregarious figure, eager to ensure the team enjoyed itself. Bohrsmann, a controversial figure who loved making public statements and eagerly stressed his team's special qualities, was actually delighted that league had rid the game, and the Australian team, of its bad influences. '[T]he cleavage had acted on Rugby like a spring cleaning, and the game had emerged cleaner and better in every respect,' he said. 'Any man who had the slightest trait in his character towards playing the League game was absolutely worthless to the Rugby Union. Afterwards he would become worthless to himself. Professionals became wastrels on the sea of society forever.'

This jaundiced view was part of the rugby union mantra for many years. Thankfully in other areas Bohrsmann was more understanding, in particular allowing the Wallabies, who again wore the Waratah emblem on their jersey, to mix business with pleasure. As their five-eighth Bob Adamson later explained: 'We were never in bed. That was the trouble. I never had such a time in all my life.'

The Wallabies were often billeted on a university campus, and revelled in the wild student life. They became notorious for playing up. According to one report in the *San Francisco Examiner*: '"Late to bed and early to rise" was the motto of the Australian Rugby players yesterday. The naughty boys stayed up until after midnight with their hosts at the British residents' smoker on Thursday evening, and they jumped out from under the covers at the stroke of seven.' One newspaper cartoon showed a dazzling American beauty pulling the petals off a waratah bloom while gazing longingly at an Australian player who bore an uncanny resemblance to the team's forward leader, Tom Richards. She was saying: 'He loves me, he loves me not, he loves . . .' The caption read: 'All our girls are doin' it, doin' it, doin' it.' With so much social activity, it was hardly surprising that the Wallabies came close to being beaten by the United States in the one-off Test held in Berkeley.

This Wallabies squad was rich with great characters and men of resolve, in particular their fullback Larry Dwyer, who the following year, despite his humble background, captained his country. Nothing was easy for Dwyer. The son of poor Irish immigrants, for some years he was unable to afford football boots, instead wearing his school shoes to play. He lived in the New South Wales country town of Orange, 260 kilometres west of Sydney, and was forced to endure the most exasperating of travel arrangements to just play a representative game.

He left school at twelve to work as a clerk in a solicitor's office, and whenever he was selected for New South Wales or Australia he would have to take leave from his Orange employer, who permitted him to work late on Friday night, before catching the overnight train to Sydney. Upon arrival at Central Station, he would then trudge up the hill to the Sydney Cricket Ground, introduce himself to his teammates, play the Test or state game and then head straight back to the railway station for the return trip to Orange so he could be back in time to start work on Monday morning. But not even such stout characters as Dwyer could stop New Zealand from dominating every time they faced Australia. After the First World War it was an even easier task for the All Blacks because Australian rugby was once more in disarray.

•

Between 1919 and 1929 rugby virtually disappeared in Queensland. New South Wales alone held a flickering rugby flame and became Australia's representative side, which often meant its teams were the whipping boys for New Zealand and South African sides. There were the occasional triumphs, but these were interspersed with moments when Australia struggled to just remain competitive. And while rugby league continued to attract the big numbers, rugby Tests were moved from the Sydney Cricket Ground to the less prestigious Sydney Sports Ground next door. There were some diabolical tours during this period—including the 1923 trip to New Zealand when the New South Wales team was decimated in the three-Test series. One player was prompted to gloomily remark on return to Sydney: 'We would enter each town with a raucous blare of trumpets, and sneak out again in the dead of night.'

This grim decade thankfully ended in triumph. The Queensland Rugby Union's demise had ended any hope of a second Wallaby tour to Great Britain, so a New South Wales team was organised instead. When the 1927–28 Waratahs, comprising Australia's best players who were all now playing for Sydney clubs, embarked on their eight-month tour of Britain, Ireland, France and North America the blueprint for the exciting, at times outlandish Australian attacking game was established. The Waratahs succeeded in changing the country's playing style to an all-encompassing fifteen-man formula where attack was imperative, thus ending the long period when New Zealand and South Africa's safe, forward-based football was mimicked.

Some of the Waratahs struggled to take themselves seriously, with three players telling the British newspapers they were 'full-time surfboard riders'. But by the end of the tour these 1927–28 Waratahs, unlike the 1908 Wallabies, had won over their British critics. *The Daily Express* editorialised: 'They played the game in the same spirit for over six months, and when the tour was over left an indelible memory of 15-man rugby not seen before in the United Kingdom.'

One of the architects of the radically different Australian running game was captain and coach Johnnie Wallace, who had spent a number of years in the United Kingdom studying at Oxford as a Rhodes scholar. His Scottish heritage saw him represent that country in the Five Nations championship, where he was part of the most expressive of backlines that included Eric Liddell of *Chariots of Fire* fame. Scotland's success in being so attack oriented and in playing the full width of the field convinced Wallace that this style would work in Australia as long as he had forwards and backs who were all as eager to play with expression. Ball skills and an open mind were imperative.

He demanded the Wallabies selectors pick players committed to this philosophy. He wanted skilful, fast forwards who loved playing with the ball in hand, and backs prepared to perform with initiative and adventure. 'Give me a man with skill, pace and pluck rather than a bonehead,' he said. The selectors acknowledged Wallace's demand and chose an extravagant and creative bunch; most importantly they included a man who became one of the professors of the game, especially at his club domain of Randwick, Cyril Towers.

Together with fellow Waratah tourist Wally Meagher and Randwick identity Arthur Hennessey, Towers was instrumental in devising a successful flat backline alignment and direct running style. This philosophy, which first emerged in New Zealand during the 1920s and turned his club the Randwick Galloping Greens into the most dominant of club forces, was still being used more than fifty years later by Australian coach and devoted Towers disciple Bob Dwyer, who revived it as the Wallaby style.

Towers was a dogmatic character who did not suffer fools. Overlooked for the 1933 Wallaby tour to South Africa, the team manager Wally Matthews explained that Towers was too forthright and that this would disrupt team morale. There was a fear he would take over the team.

The single-minded Towers had his detractors. He was prone to haranguing people, dominating conversations and sometimes appearing to have little interest in what anyone else had to say. He had some extremely dim views of others, including one notable Australian coach whom he brushed off with: 'If he's got a bright idea on rugby it would die from solitary confinement.' However, Towers' rugby knowledge was unsurpassed, and for those with the patience to shut up and listen he was a mine of information. Using coins and salt shakers on a dining room table, in the 1970s Towers taught Dwyer how the doctrine of great backline play revolved around the attacking alignment not standing deep and each player always running straight.

Linking up with Wallace on the Waratahs tour confirmed Towers' attacking beliefs, and convinced him of the value of the timing of the pass. It became a hallmark of the Towers game. In one of the few times that Towers took orders, Wallace told him: 'Give me the ball when I call for it.' Wallace would scream 'Now' from the wing, and Towers would respond with his skipper invariably making the break, often to score. Towers never forgot that lesson.

Playing alongside maestros such as Wallace and Towers were other creative rugby minds such as Alec Ross, Tom Lawton and Syd King. The team lost only five of its thirty-one matches—defeating Ireland in Dublin, Wales in Cardiff and France in Paris but losing to Scotland and England—while averaging more than three tries per match.

While the tour ranks as one of the most important undertaken by any Australian sporting team because it provided the successful template for future generations there were still some testing moments, such as when the press was told that Allan 'Sheik' Bowers wanted to go home because of injury, that he was homesick and missing his wife whom he had married two weeks prior to leaving Sydney. The real reason for his sudden departure, however, was that he had been involved in a scuffle at the team hotel with vice-captain Charlie Fox. What actually occurred between Bowers and Fox remained a tight secret, but not for the last time in Wallabies history was there the whiff of a cover up.

Not that the captain was without problems. Wallace suffered at times from the demon drink, which according to several players affected him during later coaching stints. He even ended up in court several decades later, when a New South Wales selector, after assaulting Kenneth Archer from the *Truth* and *Sportsman* newspapers following a match at North Sydney Oval. An agitated Wallace had abused Archer saying that the journalist 'fucking well stinks'.

Archer told the court that Wallace 'had been drinking, for I could smell it. I said "if there is any stink, it comes from you".' Wallace punched Archer on the jaw, knocking him to the ground. He was subsequently fined £53.

But when on top of his game Wallace, like Towers, pushed the view that Australian rugby had to remain a fifteen-man game. And there were enough apostles out there to ensure that the Wallace–Towers–Meagher doctrine was never forgotten and became Rugby—the Australian Way, although there was a period when rugby fans could have been forgiven for thinking otherwise after the teams of the late 1930s, 40s and 50s became far too predictable in their obsession with their supposedly match-winning backlines. Their eagerness to push everything towards the wings made them easy targets for the All Blacks, who simply shoved them over the sideline.

Instead, Australia began to focus more on defence, playing field position, kicking every penalty possible and preying on opposition mistakes, a tactic that became the norm in the mid-1990s and led to World Cup success. At other times, due to lack of quality either up front or out wide, Australian coaches had to make dramatic adaptations—including in the mid 1960s when Des Connor introduced the short lineout as a way of giving Australia some chance of thwarting New Zealand's overwhelming dominance in that area. That almost worked. In the 2000s Australia became obsessed with structure and regimentation, relying on precise and endless phase play that revolved around forwards putting their heads down and barging away at the defensive line until holes eventually appeared.

Forward obsession became a necessity at times, as did the acts of outright violence (which verged close to terrorism during the outlandish David Brockhoff era) to bring some mongrel back to a national team when it had become too soft. But it was when the team pursued the running game developed by Towers and Wallace that Wallaby fans were most at ease, and it happened with enough regularity for the teams to retain a solid supporter base.

The crucial and unique element to the Australian game established in this early period was that most players had a touch of the mug lair. From the late 1920s to the start of the Second World War the team's eccentric characters, such as non-conformists 'Wild Bill' Cerutti and Aub Hodgson, the extrovert Myer Rosenblum and fearless combatant Weary Dunlop, provided colour and vibrancy. There were also celebrated madcap selections, none more so than that of John Young.

Rugby historian Jack Pollard, in his encyclopaedic tome *Australian Rugby Union: the game and the players,* reserved his best paragraph for Young. Pollard wrote: 'He [Young] proved a poor tackler, and abominable handler, who made breaks without the ball, but he was a very popular member of the team, who later became a close friend of other members of the 1933 touring team [to South Africa], when they played lawn bowls. He had a resounding voice, and in partnership with Jack Steggall, enlivened many a bowling club discussion.'

Dunlop, who became one of Australia's most honoured war heroes, was far more on the pace and typified the toughness of the Australian forward. He only played two Tests, but certainly made his mark in the 1934 series against the All Blacks. For this Test in

Sydney both teams were accommodated at the Wentworth Hotel, but the All Blacks were their usual surly selves, refusing to fraternise with the locals. Each morning Dunlop attempted to be cordial, but the New Zealanders shunned him. Finally one of their players, Beau Cottrell, pulled Dunlop aside and said the team had been told by the manager not to be seen in the company of the Australians. 'You'll find us very friendly after the match,' Cottrell said in the hope of soothing Dunlop. 'OK, Beau,' Dunlop snarled. 'You go and tell your manager that the fact I say good morning to you doesn't mean that I won't try to knock your bloody heads off on Saturday.'

As expected the Test was wild, with several All Blacks taking it as their duty to pulverise Dunlop. One All Black pinned Dunlop to the ground, while another elbowed him in the face. According to his biographer Sue Ebury, in the dressing rooms after the match Dunlop set 'his freshly re-broken nose by inserting a toothbrush up each nostril—after draining the usual two bottles of beer awaiting him on top of his locker—by way of an anaesthetic'.

Myer Rosenblum also led a full life. Having headed to New Zealand with the New South Wales team in 1928, he was so delighted with his first major appearance that he decided the night was the occasion for him to lose his virginity. 'We were staying at the Waterloo Hotel, down by the Wellington Railway Station,' Rosenblum told journalist Spiro Zavos. 'I had a room to myself. So I made a proposition to one of the waitresses. "You'll be number 13 in line", she told me. "I can't wait that long" I told her.'

Zavos described Rosenblum as 'something of a Renaissance man, a man for all seasons'. Rugby was just a small part of Rosenblum's life: he had also represented Australia at hammer throw, played the bassoon in the Sydney Conservatorium orchestra and was a master pianist, a champion hurdler and the most passionate of tennis players. Apart from being a Latin scholar, he also spoke German, Yiddish, French and Italian. The late broadcaster Brian White once remarked he had met only three true intellectuals in his lifetime: Francis James, Gough Whitlam and Rosenblum.

After a successful career in law, where one of his articled clerks was the future prime minister John Howard, Rosenblum lived well into his nineties. In his final years he took great pride in being tagged Australia's oldest living Test player.

The 1928 tour also introduced 'Wild Bill' Cerutti to the international rugby world. From day one this mad dog and crazed prop forward loved nothing better than belting an opposition on the field and then getting drunk with him that night. He had the face of a one-bout-too-many boxer, the physique of a wharfie and the demeanour of a knockabout. He loved to punt, losing money on the horses and cards, was a heavy smoker, emptying rooms with his pipe smoke, and was the team's entertainment officer, leading its sing-songs. And for well over twenty years this pugnacious, cheeky, fun-loving lug was Australian rugby's most renowned figure. In New Zealand he was better known than the Australian prime minister.

The son of Italian immigrants who were involved in a wood-turning business, Cerutti was known as Wild Bill from virtually day one. Considered by some to be too young to tour with the 1927–28 Waratahs, Cerutti had been picked for the Rest of New South Wales. Irked that he hadn't been selected for the touring team, the teenager decided to make his mark by chasing the returned Waratahs' leading players around the field and belting them whenever he got near. In the press box one scribe asked: 'Who's that wild bastard running around out there?' That wild bastard became 'Wild Bill' in the next morning's newspapers.

When he made the New South Wales touring team, he became even punchier. In the opening match of the 1928 Waratah tour of New Zealand, Cerutti was assigned the task of upsetting Auckland forward Bubs Knight by 'bopping him'. Wild Bill spent the whole match doing just that, and then sprinting around the field being chased by Knight. The selectors liked what they saw, and picked Cerutti in the Test team.

Cerutti and Knight met up at kick off for the second Test. Knight grabbed Will Bill and asked: 'What are we going to do, Cerutti? Play football?' A truce of sorts was sought, but a few years later before another Australia–New Zealand Test Knight, a butcher, decided to send Cerutti ten pounds of prime beef. The team ate nine pounds, but left the final pound sitting in the sun on the hotel roof for several days. By game day the meat was putrid. When the first scrum was set, Cerutti pulled the meat out of the pocket of his shorts. 'Here's your bloody steak, Knight,' he uttered while ramming it into Knight's eyes. Yet again Knight spent the rest of the game chasing Cerutti around the field.

One of Cerutti's closest colleagues in the Wallaby team was fellow forward Aub Hodgson. Hodgson was even crazier than Cerutti. Countless punches were thrown—all of which connected—during their first meeting at a Sydney club match. In the first lineout Cerutti decked Hodgson; Hodgson pole-axed Cerutti in the second. As Hodgson got to his feet, Cerutti suggested a truce: 'A young GPS fellow like you shouldn't start this sort of thing. Let's call the whole thing off.' Hodgson readily agreed. However, during the first lineout of the second half Cerutti belted Hodgson. A groggy Hodgson got to his feet, nursing a battered jaw, and yelled: 'I thought you said we'd made a truce.' Cerutti leant back and roared with laughter. 'That's lesson number one, never trust the opposition.'

Even as Test teammates neither could resist the temptation of putting one on the other's chin. During the 1936 Wallaby tour of New Zealand they became bored at an official function and decided to adjourn to a back room to test each other's slapping abilities. The good hearted slaps turned into nasty uppercuts and hooks, and teammates had to pull them apart.

The most celebrated Cerutti story comes from the Australian tour to South Africa in 1933. The early matches involved many fiery moments so team officials, concerned that the Test series could lose its way by becoming overly volatile, decided to get the teams together for an official dinner to calm the situation. The South African Rugby Union president was the first to speak, telling his players that if they did not play in the right spirit they would never again appear in the

Springbok colours. The Australian manager followed, stating that any of his players who misbehaved would immediately be sent home. Cerutti was sitting next to the famous South African brothers Boy and Fanie Louw, who whispered to him as they left the room, 'It'll be on tomorrow.' 'Why wait for tomorrow,' came the reply. It was on—the Louw brothers scuffling with Cerutti and Hodgson, who had become near inseparable friends. The Test was even more volatile.

Cerutti's involvement in the game lasted decades and he became a mentor to future generations of Wallabies, acting as a manager and tour liaison officer. In the late 1950s he told Wallabies hooker and future Test captain Peter Johnson during a New Zealand tour: 'You can go a long way in the game, sonny. Just be patient and give away the beer and smokes.' Reaching into his pocket, Cerutti handed Johnson a handful of Havana cigars. He also suggested that Johnson try gin and tonic instead of beer. 'All in all, the experience lasted two minutes, tops, and I don't recall saying anything. But it set the agenda for the remainder of my rugby career,' Johnson recalled years later.

Cerutti also had an impact on Nick Shehadie who, after a decade in the Australian pack, became Lord Mayor of Sydney, Australian Rugby Union president, one of the masterminds behind the first World Cup and, after Weary Dunlop, the second Wallaby to be knighted. As a team assistant manager he took special care of Shehadie during his playing days—even once piggy-backing him to and from a party in New Zealand.

Not surprisingly countless friends and colleagues wept openly at Cerutti's funeral in 1965. Aub Hodgson's death seventeen years later prompted a similar response, and he was given a standing ovation as his body disappeared behind the curtains at Sydney's Northern Suburbs crematorium. Both were the heart and soul of the local game. Like Cerutti, Hodgson was forever surrounded by revellers, who were charmed by his reminiscences, his outlandish behaviour, his vast football knowledge and his eagerness to be the ultimate host to any visiting rugby player.

Hodgson had thousands of stories to tell, including the time he struggled to get through the All Blacks defence in a Test match. Whenever he got into the clear an All Black would appear from nowhere to mow him down; that is, until Hodgson came up with the smart idea of holding up the ball, putting up his hand and shouting, 'Stop'. Surprisingly, the All Blacks did stop, and Hodgson was able to sprint towards the line.

Like Cerutti, Hodgson had a legion of friends from around the world. He would entertain them either at 'Aub's' bar in Kings Cross or the Rugby Club in Sydney, where he had a special spot at the end of the main bar. He was renowned for organising wild parties, including one that is still talked about by the 1966 British Lions team as the bath tub was filled with champagne.

He was also the master of winning bets, especially when someone questioned his rugby knowledge. The loser inevitably had to buy Aub lunch, which often turned into dinner and then a party. Hodgson even secured lunch out of Test cricketer Sid Barnes, who was known as a tightwad, after he bet him that if they stood side by side in Martin Place on a Monday morning more people would stop and say hello to him than Barnes. Aub won that bet by about fifty people.

Sadly Hodgson did become a bit dotty in his old age, welcoming visiting teams at Sydney Airport in his pyjamas and donning his dressing gown when he flew to interstate matches. Just as sad was his expectation that he would be the star of the 1939–40 Wallaby tour. Unfortunately, a devastating world force ruined his chance.

3

FLYING PIES AND MILK-SOAKED EARS

On the day war was declared in 1939, disconsolate Wallabies manager Dr Wally Matthews stood in the middle of Twickenham fighting back tears. He had just left a meeting with the English Rugby Football Union where it had been decided that without a game having being played and just two days after the team had arrived in Plymouth following six weeks at sea, the Wallaby tour was over. Matthews was dreading the drive to Torquay, where he had to inform the players that due to the dangers of war they had to return to Sydney as quickly as possible. Matthews wrote in his diary: 'Tour then is finished and have therefore decided to get team home as soon as possible. One cannot help worrying and what a disappointment it will be to the boys. Stood in the middle of the empty ground on the first day of the war.'

It was all in such dramatic contrast to the scene two months earlier when the chairman of selectors, W.W. Hill, announced following a six-hour meeting the Wallaby team to tour the United Kingdom, the first to do so since 1908. This was a team, he declared, superior to the Wallabies who toured South Africa in 1933 and 'better all round than the Waratahs of 1927–28'.

Not for the first or last time in the history of the Wallabies did rugby ability mean little in the selection of Test players. Big names missed out, including Cyril Towers and Bill Cerutti. Towers later pondered whether his omission had something to do with a serious personality clash with the manager, after all the last time Matthews took a team away to South Africa six years earlier the Test centre had been overlooked. At that time Matthews had made it known he thought the headstrong Towers was a divisive influence. Cerutti on the other hand wondered whether anti-Italian sentiment in the lead up to the Second World War had made him expendable.

Cerutti and Towers both attended the selection announcement. While Cerutti immediately congratulated the forwards picked ahead of him, Towers was visibly upset. He could not speak and left shortly after, refusing to comment on his non-selection. As former Wallaby and *Daily Telegraph* rugby writer Sid King reported: 'Towers was jotting down the names of the team. "Centre-threequarters" called the chairman, and then read the four selected. The pencil in Towers' hand moved rapidly, then paused and trembled. He closed his eyes momentarily, and swayed slightly. He could not hide his disappointment, for here was smashed an ambition harboured for years.'

Towers retired a year later, telling the *Daily Telegraph*: 'I'm tired of the Union's petty meddling and stupid administration. They've killed my enthusiasm for football.' He was, however, lured back to Randwick in 1951, even making a cameo appearance in reserve grade when at age forty-five he scored two tries.

The Australian selectors picked an eclectic mix of players, including four Victorians—Max Carpenter, Andy Barr, Stan Bisset and George Pearson—who they described as the 'Lucky 29'. The Lucky 29 soon became the Unlucky 29.

The early weeks of ship life were a delight, but as Europe approached life on board became increasingly unpleasant. While some of the players fought pneumonia and food poisoning, a number of the younger players became increasingly unimpressed with the team elder Hodgson, who threw his weight around at team meetings and gym sessions to such an extent that at least one other forward came close to belting him. But as the ship approached the French coast in late August 1939 all personal rifts were forgotten.

As the ship departed Marseille, Matthews wrote in his diary: 'This morning we find all the windows painted black, learn that all lights will be out at night, and no smoking on deck. We must be at war. What a tragedy! The team wonders and disappointment is written on their faces. What an ending to it all.' The players were worried they would not even get the chance to stand on English soil. 'Will England be at war and what is our next move?' Matthews asked.

When they arrived in Plymouth five days later, the players were allowed to leave the ship and head to a hotel in Torquay. In the billiard room they heard Neville Chamberlain's radio broadcast telling the world that England was now at war with Germany. They knew they would be going home.

The next two weeks were a haze—filling sandbags to protect their Torquay hotel, a visit to Buckingham Palace to meet the King (where Bisset took delight in using the King's private toilet), photographs at Twickenham wearing gas masks and then preparing for the dangerous trip home with the threat of enemy craft.

'The tour was a great disappointment,' Bisset recalled sixty-five years later. 'When our ship was blacked out in Marseille we knew this was serious. And when war was declared, a few of us wanted to immediately join up, but were told we had to return home to enlist. Then the trip home was quite hazardous, because of the threat of attack.' The return to Sydney took four months rather than the usual two because of the zigzagging course the ship had to make to avoid German U-boats.

At least the players got one opportunity to put on their football boots when their ship berthed at Bombay. It was decided all those who had never appeared in an Australian jersey would get the chance to wear the green and gold. Of the ten newcomers who played in Bombay nine never got the chance again to play for Australia, including Bisset and Barr. 'Thankfully there was one game when we were allowed to play in the Australian jersey against a team from Bombay Gymkhana, who I recall was mainly English. I remember that we hadn't done any training, and the opposition was a pretty good side. So for the first 20 minutes, it was tough,' Bisset said. The Wallabies won 21–0.

Matthews wrote in his tour report: 'Team well led by Gibbons and considering conditions (no training etc) played well. What a team these chaps would have turned out to be—Smith and McLean—are just developing and if this war permits will be great footballers.'

Matthews proved to be an excellent judge. Bill McLean, who became a captain in the AIF Commandos, was one of the few who played after the war, becoming a Wallaby captain. Len Smith played rugby league, rising to the rank of captain-coach of the Australian team that defeated New Zealander in 1948. Sadly, his career ended when he was inexplicably overlooked for the 1948 Kangaroo tour of England and France. Why Smith missed out remains one of Australian Rugby League's greatest mysteries. He believed he was the victim of sectarianism—a Catholic in a Mason-dominated game.

While McLean and Smith did get the opportunity to play again, for others surviving the war was a bigger challenge. New South Wales five-eighth Cec Ramalli, the son of an Indian camel driver who changed his surname from Ali Ram, was captured in Malaya. His captain, Vay Wilson, joined the British Navy and was awarded the DSC for his action in the English Channel in a PT boat.

Winston 'Blow' Ide, whose mother was Australian and father a Japanese silk printer, died when the Japanese POW ship he was on was torpedoed and sunk by an American submarine. Despite repeated entreaties to clamber onto an overcrowded raft, Ide kept helping his fellow POWs. His final words were said to be: 'No, mate. I'm staying here to help my mates. In any case I can swim to Australia if I have to.' Shortly after, he disappeared.

Bisset was one of a number of Wallabies to win a Military Cross. His brother Butch died in his arms on the Kokoda Track. His teammate

Nicky Barr became one of the war's most celebrated air aces, credited with bringing down at least twelve enemy planes in the space of a year. He was shot down three times behind enemy lines and escaped four times, including once from a moving train. For his courage, organising escape routes and clandestine work against the enemy, Barr was also awarded a Military Cross. Although he never played a Test for Australia, Barr remained a cherished Wallaby. Following the war he kept in keen contact with the game and played in numerous services matches.

•

Post-war times were tough and there were many shortages. Indeed, a number of Sydney club teams had to use footballs filled with paper because of the lack of football bladders. In New Zealand, life was even more rudimentary.

Eager to revive international rugby, the Wallabies headed to New Zealand in 1946 where, in their Invercargill hotel, the players were forced to sleep two to a bed. Fleeing the hotel, the players headed to a dormitory where they had to hammer nails into the wall so they had somewhere to hang their clothes. To add to their indignity, New Zealand officials suggested the Wallabies should take on a Kiwi coach. Pointing directly to a ridge close to Eden Park in Auckland known as the Khyber Pass, the Wallabies told their Kiwi opponents exactly where they should stick that idea.

Skipper Bill McLean's pre-Test speech was as brutal as the match itself: 'Listen to me. You're playing for Australia today. Your country, do you understand? Our aim is to kick the shit out of them and no one takes a backward step. Nobody! You're playing for your country! If you don't, you'll cop this from me.' With that McLean flung his fist in every player's face. They lost the Test.

In desperation, Wallaby management called a team meeting. The players feared the worst. 'I've tried everything with you blokes, taught you everything I know,' bellowed manager Dr W.H. Ward. 'There is only one thing I haven't tried. No one is to leave the room until they're dead drunk. And I mean no one.' An eighteen-gallon keg was rolled into the room, and Ward locked the door. They went on to lose the Test series 2–0.

The hard luck story of that tour goes to New Zealander Jack Finlay. On his way to Auckland for the Test, a hungry Finlay hopped out at a railway station to buy himself a meat pie. Eating it while standing on the platform, a train accelerated out of the station and Finlay was hit by an open carriage door. Shortly afterwards, he announced his retirement.

Three years later, in 1949, the Wallabies really told their Trans Tasman foes where to go when they succeeded in being the first Australian team to win the Bledisloe Cup on New Zealand soil. What this meant became very clear when the brash young forward Rex 'The Moose' Mossop grabbed the radio microphone after their Test triumph in Auckland and shouted down the line: 'Hi, Dad! Hi, Mum! Hi, Kirk! We've beaten the bastards! You beauty!'

Thus began the flourishing and often controversial media career of big, bad Moose, who on that tour discovered the ultimate cure for cauliflower ears—bathe them in hot milk several times a day. With a gift for entertainment, he definitely fitted in with the Wallabies. The star of the 1946 team, however, was its fearless prop and legendary singer of dirty ditties 'Wallaby Bob' McMaster, who in later years was watched in virtually every living room across the country as the most famous TV wrestling referee of them all, keeping apart the likes of Mario Milano, Spiros Arion, Tiger Singh, Big Bad John and Larry O'Dea in TV's *World Championship Wrestling.*

As for the big silver monstrosity Moose and Wallaby Bob were playing for, and proudly had their photograph taken with, like the rest of the Australian team they were not aware of its odd history. It was originally presented in the early 1930s by the Governor-General of New Zealand Lord Charles Bledisloe, nicknamed 'Chattering Charlie' because of his eagerness to wear cravats and spats and his tendency to make boring speeches at agricultural shows. According to those who knew him, Chattering Charlie was an upper class fool who didn't know 'one end of a rugby ball from the other'. 'He is never happier,' one journalist wrote, 'than when he is discussing ephemeral fever or Berkshire shows.' A persistent whinger to newspaper editors, Lord Bledisloe had one journalist sacked because the caption underneath a photograph of him and his wife referred to a prize winning ram at the Canterbury Show.

The donation of the Bledisloe Cup was simply a public relations exercise. It first appeared at the Australia–New Zealand Test in Auckland in 1931, but so enthusiastic was Lord Bledisloe that on the day of the game he went to a travellers' smoke night at the other end of the North Island.

It also took the Wallabies and the All Blacks some time to embrace the cup because a short time after Australia won the trophy in 1949, it disappeared. For well over a decade no one knew, or even really cared, where it was. Eventually someone remembered it had been given on loan to the New Zealand Tourist Bureau in Melbourne as part of a promotional display. That is where a cleaner found it, on its side hidden away behind cardboard cut-outs of sheep and Maori huts. It was only when the Wallabies began beating the All Blacks on a regular basis in the late 1970s and 1980s that the Bledisloe Cup again became an important sporting icon.

The Australians probably purposely ignored the cup, because it was too much of a reminder of how close the local game had come to collapse. The 1950s and 1960s were grim times for the code, which was deep in the shadow of rugby league. In 1951 the Australian team played in front of virtually an empty house at Brisbane's Gabba. Only 4800 spectators could be bothered attending to see the Wallabies lose once more to the All Blacks.

The following year the Fijians revived a flagging game through a most spectacular of Test series, which also brought much needed revenue to the cash-strapped Australian Rugby Union. The series was exciting and volatile, attracting near capacity crowds. And the Fijians were as direct as their better known Australian opponents. In one match, when a Fijian player was injured at the bottom of a ruck, an accusing finger was pointed at Australian back-rower David Brockhoff. 'Fifty years ago we would have eaten you for less than that,' the Fijian declared at the astonished Brockhoff.

The ARU was delighted by the monetary return, but the Wallabies themselves remained paupers. They were definitely playing for love. For many years players could be seen outside Test grounds mingling with the scalpers, hoping to sell their allocated tickets to get some extra funds. Their playing expenses amounted to virtually nothing.

Australia, which had for so long struggled to overcome the never-ending loss of its key players to rich rugby league clubs, also relied on New Zealand to act as a charitable big brother. When the ARU had virtually nothing, its New Zealand counterparts provided funding for jerseys and took on some of the costs of getting the All Blacks to Australia. The situation was so dire that in the early 1970s, the Australian Rugby Union often struggled to find the funds for tours. In 1977 there were no Tests because the ARU was near broke.

However, when Australia finally became prosperous, there were times when it was nowhere near as charitable as its New Zealander brothers had been. The Kiwis never forgot this. Nor did they forget the pot shots certain ARU officials took at their New Zealand counterparts, in particular the crusty International Rugby Board delegate Wylie Breckenridge, who was infuriated that New Zealand officials would crawl to northern hemisphere bodies at the expense of Australia. This prompted a blistering series of letters in 1968 between the Australian and New Zealand Unions about 'unprovoked' attacks.

•

In the 1940s, 50s and 60s there were good, average and appalling Wallabies line-ups, great wins, terrible losses and strange moments. It was a time when the Australians sat deep in the shadow of the two more powerful southern hemisphere nations—New Zealand and South Africa—who, like the northern hemisphere unions, believed it didn't take much to distract the Wallabies. The Irish would try to ply them with champagne and stout before Test matches, while on one occasion on the South Island of New Zealand the Australians were convinced that over-imbibing on the famous Bluff oysters, Worcester sauce and whiskey was the best way to overcome pre-match nerves. The following day they struggled to crawl, let alone run, onto the field.

But despite its far smaller player pool, Australia still had the ability to produce the most spectacular, unpredictable and memorable of players. And, as always, the Wallabies succeeded in being a home for the most hilarious, the most outspoken, the most engrossing of personalities. Being a prankster almost became a prerequisite to being called up. Fullback Brian Piper even took his life into his own hands when he decided to upset the nightly romantic meanderings of one of his 1949 Wallaby teammates. Aware that the Wallaby Casanova had a woman in his room for the umpteenth night on the tour, Piper filled a bucket with water and scaled a third floor hotel ledge until he was outside the flashy forward's window. According to fellow Wallaby Max Howell in his book *Bledisloe Magic*, Piper opened the window and yelled 'I've got you at last' as he attempted to fling the water at the couple. Losing his balance he crashed to the ground, sustaining injuries so serious that he missed the rest of the Test series.

Others, such as one of Australia's first post-war captains Dr Phil Hardcastle, were enlightening players just through their vitality. A pest of a forward, Hardcastle loved niggling opponents at the set pieces, obstructing them and throwing the sneaky punch. He could also irritate his fellow Australians. Forward Graham Cooke was so annoyed during a Test trial match when Hardcastle stepped on his feet and held him down during lineouts that he finally moaned: 'Do that one more time and I'll belt you.'

At the next lineout, while tugging on Cooke's jersey, Hardcastle tried to ask what was wrong. He had a terrible stutter and as he started to ask the question with 'W-w-w-w', a frustrated Cooke threw a wild right at Hardcastle, who ducked at the perfect time. The punch instead knocked out Eric Tweedale, who had to be stretchered from the field.

Then during a fiery Australia–New Zealand Test, Hardcastle was having a torrid time against All Blacks front-rower Johnny Simpson. Simpson was infuriated that a Wallaby had king hit him. Hardcastle attempted to protest. 'F-f-f-f-fair dinkum, J-Johnnie, it w-w-w-wasn't me.' 'Doesn't matter,' Simpson replied, 'you'll do,' and hit him with a right cross.

And it was a Hardcastle after-match speech that many regard as the greatest of all time. Beckoned to the microphone after a game in Wales, he grabbed the microphone, blew into it and said: 'Gee-gee-gee-gee-gentlemen, w-w-w-words f-f-f-fail me.' He then sat down to a standing ovation.

Like Hardcastle, Dick Tooth hailed from Sydney University and became one of Australian rugby's most renowned midfielders. And like Cyril Towers and Len Smith before him, he discovered that the power of the rugby official was all encompassing. Getting off-side with the rugby blazer brigade could lead to inexplicable humiliation.

Even more than fifty years on, players from that time claim that Tooth's omission from the 1957–58 Wallaby tour of Britain, France and North America was the biggest selection bungle in Wallaby history. His selection credentials were overwhelming: he was a masterful five-eighth, fullback, centre, capable goal kicker, a skilful tactician, a courageous defender and a widely admired skipper who had been in charge in the two Tests leading up to the tour. He made one cardinal mistake, however. At the after-match function following the final Test against the All Blacks in Brisbane in 1957 Tooth had a disagreement, not entirely about football, with the chairman of selectors, Tom Pauling. Clearly wanting to remind the Australian players they were best seen and not heard, Pauling overlooked Tooth for the twenty-seven-man party.

There was an immediate outcry. Col Windon, one of Australia's most notable back-rowers, retired from coaching at Randwick in protest, while the club stalwart Wally Meagher said, 'The whole thing is too stupid for words'. At the time, the Gordon rugby club ran a competition on who would be in the Australian team. Out of 2000 entries, only two didn't pick Tooth.

As expected, the tour was a fiasco. Without Tooth, the Wallabies lost all of the five Tests. And the new coach Dave Cowper, who was appointed the day the team left for overseas, was not up to it. The Wallaby practices ran to clockwork but became tedious. The players soon lost interest. Cowper, according to the players, had only two moves and he wanted them perfected. By the time the team was in the north of England, several leading players had had enough. When Cowper shouted 'Ruck it here . . . ruck it there', one forward grumbled back 'Ruck it your bloody self' and walked off the ground.

Just two years earlier the team dynamics were very different. Bill Cerutti, who was in charge of training during the Wallabies' New Zealand tour, would throw players into an icy mountainous stream if they dropped a pass. On the same tour, Cerutti agreed to winger Eddie Stapleton's plan to lose weight before the final test. So enthused was Cerutti with Stapleton's decision that he would not eat for two days, he did the same 'to keep Eddie company'.

This was also a period when touring Australian teams became accustomed to being described as either the Woeful Wallabies or the 'worst side to leave Australia', a line first used in 1958 by Sydney journalist E.W. Kann and with good reason. After a lamentable northern hemisphere tour where they were beaten by all and sundry, the Australians had struggled against the New Zealand Maoris at home and in the first Test of their New Zealand tour were swamped 25–3 in Wellington. But as so many rugby writers have discovered over the years, when a Wallaby is provoked he invariably comes out fighting. Two weeks after the Wellington debacle, the transformed Wallabies won in Christchurch 6–3.

So irritated were the Australians by the constant sniping, especially by the press, that in Christchurch they weren't going to let anything upset them—even prop Keith Ellis kept on playing while choking on his false teeth, which he'd forgotten to take out before running on the field. At the first ruck they broke in two, something Ellis realised when one half went down his throat. Strange on-field occurrences were not uncommon for the touring Wallabies. Hooker Jim Cross was reputed to have once played an international against the All Blacks wearing a wrist watch. So vague was he that teammates are adamant he would arrive at games with either two right boots or two left boots.

•

During the 1960s, the Wallabies' form swung as wildly as the times. Swinging sixties. Swinging Wallabies. They would peak, enjoying spectacular triumphs (none more so than when they twice beat South Africa on Springbok soil in 1963) but would suffer drastic and extensive losses as well. This was not surprising considering how relaxed overseas tours could be. Before one tour, a leading forward who was about to have his fitness test to confirm he could travel to South Africa was sighted at the main bar of the Rugby Club in Sydney downing a gin and tonic while sucking on a cigarette. He passed the test soon after.

As future Wallaby skipper Peter Johnson wrote in his self-published autobiography of the 1961 Australian tour of South Africa: 'Training sessions resembled "buffets" where we tried a bit of this, then a bit of that. Not only were these runs unstructured but usually so laid back it was difficult to tell when they started and finished. And the menu never contained serious scrummaging or lineout work.' And, as strange as it seems, they thought the best way to overcome playing at altitude in South Africa was by cleaning their teeth before running out to play.

The actual menu on that tour wasn't anywhere near as exciting, with reports that the South African hosts were starving the Australians with meagre portions. Sitting in his Sydney office, New South Wales Rugby Union president Arthur Henry fobbed off the reports: 'After all the Wallabies are there to play football, and not to eat off the fat of the land. They have to keep fit.'

If the opinion of the then Wallabies manager Bjarne Halvorsen is any guide, they also didn't think they had much chance of winning.

After losing the series, Halvorsen said at the official function: 'It's no disgrace to lose to this wonderful Springbok team. We did not expect to win the Tests anyway.' The players were aghast.

During this period the Wallabies became accustomed to standing behind their own goal posts, observing an opposition kicker attempting another conversion. Calling his players around him for a deep and meaningful, captain John Thornett pleaded with his team: 'Listen, fellas, this just isn't us.'

'All right,' interrupted forward Dave Shepherd. 'Well, let's get the hell out of here before somebody thinks it is.'

Adding to the uncertainty was player concern about the sanity of some of their coaches of that time. Wallaby skipper Peter Johnson recalled first meeting the newly appointed Australian coach Bryan Palmer in 1962. 'All I could think was, What sort of nut have we got here?' Johnson said of the bombastic, excitable Palmer.

So desperate were the 1963 Wallabies that forward Peter Crittle, sidelined with injury for the first Test, was told by Wallabies manager Bill McLaughlin to spy on a Springboks training session in Pretoria. Crittle turned out to be only an average spy. First, he was sighted by the local newspaper, which plastered his photo over the front page, and then his observations were found to be faulty when two of the South Africans whom Crittle thought were ponderous and easy to target cut the Australians to pieces a few days later in the second Test. Crittle was ridiculed by his teammates because of McLaughlin's actions, but the players got the manager back when they let a chimpanzee loose in his hotel room while he was in the bath.

But not even having the world's best halfback Ken Catchpole could turn the Wallabies into the world's No. 1 team. Still, Catchpole allowed them to enjoy their best decade since the 1930s—which was admirable considering union continued to be gutted as rugby league lured away so many of the code's best representatives, including Dick Thornett, Kevin Ryan, Phil Hawthorne, John Brass and Michael Cleary.

And once again the Bledisloe Cup was lost—this time in 1968 when it was sent to Port Kembla instead of Sydney. The Port Kembla wharfies, entrenched rugby league fans, had no idea what it was. The glory of Trans Tasman rugby came close to being sent to a scrap metal dealer. It was eventually retrieved by someone with a faint interest in rugby and sent to the Sydney Cricket Ground in time to be on display on the Test halfway line.

Rugby also appeared to lose some of its innocence during the 1960s, with the game making newspaper front pages for all the wrong reasons when the first Wallaby was sent home from a tour and the captain had his career prematurely ended because of a wild All Black act.

From the first tour in 1908, the Wallabies had grown accustomed to being castigated by the home media for supposedly dirty play. A concerned Wallabies management pushed for a policy of clean play for the 1966–67 tour of the United Kingdom that even forbade players from retaliating when provoked. Manager Bill McLaughlin, mindful that recent Australian teams had been criticised in the British press for several unsavoury kicking incidents, assured the the English union that he would deal heavily with anyone guilty of nefarious play.

The players were dismayed when they heard this, believing they would become easy targets. But McLaughlin ignored their protestations. 'That's the policy, and we're sticking to it,' he said. There would be an 'automatic four match suspension for dirty play'. And to assert his authority even more, he demanded that players be barred from accepting free cigarettes so as not to compromise their amateur status.

Ross Cullen, a forward who had never played a Test, became McLaughlin's prime target. He soon discovered the Wallabies' manager hadn't been joking. Just before full time in the third match of the Tour against Oxford University, Oxford prop Ossie Waldron left the field with blood streaming from his left ear. As he passed the referee, Waldron said he had been bitten by Cullen. The referee took no action.

In the dressing rooms a flustered McLaughlin rushed up to Cullen. 'What happened out there? Did you bite that bloke on the ear?' Cullen admitted that it appeared he had bitten his opponent, but before he could fully explain the episode McLaughlin had turned and left the room.

Cullen told teammate Peter Johnson straight after the game that 'The bastard was boring in on me, so I told him I'd bite him if he didn't stop.' Asked by Johnson if he had actually bitten Waldron, Cullen replied: 'No, I didn't. He pulled his ear away as he sensed my teeth and that must have done it.'

The next morning, following an all-night meeting involving McLaughlin, John Thornett and assistant manager Alan Roper, Cullen was told he was being sent home. So shocked was he, he didn't even attempt to explain to McLaughlin the legitimate excuse he had for retaliating. For years he believed had been made a scapegoat. He disappeared from the game for a long time and did not bother turning up to Wallaby reunions.

There were ramifications from Cullen's departure. Many of the Queensland players were incensed he had been sent home, believing the treatment meted out was overly harsh. The players were also aware that Roper did not agree with McLaughlin and Thornett over the 'no rough play' rule. Jules Guerassimoff, a pugnacious and forthright forward, came out in defence of Cullen, fronting both Thornett and McLaughlin. It wasn't a smart move; rugby administrators don't like being told off by players. Guerassimoff had played his last Test.

McLaughlin did not help himself when he returned to Australia. After explaining to the media that he had told the players they were ambassadors for Australia, so punching was barred from any game, he added that, 'After a couple of games I told the boys they could punch back if they were hit.' Later that day McLaughlin lost his spot as a New South Wales delegate on the Australian Rugby Union. Alan Roper lost the ballot to be coach.

Another Australian player to suffer unfairly during this period was Ken Catchpole. His demise was not the result of his own team's lack of faith, but due to the aggression of the most rabid of rivals.

For years Australian rugby had relied on scrappers, part-timers and enthusiasts. It lived off the smell of an oily rag. (The 1967 Sydney representative team suffered the embarrassment of its jerseys falling apart when playing Ireland because someone had used too much bleach. Some players even had to finish the game bare chested.) Only rarely did Australia boast of players of World XV quality. Catchpole was one of the few. He was described by England's Rugby Football Union president in 1967 as 'the greatest scrum half the world has known'.

Catchpole was the complete player, and one of the few Wallabies the All Blacks were sincerely worried about. They got their chance to do something about that threat in 1968 when, during the Sydney Cricket Ground Test, Catchpole was buried at the bottom of a maul with the ball underneath him. One of his legs was protruding from the confusion of bodies and for Colin Meads, the All Blacks' most famous player, that was too irresistible.

Meads, of Pine Tree and sheep under both arms fame, pounced on Catchpole's leg and yanked it with all his might. The Australian was defenceless, and in agonising pain he saw his 'muscles stretched like rubber bands until they snapped'. His hamstring was torn from the pelvic muscle, and groin muscles were damaged together with his sciatic nerve. Catchpole's last Test ended with him being carted off the field on a stretcher.

Meads' actions angered the Wallabies and their supporters. Former Test forward Keith Cross was so incensed that he sent Meads a newspaper cutting describing Catchpole's injuries. With it was a note that read: 'Colin, are you proud of this effort?'

Meads was never allowed to forget what he had done. 'The referee did not penalise me, but in the eyes of the Australians, I was just a dirty big bastard,' he wrote shortly afterwards. 'All Australians thought I was a bloody criminal and I know Australia has still got this against me.'

The end of Catchpole's rugby career just added an extra edge to Australia's pursuit of the Bledisloe Cup, which the rugby public suddenly found captivating. For this, blame John David Brockhoff.

4

IT'S JUST A TEA PARTY

In 1973 the Australian players sat in the dressing room sheds behind Ballymore, scared even to look at each other. Their eyes trawled the concrete floor in search of an escape hatch. The atmosphere was dark, the feeling one of disbelief. As fullback Arthur McGill explained years later: 'No one said a word. No one could speak. It was total shock.' Making an almighty racket, hundreds of Tongan kids had clambered up onto the roof and were jumping up and down on the galvanised iron merrily giggling away. The walls, the small windows, the shower recesses all shook as the noise reverberated.

Surely, it couldn't get any worse than this. Australia, supposedly a world rugby power, had been decimated by a bunch of nobodies from a tiny Pacific Island. And this was the same mob of nobodies who had been beaten by the part-timers in Victoria, and arrived for this tour with barely any gear and had to go searching for football boots because they were more accustomed to playing in bare feet at home.

All the worrying signs of a big country taking a minor opposition for granted were there. The previous week at the Sydney Cricket Ground the Test had ended in hilarity when bulky forward Garrick Fay decided to kick an ungainly, unnecessary and mocking field goal in the final minutes. The kick went over, but an infuriated Wallaby coach Bob Templeton grabbed Fay after the game and scowled: 'Don't ever bloody well do that again.' Earlier in the game Mark Loane, making his first Test appearance, had had enough time to peer down and pick up a 20 cent piece on the SCG cricket wicket and hand it to his stunned skipper Peter Sullivan.

A week later the Wallabies were the embarrassment of the nation. They had been beaten by Tonga 16–11, who basically tackled them out of the game. A few days later, journalist Norm Tasker in *The Sun* asked, 'Where do we go from here?' For weeks, months and even years later, Australian rugby was a laughing stock because of this impossible to believe moment. There was an upside, however: it forced embarrassed administrators and players to seriously look at why the local game had slumped so badly and to do something about it.

The previous two seasons had already placed Australian rugby in a terrible predicament as it had lost the support of much of the general public, including a fair share of long-time supporters. This had a lot to do with the ARU readily assuming the role of a backward, out-of-touch organisation. During the 1971 Springbok tour of Australia, the ARU and the state unions came across as regressive and ultra-conservative bodies. To defend its actions, it latched on to the naive notion that politics should not interfere with sport. This policy was hardly surprising, though, as the private school brethren who had controlled Australian rugby for so long were turning it into a fossilised organisation. It had a taint of cobwebs and the smell of decay.

The ARU fervently believed Australia should continue to play the Springboks even if it meant it was condoning South Africa's apartheid regime. The essentially conservative and subservient Australian rugby media of the time also gave the ARU unstinting support by avoiding the tough questions, with some journalists even castigating those players who were wary about either playing against or touring South Africa.

The ARU's eagerness to ensure that the Springbok tour continued despite widespread protests—one protestor was Fred Hollows, who later gained fame as a renowned eye surgeon—turned the Test matches in a battle ground. The ARU lost in the public relations stakes and the Wallabies lost on the field, with the Springboks winning the three-Test series easily. At the time the Australians were having enough trouble catching the high up and unders from the relentless Springbok attack without the extra pressure of a smoke bomb about to hit them as well.

The issue of South Africa led to division in the Wallabies ranks. While many of the players had no qualms about becoming protest targets, believing like the ARU that they should be exempt from political and social pressures because they were amateurs, some of the more progressive players made their opposition to the Tour clearly known. Wallaby forward Tony Abrahams, who had toured South Africa in 1969, became an outspoken critic of the apartheid regime, calling for an end to sporting contact with the republic. He was supported by fellow Wallabies Jim Boyce, Paul Darveniza, Terry Forman, Barry McDonald and Jim Roxburgh, who argued that hosting all white Springbok tours was condoning 'the racial policy of South Africa'.

The players' bold stand, which included distributing anti-tour pamphlets outside grounds and speaking at protest meetings, helped bring the issue of South Africa to a head and for the first time forced Australia to seriously consider the ramifications of a Springbok tour and its own problems with Aboriginal Australians. The demonstrations also saw support among the Australian public for continued contact with South Africa slump from 85 per cent at the start of the tour to 63 per cent by the end. This daring move by the players, who knew they would be shunned by teammates and administrators, remains the most rousing and telling Wallaby moment in an otherwise gloomy era.

Despite the 3–0 Test drubbing, matches being played behind barbed wire fences and more than 750 arrests, including in Canberra that of a deaf mute, boneheaded ARU officials still publicly argued that the Springbok tour was worthwhile. They just didn't get it.

They did get it later that year, however, when a squad described by Norman Tasker as 'one of the softest teams in history' embarked on a haphazard tour of France and found itself housed in a mental asylum near Strasbourg that had bare floors and no showers or toilets. Angry threats by the legendary Wallaby manager 'Smokin'' Joe French to the French rugby union administration that the team would go home the following day saw them moved to slightly better accommodation. At least the walls weren't padded.

Then in 1972 the Wallabies were once more made to look like fools, when during a tour to New Zealand the All Blacks thrashed them time and again. New Zealander Chris Gaskill wrote: 'The Wallabies aren't a team, they're a scream.' There were even calls in New Zealand to cease playing Tests against the Wallabies because it was a waste of time, and the All Blacks were gaining bad habits from beating bad opponents.

It was not as if the Wallabies were without good players; there was just a distinct lack of depth. Too often selectors were forced to choose players who were well short of Test standard. And there were also players who took it all as a bit of a lark. Following their first Test drubbing, one player arrived at a team meeting dressed as a woman and arm in arm with a girl wearing team gear and a Wallaby blazer. French, a crusty, hard Queensland official, looked the player up and down and growled: 'Take it off or you'll be on the next plane back to Sydney!' The player and the girl fled.

At least the girl had the right blazer on, unlike the 1973 Wallabies who went to Wales and England with the wrong national emblem. Instead of a kangaroo and emu, their Monty Pythonesque blazer had two kangaroos carrying the Commonwealth Shield. But by then it appeared the general public cared very little about rugby union at all, as the interstate match between New South Wales and Queensland that year attested. This Wallaby trial lured just over a thousand spectators to North Sydney Oval—there were more at the greyhound races that night. Rugby was in a mess.

The bungling and constant mishaps put enormous pressure on the capable players, such as skipper Greg Davis, to perform well. The Wallabies opted against taking up the New Zealand offer of a coach back in 1946 but when Davis, a New Zealand wool classer, moved to Sydney Australia embraced him. At the time the Wallabies lacked hard men and Davis, the most fearless of forwards made even more threatening with a near-bald dome that made him appear half mad, was able to give the pack some sort of edge. And this back-rower, who had learnt all his tricks in the hard school of New Zealand rugby, was prepared to go to extremes, making him one of Australia's most inspirational captains.

Davis' boldness came to the fore during the 1971 French series; while being cautioned by the referee, he was hit with a wild round arm punch by an opponent. As is the way of one-eyed French referees, the official simply ignored the king hit even though Davis was bleeding profusely from a shattered nose. That night Davis had to decline making a speech at the after-match function. He stayed in his hotel room with a spoon up his nose, which he tapped gently with a Coca-Cola bottle in the hope of straightening it. But Davis couldn't play forever, and as soon as he retired standards again fluctuated wildly.

•

Alarmed by Australia's inability to compete against the best like the All Blacks and the minnows like Tonga, the ARU was forced into action. Conferences were organised, All Blacks Colin Meads and Wilson Whinerey were beckoned from New Zealand for their thoughts and a report was commissioned. The report, written by rugby officials John Howard, Bob Templeton and Bill McLaughlin, called for reform at all levels, a better representative program, greater emphasis on schoolboy football and improving the level of coaching in Australia. A national coaching panel was set up and overseas fact-finding missions were organised, which saw the then Wallaby coach Templeton head to the United Kingdom on a tour that had to be funded by Claude Fay, a successful Sydney hotelier and father of Wallaby Garrick. Fay's involvement was crucial, because at that time a proposed Wallaby tour of Canada and Argentina was called off due to a lack of money.

As crucial as the ARU revamping itself, the other critical reasons for Australia's eventual rise out of the mire was the revitalisation of Queensland rugby and the radical move of handing the Wallaby coaching reins to one of the most extroverted, ardent, animated rugby men of all—the one and only David Brockhoff. For too long New South Wales rugby had dominated the local scene, providing most of the Test players and its off-field leaders. Finally, in the mid-1960s Queensland officials purchased that state's own ground in the inner Brisbane suburb of Ballymore and, taking a chip-on-a-shoulder attitude to the heights of paranoia, focused on beating the Sydney spivs.

Queensland administrators fervently believed they did not get a fair deal from their New South Wales counterparts. This worked in turning Queensland into a major rugby power, and for several decades the prime breeding ground for Wallabies. Whereas down south the fighting between New South Wales and New South Wales country officials caused division, the administerial ranks in Queensland appeared solid, aimed at being progressive and focused on supporting the state team. The other clear difference was that, even though the leading Catholic schools provided many representative footballers, there still appeared to be a Protestant dominance in the running of the game in Sydney. Queensland rugby was influenced by the Catholic brethren. The Brothers club, founded by the old boys from two of Brisbane's premier Christian Brothers colleges, Nudgee and Gregory Terrace, was a Queensland rugby stronghold. That didn't sit well with New South Wales powerbrokers, who understandably looked upon the Queensland resurgence as a major threat to their own powerbase.

What all of this meant was that Queensland was breeding the right type of Wallabies—hard, mean mongrels who delighted in proving they were sick of being downtrodden. All they needed was the right type of aggressive coach. David Brockhoff was that man—and he used Ballymore as his arena to show it was time for the Wallabies to stand up and be counted.

Each football code has its unforgettable breast-beating, pulpit-thumping, hot gospel evangelist. In AFL it was Butch Killigrew, who worked on the theory: 'What is a football club? It is grass in the middle, posts at the end and bricks and mortar. It is people that give it soul. A football club is a living body.' In rugby league Roy Masters worked on the theory: 'It is time for the fibros to rise above the silvertails.' In rugby union it was Brock, who said: 'I know every back should be drowned at birth, but look . . . first five minutes, men, we lock the bully out of the gate . . . and then for the rest of the afternoon we play in the field. You have to be everywhere, breakaways. Everywhere! No excuses . . . cause havoc at the breakdown like sharks in a school of mullet. As for the tight-five, all day like wind through wheat. Not scattered rocks here and there, but like wind through wheat. And when you're through the other side we're like crowbars through the Opera House window. We get in, loot the joint and get out. And remember, no height in the lineout is no excuse; we must have the fruit, so every lineout is a dockyard brawl. Except our twenty-two—row of ministers—no easy penalties. Five-eighth . . . Kick this slippery pig to those mongrel dogs. And halfback listen to me. No Harbour Bridges. For Christ sake, no Harbour Bridges or the pigs will slit your throat. Now follow me.'

Brockhoff, who hailed from the high-profile Sydney flour-milling family that saw him become a master of making biscuits, was flamboyant, both as a player and as a teacher. He could be raucous, dominating proceedings with his deep, loud voice and the most vibrant, booming of laughs. He knew how to use animated facial expression, humour, language and body movement. His beaming smile and the most stern of glares had the same impact: they were hypnotic. His arms were forever waving this way and that and he would stand erect, using his tall, thin frame to great effect.

Around his neck at training would hang a big bath towel or even a tartan scarf. A whistle was cradled in his right hand ready to be blown with screeching intensity at those he perceived as idiots—and they were many. He'd bang his hands, pound his fists, demand concentration and attention. He would enthuse the troops with his rasping calls to battle, urging his battalions to climb over the trenches and kill anyone or anything that stood in their way.

His boundless enthusiasm as a player won him selection in eight Tests, and his extroverted behaviour put him immediately alongside Cerutti and Hodgson as unforgettable Wallabies. As a player he was accused of 'sea gulling'—as a back-rower hovering away from the action, but always there to take the telling pass and make the break. In New Zealand he was known as 'Offside Brockhoff' because he could always be found near the advantage line, causing trouble.

His playing day tales included his colourful relationship with forward teammate Jack Baxter (known as 'Tarakan Jack' because of the extensive burns he suffered several years earlier when trapped during an explosion on the HMAS *Tarakan* at Garden Island). Brockhoff explained to Peter Jenkins in *Wallaby Gold*: 'I was packing behind the bastard [during the 1949 Wallaby tour of New Zealand]; it was against Canterbury or something. They hit him with everything and his eyebrow came off. It was twitching on the ground, the whole eyebrow; you've never seen anything so ugly. Of course I vomited out of sheer disgust. But he smacks me on the jaw, this tough guy who'd been through the war in the navy, and says: "Listen you, put it back or you're off." So I grabbed the eyebrow and slapped it back on his face and went down in the next scrum sick with fright and terror. That was Baxter.'

But it was as a coach that Brock made his real mark. He was a winner, initially with Sydney University where his unusual methods brought success. His philosophy, inspired primarily by New Zealand coach Vic Kavanagh, who pushed the powerful rucking game, was concise: get a fierce, dominant pack; make them brutal at the ruck and scrum; ensure they are intimate with something called the 'famous Vickers machine-gun tripod defence'; and, in a variation of the Kavanagh philosophy, make certain you have a kicking five-eighth. For Brockhoff, kicking was usually the first option. The five-eighth would kick the ball in front of the forwards, and these eight mighty heathens would drive, smash and decimate everything in their way.

Getting his players in the right frame of mind was Brock's specialty; his pre-match speeches were famous, and players soon had their favourite examples of a special rugby language known as Brock-speak. As Wallaby coach Alan Jones said at a celebration for Brockhoff's eightieth birthday in 2008: 'Statistics are only part of the Brockhoff story. What they don't highlight is the verbal imagery, the cryptic and almost Delphic utterances of Brock.'

Stories abound about Brock, with one of the most notable involving the day in the 1970s when he was coaching University against arch rivals Randwick at Coogee Oval. The match was set down for 25 April and Brock, the master motivator, based his pre-match speech around Anzac Day and the Australian soldiers' bravery during the Gallipoli campaign. Unbeknown to the players, Brock had arranged for the University dressing room door to be loosened on its hinges.

Ten minutes before kick off, Brock was in a lather. 'This is Anzac Day, men—we are playing Randwick, the outright enemies. This is Turkey for us. If it was good enough for the boys at Gallipoli, it's good enough for me, and today, fellas . . . WE DO BATTLE!' Then Brock strode towards the door, ripped it off its hinges and slammed it onto the concrete floor. He then screamed, 'Follow me out; over the top!'

At half-time it wasn't certain whether Brock's message had sunk in. University were 17–3 behind, prompting Brock to give his players another patriotic blast during the break. University won 18–17.

Other celebrated club moments with Brock included the time when he climbed a tree at University Oval in an attempt to distract the kicker. As the Randwick player lined up for the conversion there was a sudden rustling of the branches in a tree just behind the goal posts that built up as if a hurricane had hit the ground. Some seconds after the successful conversion a sheepish Brock was sighted clambering his way out of the tree.

The players always knew where they stood with Brock. Wallaby forward John Lambie was selected to play for New South Wales agains Tonga, with Brock being seconded to take charge of the Waratah forwards. At New South Wales' first training run Lambie was struggling with the team's defensive patterns, which saw him way out of position. Brock beckoned the team, and focused on Lambie. 'When I tell you to do something you bloody well do it,' Brock bellowed. 'Lambie, it's not your fault . . . It's the selectors' fault, you shouldn't be here.'

When Brockhoff took over as Wallabies coach in late 1974 he applied a 'step forward' policy that had immediate impact but also almost saw him sacked within months. Brockhoff had decided to revamp the Wallaby culture. They were too soft, and had no idea what was required up front. It was time to apply a bit of muscle.

It was to Brockhoff's advantage that the players available in 1974 were a formidable group, including fire and brimstone men like prop Stu Macdougall and willing supports such as Mark Loane and Tony Shaw. That year also saw the rise of Ray Price, an antagonistic, cocky forward who had no interest in reputations and was renowned for his brutal Cumberland throw tackle that was as devastating as anything from the halcyon days of World Championship Wrestling. Price came from the tough Western Suburbs of Sydney, and looked like a long-haired lout. He was the aggressor the Wallabies had been waiting so long for.

Brockhoff knew he could fire up Loane. Before their first Test together, Brock handed the powerful Queensland No. 8 a note that said: 'Mark. Today I want you to run like a train without a station.' Macdougall was a bit harder, especially as he liked to stand up to Brock. On one celebrated occasion just before a Test, the coach decided to inspire the troops in the dressing rooms by playing a tape recording of a speech by Winston Churchill. After several minutes,

Macdougall queried: 'Does it get any better, Brock?' The moment was lost and the players found themselves in fits of laughter. An angry Brock stormed from the room.

•

As countless Wallabies have explained, while they have an aversion, indeed a near fear about confronting the All Blacks, it is nothing compared to the hatred they feel towards England and its attitude that Australians were nothing more than convict colonials. It was never hard to get a Wallaby team inspired before playing England in a Test, but Brockhoff took it to the next level for the 1975 series.

After winning an edgy, sometimes volatile Test in Sydney, Ballymore became the ground for Brock to introduce some real rough and tumble tactics. The ARU, in particular its president Bill McLaughlin, was concerned that Brockhoff was up to something for that game. Former Wallabies enlisted to go into the dressing rooms to assess the scene were astounded by what they saw, an animated Brock screaming: 'You'll run out, you'll line up on the other side of halfway, you'll see those dirty, rotten Pommy bastards, you'll sing *Advance Australia Fair,* and then you're going to go through them like a madman in a glass factory with a crowbar.' It was no surprise the players were somewhat animated and that a pact had been made that if there was a brawl it would be one-in, all-in. The code word for the calling of arms was 'Bondi Beach'.

Australia kicked off, England caught the ball and then Macdougall kicked everything in sight, but in particular England prop Barry Nelmes' head. The rest of the Australian pack joined in, throwing punches every which way. Peace was momentarily restored, but as the two packs of forwards ran to the first lineout of the match the other England prop, Mike Burton, sidled up to Macdougall and told him he had better be ready for the get-square. Macdougall yelled out to his teammates: 'Right boys, Burton's got the biff on.'

The lineout turned into an all-in brawl, with every Australian forward taking on his opponent. Despite Australia appearing to start the brawl, Queensland referee Bob Burnett, struggling to keep control, singled out Burton and penalised England. Burton was in a state of disbelief and, losing his senses, almost took off Wallaby winger Doug Osborne's head with a wild elbow charge from the kick off. Burton suffered the indignity of being the first England Test player to be sent off by a referee.

Up in the main grandstand a seething McLaughlin, surrounded by tut-tutting English Rugby Football Union officials, wrote a note that he had delivered just before half-time to Brockhoff. It said: 'You have brought the game into disrepute. Call your dogs off. Otherwise you will be sacked.' Brockhoff read the note. He passed the message on to the players during the break, and five-eighth Ken Wright just laughed. 'Don't worry, Brock. This is a tea party.'

Although the mayhem inspired England and saw it take the lead before the break, Australia eventually won all the fights and all of the football to record its first Ballymore triumph. But the ARU wasn't happy. Nor was Burton, who was given a lift by Brockhoff to the after-match function. The conversation in the car was terse.

But the Wallabies and Brockhoff found no peace by at last becoming the aggressors. The British media had the scandal it had been waiting for. The *London Times* said that Australia's tactics were 'a disgrace to the Rugby Union game and the sort of thing which, if allowed to continue, will encourage parents to point their children towards different games . . . Unions have to ensure that their international teams are not coached and encouraged to behave like animals.'

For some months the tour at the end of that year to the United Kingdom and Ireland was in serious doubt because the Home Unions were concerned about Australia's rough play. McLaughlin was pressured by British officials to get rid of Brockhoff, especially after the Fleet Street press relentlessly reported his instructions to 'kick everything that moves above grass level'. *The Guardian* described Brockhoff as an 'undesirable element'. Leading English officials met in London, and in a press statement said that 'if the illegally aggressive approach were maintained in England we should not want them there . . . Fortunately, the Australian authorities seem as disturbed as us and assured us that they would take steps to put their house in order.' The House of Brockhoff was under serious threat.

It was only after McLaughlin again kowtowed to England and promised the hosts there would be no repeat of on-field violence that the tour went ahead. McLaughlin also warned all potential Wallabies that anyone involved in foul play would not be selected in the touring party.

The ARU brought in Ross Turnbull, a cunning political operator, to be tour manager but most importantly to put the brakes on Brockhoff. Turnbull, who during his football career went by the nickname Mad Dog—a tag he hated—was made the tour spokesman and Brockhoff was barred from talking to the press. Being a master of self-promotion, Turnbull took to the role with relish. He charmed the British media, bombarding it with information, later confirming that his prime task was to restrict Brockhoff from speaking so that relations with the Rugby Football Union were not jeopardised.

Brockhoff abhorred Turnbull's power, and his relentless use of it. He clashed with Turnbull on numerous occasions, including when he wanted the new captain Geoff Shaw on the selection panel, a move immediately opposed by Turnbull. Brockhoff won that battle by telephoning McLoughlin, and threatening to resign if Shaw was left out of selection meetings. Shaw was put on the panel, but from then on Turnbull and Brockhoff hardly spoke to one another.

The players were similarly unenthused with Turnbull's autocratic approach and obsession with discipline. Many admitted to being frightened of him and worried that if they did anything wrong, however minor, they would be immediately sent home. According to Stan Pilecki, Turnbull was 'a real schoolmaster type, who imposed rules for everything, no smoking, no gambling etc. Treated everyone like young kids . . .'

Before the team left for England British referees were brought across to explain the dangers of rucking, while the players had to undertake psychological tests aimed at assessing their reactions to stressful situations. Not surprisingly the Wallabies lost their edge on that tour. The players were inhibited because they were unable to be aggressive and they won only one of the four Tests.

But there was at least one schoolboy moment on the Tour as the team flew from Liverpool to Dublin. Shortly after take-off a voice screamed over the cabin intercom, 'Mayday! Mayday! We've lost power. I think we'll hit the flats at the end of the runway.' The passengers, including the Wallabies, were shocked, to say the least. 'Adopt the crash position,' the voice continued. 'Head between your legs and kiss your arse goodbye. Especially you, Ross.' Turnbull sentenced Macdougall to three days as duty boy.

Brockhoff on a leash was also an hilarious commodity, especially when the team went to Buckingham Palace to meet the Queen. It was 13 November, two days after Governor-General John Kerr had sacked Prime Minister Gough Whitlam. Brockhoff introduced himself to the Queen with the words: 'I met you, ma'am, in 1953. You were wearing a big hat in Martin Place.' Continuing, he said: 'Ma'am. When the Governor-General sacked Gough Whitlam, I understand he rang you in the middle of the night. Did you know what the Governor-General said to you?'

Her Majesty courteously replied, 'No!'

'The Governor-General said, "Whitlam out. Fraser in." And you know what you said then?'

'No, what did I say?'

'Don't ring me in the middle of the night with the cricket scores.'

5
GROWING UP

It had an innocent enough front cover, a group of players seemingly practising the rumba. Its title, *The Game they Play in Heaven*, was hardly going to incite a riot. However, Wallaby prop Steve Finnane's biography was certainly true to its sub-title, *Australian Rugby from the Inside*. With the help of fellow Wallaby and journalist Mike Jenkinson, Finnane had provided an in-depth look at Australia's most volatile rugby years. He admitted he was the 'Phantom Puncher' and listed those illustrious opponents he had belted, including Welsh prop Graham Price, whose jaw he broke in the 1978 Sydney Test. 'After five minutes, Graham Price bored in at a scrum and a fight followed as the two packs separated,' he wrote. 'I stepped into him and threw a short right. The impact sent my name hurtling around the world with a label attached that said—often in 72-point type—"thug".'

Finnane, who became a Sydney barrister, took delight in his playing days in being an enforcer. Boasting a Zapata-esque moustache, large, swarthy and always keen to hold his ground, he was known as the Gunslinger. He knew how to strike fear in opposing front-rowers through standover tactics and the judicious use of the short arm jolt. As the dust cover of his own book confirmed, Finnane was a 'feared and sometimes reviled opponent' for overseas players. He also had his enemies in the local ranks.

Finnane was a perfect exponent of Brockhoff's step forward approach, making his mark playing for Sydney against England at the Sydney Sports Ground. 'A tall English forward lay stretched across the turf at my feet, the third one to end up that way in not more than ten minutes—three big names and me a novice in international terms. [His victims included Bill Beaumont and Mike Burton.] I looked down at my hands and thought: "Good God, I'm in the wrong sport!" It was an amazing moment and out of it the press created the legend of the Phantom Puncher. It also led to my selection in the Australian Test team.'

Finnane's first Test was typically rough and tough, but his ankle eventually gave out so he had to wait another three seasons to make his international mark. He did, however, make it patently clear he didn't like the tourists, describing the England captain Tony Neary as 'one of those condescending, upper crust solicitors who abound in English sport'.

This was a strange time for Australian rugby. In 1976 Fiji staged a walk-off in the middle of the Sydney Test believing that Australia was playing as dirty as them and that they were being unfairly targeted by the referee, especially when their prop Jo Savau was sent off for kicking halfback Rod Hauser. They eventually returned to the field under threat of forfeiting the game and being kicked out of international rugby. For Wallaby reserve Mick Ellem it was the most surreal of moments because as he ran onto the field to replace Geoff Shaw the Fijians were marching off. 'I couldn't believe it,' Ellem said. 'I got onto the field and I wondered, "What's going on here?" because the Fijians were storming off. I thought my Test appearance was over after just a few minutes, especially as the referee [Warwick Cooney] was running around saying, "What do I do?"' This was Ellem's only Test appearance.

This was also the time when a high-ranking ARU official on one tour discovered a leading player and a member of management in bed together. Even decades on this remains one of the tightest kept secrets in the Wallaby annals, and is held as tightly as the story of an All Black coach who decades ago had to be bailed out of a French jail by several of the players after he was arrested for fraternising with local youths.

On the field, however, the Wallabies stuck to a more familiar pattern of belligerency. In 1978 Brockhoff had been replaced by New South Wales Country coach Daryl Haberecht, a master innovator who was the genius behind numerous brilliant offensive moves including the up-the-jumper tactic, which in 1975 saw New South Wales Country beat Sydney. Seeming to have come straight from a Barnum and Bailey show ring, one of Australian rugby's most famous tries had the players forming themselves into a V-shape with their backs to the opposition. After taking the tap they made out as if they had hidden the ball under their jersey, creating complete confusion. As the opposition attempted to find the ball carrier Greg Cornelsen, who actually had the ball, took off along the sideline, offloading it to Brian Mansfield, who went over for the try. Adding to the moment was the television commentary of Norman May and Trevor Allan, who both broke down in fits of laughter.

But those dim, grim monsters of the game, the International Rugby Board, found nothing funny in the Haberecht innovation and banned it, as they did with another of his innovations in the late 1980s when New South Wales Country winger Dwayne Vignes ran with the ball in hand over the top of a touring British Lions scrum. If the moment when Vignes leapt up and bounded over the opponents before losing his footing between two of the back-rowers wasn't hilarious enough, adding to the farce was the loud tut-tutting from the fossils in the British media, who immediately demanded the move be banned. Which is exactly what the IRB did, taking all colour out of the game.

Haberecht inventiveness, and a classic Country win over England in 1975, catapulted him from being an obscure bush coach to a Test coaching candidate and the ideal successor for the too hard to handle Brockhoff. Haberecht gave the Wallabies a varied game plan, but one that still revolved around a menacing pack. Forward might was required as the world champion Welsh would be touring in his first season as coach.

Wales knew what to expect from the Wallabies and their new, keen to impress coach, so they opted to match the Wallabies in the punching and kicking department during an unsavoury few weeks. But it was the sight of Welsh prop Graham Price walking off the ground with blood pouring out of his mouth and holding his broken jaw in the opening minutes of the Sydney Test that ensured that the Wallabies were again marked as the low dogs of the international game.

In the first Test in Brisbane the Welsh had attempted to upset their Australian opponents by using their boots and fists. Finnane, in particular, had been targeted and was repeatedly kicked by the Welsh second-rowers. The Wallaby forwards realised that if they did not stand up to the blatant thuggery of the Welsh in the next Tests they would be kicked and punched out of the matches. So they made a pact, and it was in the second Test in Sydney that Finnane took the first big shot by belting Price after the celebrated Lions prop had attempted to bore in on him.

That night the Welsh manager Clive Rowlands went on the attack, having earlier complained about the referees and in particular Queenslander Bob Burnett. Rowlands questioned Burnett's partiality and his reason for wearing Queensland socks. The Welsh even threatened to go home if Burnett was appointed: 'We do not want him at any cost and if I live to be 100 I shall not alter my opinions about his refereeing.' The ARU did stand up to Rowlands and Burnett was appointed to the first Test.

To divert attention away from his team's poor tour results, Rowlands, a master whinger, blamed the Australians for everything. He conveniently ignored what his own team had done. He also insinuated that the Australians should look after the Welsh because they were helping them out of their financial difficulties by travelling to Australia.

Rowlands used the after-match function following the second Test to abuse the Wallabies, in particular Finnane, who he was careful not to name. 'One of my players is in a hospital bed tonight with a double fracture of the jaw. If we are rugby people and condone thuggery, then I don't want any part of it.'

This was the moment when the ARU should have publicly defended its team. It didn't. Instead, McLaughlin got up on two occasions to back Rowlands. Finnane wasn't the only Wallaby to be 'sickened and ashamed to be associated with the ARU'. Later, McLaughlin backtracked somewhat but the damage had been done.

Still, there were a couple of moments of amusement during the Test series. The first involved a parsimonious Wallaby forward who found a five-cent piece on the ground and held onto it for the entire match because he didn't have pockets in his shorts. The other followed Price's decking. An Australian back suddenly ran into the melee, stopped abruptly about ten metres from the action and exclaimed: 'Shit, I left my keys in the door.'

•

Shortly after the Welsh Tests, the Wallabies left for New Zealand to encounter different dramas. But if one squad was up to this enormous task it was the 1978 Wallabies—a team of remarkable personalities. Never in its history did the Wallabies comprise such a great collection of characters at the one time, especially the four Queensland jesters Mark Loane, Tony Shaw, Stan Pilecki and Chris 'Buddha' Handy.

Loane was the intellect. Like his 1960s Wallabies counterpart Peter Crittle, Loane does not believe in barriers. For this scholar life is an adventure, a constant journey. He pushes the boundaries, from climbing in Nepal to exploring the Antarctic. The arts enthral him, as do architecture and countless other subjects. As someone who devoured encyclopaedias as a child Loane was destined to provide the most intriguing, even if at times somewhat mind-bending, rugby theories.

When he was named one of the ARU's elder statesmen in 2008, Loane explained the fundamental problem with rugby was that the defensive line was so close to the advantage line. 'The game has evolved like Julius Caesar's thirteenth legion. They had a wonderful win–loss record—undefeated in fifty scraps or so—because they were very tight on the flanks and forced opponents into the middle where all the good fighters were. It was the "horns of the bull" theory. We had good success in Australian rugby when we started running big forwards at angles to cope with that . . . the Willie Ofahengaue strategy. But defenders learned to counter that too. Players don't tire and leave holes any more. That is not to say the game is better or worse. Just different.'

He was so proud to have the No. 8 on his back, telling writer Peter Jenkins that 'to me No. 8 was the supreme position on the field . . . You had seven players in front of you, seven behind. It was a role that combined anticipation—predicting things before they occurred—while also having a mathematical element. You had to learn the lines of running to the breakdown, the lines for support and for cover defence. That had intellectual appeal. And on top of that was the athleticism of the contest. The strength, speed and stamina.'

While Loane was not your ordinary back-rower he remains one of Australia's finest No. 8s, matching fearless play with peerless ball-in-hand skills. He hurtled and hustled, and in tandem with Shaw was a big game hunter. After football, he became one of Australia's most respected ophthalmic surgeons.

Known as 'Crazy Eyes' for his intense, wild glare, Shaw was the extrovert. On the field, he was fearless. Off the field he was a friend of all and relished the fun times. He was a true leader who led from the front and was the master of the inspirational team speech, but also knew how to be the ratbag aggressor. Stan Pilecki maintains that Queensland coach Bob Templeton told Shaw to king hit him in the first ruck of every match they played in, even though they were teammates, to get Pilecki 'fired up' for the rest of the game.

Stanislaus Pilecki was a throwback to another age. Hailing from Augustdorf, Germany, he was known as 'the Pole' because of his Polish heritage and was the subject of probably more stories than any other Wallaby. Although nowhere near Australia's best, the man with the gargantuan moustache was a more than reputable prop, but where he surpassed all was in the endless hilarious situations in which he found himself.

The working man's player infuriated his colleagues by being the 'worst roommate in Wallaby history'. His roommates spent most of their nights awake as this insomniac either wandered around the room or lit up one smoke after another. If the lack of sleep didn't get them, the stifling cigarette smoke did. Roger Gould once described Pilecki's snoring as resembling Mt Vesuvius, before deciding to spend the night attempting to sleep in the bath tub.

'Stan the Man' was the team comedian although teammates sometimes didn't know whether he was serious or just playing the fool, such as the night Bob Templeton used rhyming slang to Pilecki after being bored by a drunk New Zealander.

'Stan, this man's Oliver Twist.'

'Hello, Mr Twist, my name's Stan Pilecki,' said Stan, offering his hand.

For this one-time oil rigger and labourer football training was a sham, match preparation a waste of time and coaching psyche up endless hot air. As his biographer Max Howell wrote: 'Pilecki had a different advocacy: piss, physios and parties.' He was his own man, as Templeton discovered during one tour after Loane, who had torn his adductor, had to be replaced by Pilecki. Half asleep on the bench, he was told by a frazzled Templeton to get on the field.

'I'll be on when I'm ready,' Pilecki replied.

'Well, at least bloody well warm up,' scowled Templeton.

'What do you think this is?' Pilecki replied, before taking a final draw on his cigarette. He always said his most difficult moments as a rugby player were attempting to stub out a cigarette on a muddy field. It proved near impossible. He was also one of the few players to stand up to Alan Jones during his turbulent time as Australian coach. And he stood his ground with Australian selectors, including Sydneysider Jim Zemancheff, who infuriated Pilecki, a proud Queenslander, with the repeated claim that New South Wales had the best 'tight five' in the world. On finding Zemancheff after one game Pilecki enquired, 'You Zemancheff?'

'Yes, I am.'

'Well, you can stick your tight five right up your arse.'

Like Pilecki, the vibrant, effervescent front-rower Chris 'Buddha' Handy (so named when sighted during an Australian Colts tour of Japan cross-legged on the floor playing cards) was the life of the touring party. Always understanding the importance of publicity—good or bad—he became a media identity and a legendary mine host of several Brisbane hotels. One of rugby's most famous photographs was of Handy standing at a lineout in the middle of a Wallaby–All Black Test match with his face smeared in blood. With this intersection of rich red rivers he looked like the ultimate warrior, the ultimate enforcer. Instead, he had actually just been hit with a right-handed punch from All Black forward Andy Haden. 'The copious bleeding that followed made me appear to be some sort of legendary tough guy which was not just incorrect but manifestly wrong. The tough ones do the punching—they don't get belted,' Handy later wrote. 'I might have won something of a reputation as a hitman, but the real story was that I couldn't fight. I got belted all the time. I was the beltee, not the belter.'

Like Pilecki, Handy also struggled to sleep, prompting an unusual preparation for his first Test appearance. On the night before the Test, Handy was pacing the Auckland hotel corridors when he was suddenly grabbed by the Sydney *Daily Telegraph*'s rugby writer Jim Woodward and fellow scribe Ray Kershler. 'So began my long-term association with the press,' Handy later reminisced. 'They just said "Come with us" and the three of us headed into their room. There we demolished what was left of a bottle of Kahlua and milk (the old Brown Cow) which was Jim's favourite drink. Some two hours later I returned to my room, to sleep a very deep and peaceful sleep.'

With so many ratbags in this Wallaby party, it comes as no surprise that during the tour one well-known rugby writer recalls heading to the hotel foyer to see several of the players standing at the bar ordering drinks. One of them was naked. The nude player beckoned the journalist over, took off the scribe's glasses, rubbed them between his buttocks and placed them back on the journalist's head. The player and the scribe then embraced, and spent the next few hours matching one another round for round. Two days later he was a star in Australia's 30–16 Auckland triumph.

But it was another Wallaby forward who became the star of that 1978 tour, picking the perfect day to ensure his name will be forever remembered. As the Wallabies headed to Auckland for the final Test of the series, few gave them hope of ending the All Black domination. Although having come close in the first Test, the second Test was a one-way All Black affair with the same anticipated for the Third Test at Eden Park especially as all of New Zealand thought the Wallabies were in disarray—a reasonable assumption considering their coach was in hospital at the time following a heart attack. So ill was Haberecht that he did not leave hospital until several weeks after the tour, forcing the Wallabies players and manager Ross Turnbull to take over proceedings. Banding even more tightly together, they made a pact they would win the final four matches.

Throughout the tour Haberecht had been deliberately evasive to the New Zealand media, one of his favoured sayings to get the press off his tail being: 'The Test will be played on a regulation-sized pitch with a regulation-size ball.' The Wallabies also opted for the Hard Luck Hal approach, staying in tough suburbs in out-of-the-way hotels.

The only allowance made to the outside world was when Turnbull accepted an offer from former All Black coach John Stewart to conduct one training session, described by the team as the most innovative they had experienced. Apart from that one session the players organised all the other training sessions, ignored talk of bringing in another coach and closed ranks. Turnbull took it upon himself to give them the rousing pre-match spiel, and although he and Brockhoff were hardly friends he obviously took some notes from their testy period together.

According to Handy, Turnbull organised a meeting on the morning of the third Test, telling the players he had been in contact with the ARU which had stressed that Australia's rugby future revolved entirely on that one game. It would determine whether Australia went forward into the 1980s or remained the strugglers of the 1970s. Always one for hyperbole, Turnbull then sent the backs out of the room and told the Test forwards: 'Look, these Phantom-comic swappers and Mintie-eaters, these blonde-headed flyweights [the backs] are one thing, and we will need them after the hard work's done. But the real stuff's got to be done right here by you blokes.'

The message obviously worked for wild haired and bearded Greg Cornelsen, the Wallaby No. 8 that day, because the kid from the New South Wales country town of Jeogla almost single-handedly transformed the Test by scoring four tries. Being in the right place at the right time, Cornelsen's first try came through an All Black lineout mess up that saw the ball bounce off the goal posts right into his arms. The second resulted from him charging into a ruck and the ball suddenly appearing in front of him. The third followed an All Black knock-on, and the fourth came from textbook back-up work. For a man who never scored a Test try before or after, Eden Park offered Cornelsen the ultimate abundance of riches, including the highest number of tries scored against New Zealand in a single Test. He also enabled the Wallabies to enjoy one of their biggest wins—30–16—over the All Blacks.

Despite this extraordinary solo feat, it was in the following season that the Wallabies really made an impact on the Australian sporting psyche, and the Bledisloe Cup meant something to more than just the rugby anoraks.

•

Due to Haberecht's ill health, Dave Brockhoff was back as Australian coach in 1979 and he was ready to stir everything up. The All Blacks had agreed to a one-off Test to be played in Sydney to again help the ARU through its financial difficulties. However, it was not until the morning of the match that the players were aware that the Bledisloe Cup would be part of the bargain when they heard the All Blacks had brought it with them from Auckland.

The cup remained an unknown bit of silverware in Australia and for good reason, considering the Wallabies had not had their hands on it since 1949. So when they won it back in Sydney thirty years on by beating the All Blacks 12–6, Brockhoff wasn't going to waste the opportunity. He leapt the fence, embraced his warriors and thrust the cup into their hands before joining them in a memorable lap of honour around the Sydney Cricket Ground. This was a side of the Wallabies the rugby public had never seen before. The wildly exuberant Wallabies were suddenly celebrating as if they had won the Opera House lottery. The crowd responded, creating easily one of the most memorable scenes of Australian rugby history. As New Zealand rugby journalist Don Cameron wrote: 'It will remain one of the vivid memories of sport—15 jubilant Wallabies hoisting the ungainly Bledisloe Cup aloft in triumph.'

The Bledisloe Cup was displayed to the crowd as if it were the America's Cup, the FA Cup and the British Open mug all rolled into one. Suddenly it meant something. And all this came just a few years after former All Black skipper Wilson Whinerey said: 'No one ever bothered about the Bledisloe Cup in my day. It just sat in someone's office.'

As the Wallabies ran around the ground, the All Blacks watched despairingly from the SCG visitor's dressing room. Forward Andy Haden, who had given his All Black jersey to Brockhoff, beckoned his teammates to the window, pointed at the overjoyed Wallabies and made a pact that this would never happen again. Suddenly the All Blacks began to respect that rag-tag mob from the other side of 'the ditch'.

6
RODIN MEETS CAMPO

Bob Dwyer was a sometimes highly emotional showman and opportunist. You always knew exactly what mood he was in: he could be vibrant, zealous, antagonistic, hilarious and often the centre of attention. He could be very loud, especially when haranguing referees from the sideline. His blunt, cutting comments often reverberated across Sydney's Coogee Oval, where he underwent his extensive football education at the Randwick Running Rugby University, finishing with first-class honours. But he could also be quietly engrossed in analysis of the intricacies of a game that so fascinated him. And he could really throw out a handy quote or two.

At the start of his Wallaby coaching days in 1982 he told the *Sydney Morning Herald*: 'I see rugby as an extension of the arts. The spirit of the William Tell Overture in the power of the scrums, the beauty of a Rodin sculpture in the sweeping movement of the backline.' Never a truer statement has been made.

Dwyer's analysis of the game and its players was certainly perceptive. After the Wallabies slackened off once again on tour he observed: 'It must have something to do with Australians. If you don't get up them like a rat up a drainpipe they fall into bad habits.' Boiling down the game to its basics, he once said: 'Good big blokes are better than good little blokes. Then again, good little blokes are better than dud big blokes. And dud little blokes should play something other than rugby.'

Unlike some Wallaby coaches before and after, who were often swayed by blind favouritism or were just dreadful selectors, Dwyer had a great eye for talent and was a courageous selector. He could pick a great player, and was prepared to gamble on inexperience. But above all, Dwyer will always be remembered for taking the three Ellas—Mark, Glen and Gary—to the next level.

A Sydney club football trooper for many years, Dwyer played through the grades at Randwick as a reliable but hardly striking flanker. He did the job, but was never looked upon as anything more than a clubman although his many years at the Galloping Greens instilled in him the importance of a strong club culture and player camaraderie. It also enabled Dwyer to meet an important figure who helped define his future and gave him the blueprint to become a highly successful coach: Cyril Towers, the Wallaby star of the 1930s.

Towers was the seer of running rugby, and when he wandered down to his old club during the 1960s he wasn't too impressed with what he saw. Randwick had turned off the Towers/Meagher flatline attack philosophy, and had lost its way by playing far deeper in attack. Dwyer thought that Towers' hectoring about the smartest form of backline play was the 'ramblings of an old footballer'. Arguments between the pair were common, with Towers at one time exclaiming that he would never be involved in a team that had Dwyer in its line-up.

Dwyer eventually saw the light, and became the great advocate of running rugby. All he needed were wizards to make it work, and they came in the form of three Aboriginal kids from the rough Sydney suburb of La Perouse—the remarkable Ella brothers. It was the start of a vibrant, memorable but at times flighty partnership.

For several years the Ella brothers had been the phenomenon of Sydney schoolboy football, turning their unfashionable, near-unknown Matraville High School into the best side around. The feats of twin brothers Mark and Glen on the all-conquering 1977

Australian Schoolboys tour had transformed them into the great hopes of the game. They just needed a club side to make the next step to true representative honours.

Towers had seen the boys at Matraville, and suggested that Dwyer track them down. Dwyer was there the day Matraville, 'a mob of skinny, little ragamuffins', humiliated the most famous rugby school in Australia—St Joseph's College, for decades the breeding ground for Wallabies. St Joseph's coach and former Wallaby fullback Brother Terry Curley was so exasperated that he yelled out to one of his players to 'tackle the black boy'.

The player screamed back: 'Which one? There's hundreds of them.'

Dwyer had seen enough. Together with Randwick Test forward Gary Pearse, he drove to the Ellas' home in the hope of convincing the brothers they should play for their local grade club. They knew when they arrived at the right house—there were ten pairs of football boots sprawled across the front verandah.

While the ever-nonchalant Glen remained in his room reading a book Dwyer and Pearse met with Mark and Gary in the dining room, putting the case for playing grade instead of colts. When one of the brothers remarked 'I couldn't give a damn whether I play colts or grades', their mother chipped in, 'Don't you use that language in this house, thank you!'

'Glen, we're playing grade,' they finally yelled out to their brother.

'Yeah, okay,' came the reply, as he kept reading. The deal had been done in the typical Ella style, with no fuss.

•

While Dwyer was courting the Ellas, the Wallabies under Templeton continued to meander. They won some games and struggled in others. One triumph was even tainted by the suggestion that their opponents had been poisoned when the 1980 All Blacks claimed they lost in Sydney because a local gambler had organised for them to be served contaminated food on the eve of the third Test. The players had become so violently ill before the game that they required injections to play. Yet the joke was clearly on the All Blacks because the contaminated food may have actually come from their shores: a batch of Bluff oysters that had been flown in from Invercargill by a fan and served to the players at a function hosted by the New Zealand High Commission. The Bluff oysters, which in decades past had made touring Wallabies bilious, had now brought down the All Blacks by 16 points.

The Wallabies' success, however, may have had more to do with an injection of youthful talent—in particular Mark Ella, who immediately made clear he was tuned to a different rhythm. Shortly after Templeton brought Ella into the Wallaby camp he asked the new Test five-eighth: 'So, how do you want to play the game?'

'I dunno. You're the bloody coach,' was Ella's reply.

The coach did give Ella his head, and allowed him to be adventurous. But when the pressure was applied too often Templeton went for safety-first tactics that sometimes stifled the Wallabies. Training sessions had also become monotonous, with players tiring of Templeton's 'Six P principle': 'Proper Preparation Prevents Piss-Poor Performance'.

The principle did not have the desired effect, and the disappointment of winning only one of the four Tests on the 1981–82 Wallabies tour of Britain prompted media reports of supposed rifts between Queensland and New South Wales players and complaints that they had become a boring, negative side. Templeton, accused of turning the squad 'into a team of Queenslanders', was dumped as coach in 1982 for Dwyer.

It was a big call, considering that Dwyer had no high-level coaching experience and his only claim to fame was three successive premierships with Randwick. The Queensland faction was unimpressed, believing that Templeton didn't have a chance with the vote weighted in favour of New South Wales (New South Wales had five votes to Queensland's two). They also believed that Templeton had been undermined by a New South Wales smear campaign that pushed the claim he had shown favouritism towards several Queensland players, split the team and caused animosity because of his coaching and training methods. And it didn't take long for the Queenslanders to exact revenge. The Queensland Rugby Union and its fawning Brisbane press pack couldn't let go of their small town mentality.

This anger had been festering for decades. Queensland never stopped believing that New South Wales treated it badly, especially in the early 1960s when it cancelled an interstate game supposedly because the northerners were too weak. The 1962 Australian Test team, which was dominated by New South Wales players, discovered how thin skinned some Queensland officials were when in the lead up to the Brisbane Test they were barred from using several local training grounds and were locked out of their Exhibition Grounds dressing room until an hour before kick off.

Years on 'Boo a Blue' became one of Queensland Rugby Union's most famous advertising slogans, and interstate matches turned into near war. Not even the New South Wales Rugby Union chairman John Howard's complaint that the slogan was 'dreadful' and 'insulting' could calm the situation. Queensland instead turned the complaint around to suggest New South Wales 'just couldn't take it'. To this day, any perceived criticism from the Sydney press is used as a way to fire up Queenslanders. And the sledging between the two states in the days leading up to an interstate match—which began in the 1970s when Queensland coach Jim Kenny said of his New South Wales counterpart Dave Brockhoff that 'he couldn't coach a choko vine over a dunny door'—still continues.

As Queensland second-rower Rod McCall explains: 'You always knew that in New South Wales sides there were a lot of big-noting, pea-hearted impostors.' Queensland forward Chris Handy turned New South Wales baiting into an art form with quotes such as: 'The only thing New South Wales can beat Queensland at is in the number of former chief executive officers, presidents, coaches and bankruptcies.' To which New South Wales captain Simon Poidevin replied: 'It was great touring with Queenslanders because it always ensured there were some terrific banjo players in the team.'

A lot of the Queensland moan was complete mumbo jumbo, but its teams genuinely believed the off-field gibberish and often rose to the occasion against their prime enemy, their only enemy, New South Wales. Even in the 1990s, Reds captain Peter Slattery proclaimed after one interstate triumph: 'It's great to be an Australian, but it's even greater to be a Queenslander.'

Queensland Rugby Union knew it could get away with such behaviour as it was actively supported by the local media. For decades the *Courier Mail*'s rugby writer Frank O'Callaghan pushed the Queensland cause, often to ridiculous lengths. He was the ultimate Queensland fan with a typewriter, believing that there was never a bad game of rugby. There were just variations of 'good rugby'. As one Sydney reporter remarked about O'Callaghan: 'A one-legged midget could be selected for the Wallabies. But he would still start his Test selection story with: "Only three Queenslanders have been picked in the Wallabies to play . . ."'

Even overseas journalists were astounded by O'Callaghan's blind faith in Queensland. In New Zealander Don Cameron's book on the 1980 All Black tour of Australia, *Rugby Triumphant,* he recalls the opening minutes of the Queensland–New Zealand match at Ballymore. 'Suddenly [Roger] Gould from about his own ten-metre line hoisted a monstrous up-and-under into All Black territory. One of the press, Frank O'Callaghan, a kindly man if a mite partial towards Queensland, jolted us awake with the bellow, "Let's see some blood on the ball" as Gould's kick boomed down into All Black territory. We were sharply awake and so were Queensland.'

Dwyer knew that he would receive no favours from the Queensland media. One of O'Callaghan's first reports about the new coach was headlined: 'Bob Who?'

•

There was no initiation period. Dwyer's first Test as coach in July 1982 exposed all of the weeping wounds. In the lead up Dwyer led with his chin, explaining that he believed the way to end Australia's rugby dramas was to return to a 'natural running game', 'fifteen-man rugby'. He stressed that the team would be entertainers, but was careful to admit that the foundation of this new game was a strong pack. As a concession to Templeton's conservative ways, Dwyer acknowledged that you can't entertain or be adventurous if the forwards aren't able to secure consistent possession.

Still, Dwyer wanted to make an immediate stand, selecting New South Wales' Mark and Glen Ella over Queenslanders Paul McLean and Roger Gould for his first Test in Brisbane against Scotland. The selections were brave but naive, especially as the Wallabies were going into the game without a recognised goal kicker and centre Michael Hawker was put on the wing. The entire Queensland pack was also selected, which seemed a cop-out.

As expected, the Queensland media lampooned the Ella selections. That was always going to happen, especially as O'Callaghan was obsessed with Paul McLean. One Sydney journalist was known to mutter how 'Frank's typewriter is always at the repair shop, as the M, C, L, E, A and N keys have been worn out through over-use.' Some years earlier O'Callaghan had described all those in the Sydney press who had preferred other players to McLean at five-eighth for a 1979 Test as 'heretics'.

However, even the Sydney media was a little hesitant about Dwyer's selections, with the *Sydney Morning Herald*'s Jim Webster writing: 'Dwyer was given the team he wanted to play Randwick style Rugby . . . it was a monstrous gamble, for Australia have never before had a team so openly picked for just one purpose.'

The barrage of complaints from the parochial Queenslanders before the game affected both Ellas. An embarrassed Glen told Dwyer he didn't want to be fullback. Mark was also unsettled after Wallaby players relaxing in the main bar at their hotel were confronted by locals, who asked: 'Why are those black fellers in the team?' This disdain for the Ellas was amplified even more when Mark and Glen ran onto the field. In a moment of disgraceful racism, the crowd booed the pair. Glen was booed again in the opening minutes when he missed a pass from his brother, prompting the chant of 'We want Gould. We want Gould.' Glen's confidence was further undermined when he muffed another try-scoring opportunity and the crowd again turned ugly on that Brisbane winter afternoon.

And it could have been even worse as Dwyer wanted to play the third Ella brother—Gary—in this Test but the coach was outvoted by the other two Test selectors—Templeton and John Bain. In the end Scotland won 12–7.

Up in the grandstand, Dwyer was discovering Queensland diplomacy Banana Republic style. One spectator approached him and said he was a traitor to his country, while Queensland ARU delegate Lyn Crowley told Dwyer he would never forgive him for his selections. True to his word, Crowley played an important role in Dwyer losing his position two years later. Queensland's power base was somewhat fragmented, but those who conspired in the Ballymore corridors knew all about revenge.

For the second Test and with the connivance of Bain and Templeton both Ellas were dropped to make way for McLean and Gould. Dwyer's reputation was hardly helped when McLean contributed a record 21 points and Gould scored two tries in a massive 33–9 triumph. The forward pack, which was basically the Queensland pack, had also put Dwyer in his place, telling him it would run proceedings at training. 'I had very little to do with it [the Sydney win]. They [the players] did it all,' Dwyer admitted later.

While relieved with the win, Dwyer's afternoon was dulled by whispers of a proposed mass exodus of players for the upcoming Wallaby tour of New Zealand. Instead of the expected outrageous celebrations in the Sydney Cricket Ground dressing rooms, there were huddled meetings of players. Dwyer had been aware of the rumblings for about forty-eight hours, but that night ten leading players delivered a statement to the selectors explaining that for personal and business reasons they would be unavailable for the New Zealand tour. Nine of the ten were from Queensland, and included Paul McLean, Brendan Moon, Mark Loane and Tony Shaw.

Their statement read in part: 'This difficult decision has been forced upon us because of the financial burden we have incurred by not receiving any significant income during the periods we have represented Australia . . .' However, Dwyer believed their decision may have also been part of a concerted Queensland protest at the overthrow of Templeton. To this day the players maintain that was not the case.

The amateur era was coming to an end and this mass withdrawal was also a blunt message to the ARU and its officials that they had to find a way around this problem. The 'shamateur era' was about to begin where officials 'turned a blind eye' to the many Wallabies who were able to stay in the game primarily because they were paid when playing for overseas clubs or were involved in hush-hush sponsorship deals.

Dwyer's problem was more immediate, however, how to rebuild a house whose foundations were suddenly under threat of collapse. With almost half a Test team unavailable for the mid-1982 New Zealand tour, Dwyer and his co-selectors had to ring around on the day the squad was being chosen to find out who exactly was available. For some positions, especially in the front row, there were virtually no candidates. Dwyer described the situation as 'farcical', especially when he had to ask a coach if one player had ever been seen on the tight-head side of the scrum. The coach lied and said yes, he would make a great Test prop, but eventually relented, telling Dwyer that he had never played as a tight head.

Eventually enough names were cobbled together, including twelve new Wallaby caps. But who would be captain? Mark Ella was almost the last man standing, so Dwyer made the bold move that if he was going to instil his new style on to the national team he needed a leader who knew exactly what he was talking about. Ella, at twenty-three, became the first Aboriginal to captain his country. As great an accolade as it was, it was something that Ella was uneasy about. His first reaction when told by a journalist that he was the tour skipper was 'Why me?'

His brothers Glen and Gary, who had both been selected, weren't going to make it easy for him. At the first training session in New

Zealand Ella decided to run the backs training while Dwyer involved himself with the forwards. Glen and Gary immediately refused to follow Mark's instructions. They were sick and tired of Mark telling them what to do, and believed that most of the moves Mark organised revolved around making him look good while they were being used as draught horses. The brothers eventually came to an agreement.

And the phenomenon of that tour? One of the real unknowns of the group.

•

He was and always will be the master of speaking before thinking. He unconsciously antagonised many with his abrasive, politically incorrect manner. He created divisions. He endlessly exasperated his peers. He often needed to be molly-coddled like an infant. He was opinionated and at times a complete shit stirrer. But underneath it all, you could not help but like him. And you could never underestimate or over-promote his football skills.

David Campese remains the enigma of the Australian game. In 1991 his colleagues laughed themselves hoarse when they read the first paragraph of a ghost-written autobiography, *On a Wing and a Prayer*: 'In that short, abbreviated hour between the fading of the winter's afternoon sun and the onset of that bitter night cold which persuades me that I could never live in the British Isles, I turned over in bed at the Surrey hotel where I was staying to take a telephone call which was to offer me the chance to change my life forever.' Those who knew Campese understood that if he had actually written the opening lines they would have read: 'Geez, it's cold here. Geez, it's dark. Who could live here? And who's this on the phone?'

When Dwyer found himself in a hole, the precocious, unpredictable, often-infuriating Campese provided an unexpected helping hand. Hailing from Queanbeyan, rugby league territory, the teenager had hardly played the amateur game. But tired of being given a tough time for missing tackles in league, he decided to try the other rugby code and immediately revelled in the local competition, where he was selected in the Australian under 21 team.

His trademark manoeuvre was on show almost immediately: a marching quick step, a flick of the legs, a wiggle of the hips, a near back pedal of his feet, the ball seductively held in both arms to one side, the defence going one way and he the other. First called the 'struggletown shuffle', this combination of John Cleese's Ministry of Silly Walks, the Nazi march and the can can—all in accelerated time—became known to the world as the Campo goosestep. No one ever did it better than Campo or came even close to imitating him. With the impetuosity of youth he was prepared to do anything, try anyone on and endlessly trust his own attacking skills.

Those who saw the Scotland Test curtain raiser in 1982 between the Australian and New Zealand under-21 teams still talk about Campo's performance. He was clearly out there to impress. At one stage he received the ball, glided around his opponent and then chip-kicked over the fullback to score. That one manoeuvre had the crowd searching its programs to work out exactly who this kid was. And it could not have been timed better. That night the Australian selectors were looking for names, any names, to add to the list of possible Wallabies.

Dwyer was always a gambler, so why not punt on Campese? The selectors really had no option. As Dwyer admitted he knew 'next to nothing' about Campese, but that was Australian rugby. Unlike its cricketing and league counterparts, whose dossier on every available tour candidate would fill a large folder, Wallabies were often selected on the say so of the rugby grapevine—someone who knew someone whose sister was once married to the barman who served drinks at a Wallaby function reckoned so and so was a good halfback—or simply because it was one province's turn to get an extra player.

To the relief of the Test selection panel, Campese was soon making an impact all over the field. His first match for the Wallabies against the New Zealand province Manawatu indicated that he was something extraordinary. And he wasn't at all perturbed by the rise in the level of play.

Mark Ella had not met Campese before the tour, but they soon discovered they were kindred spirits. Ella delighted in Campese's self-belief and fervour in wanting to do something different. Campese looked upon Ella as a near godfather. Here was someone who actually understood what he was on about, who knew how to handle his idiosyncrasies and who could quell a sometimes frustrated, prickly beast. He became almost a fourth Ella.

It was soon clear that the plan was to get the ball out to Campo and just follow. It didn't take long for several Wallabies to take Dwyer aside. Perhaps it would be a good idea to put him straight in the Test team. If they didn't know what he was up to, what chance did their opponents have? And his brashness was bound to exasperate and distract the overly conservative, overly serious All Blacks. Only Campese would remark 'Stu who?' when asked before the Test what he thought of Stu Wilson, then regarded as the best winger in the world. That annoyed the All Blacks no end as did Campese's antics in his first Test, played in Christchurch. The first time he received the ball he ran around Wilson. He did it several more times, finishing off the Test by knowing exactly where to be when Mark Ella cross-kicked a long ball towards his wing. Campese was there to gather and score. That try didn't lead to a Test triumph for the Wallabies, but it trumpeted to the world the arrival of a new phenomenon—David Campese.

Over the next two years Ella and Campese combined perfectly, but Australia continued to win some games and to lose too many for Bob Dwyer to ever feel safe about holding on to his position. Despite victories over the All Blacks and Argentina and a draw with France, Dwyer had still not been forgiven for his first venture in Brisbane, especially by Queensland officials. Even in his home town of Sydney, the factional warriors were rallying to oust him. It didn't take long before Dwyer was struggling to find any support. Most importantly, the bombastic Australian rugby king maker, Ross Turnbull, who some years earlier had gagged the most effusive of Wallaby coaches, was now prepared to anoint the most theatrical of all.

7

THE JONES TAKEOVER

'Where you from, the front or the back?' Down the telephone line boomed the always-inquisitive voice of Alan Jones. Was I from the front news section of the *Sydney Morning Herald* or the back sports department? Then working for the New South Wales Employers' Federation, it was clear Jones had no time for fools or time wasters. He seemed relieved I was from the cartoon section, but not so comfortable when I started asking him about the reasoning behind dropping Mark Ella as Australian captain.

Dealing with Jones was very different to dealing with Dwyer. Dwyer was renowned for dropping little secrets, a dollop of man's man talk and 'don't say it came from me' tidbits that could add meat to a story. Conversations would often ramble, with Dwyer sometimes taking the stance of the noisy stirrer so often found at the other end of a public bar. With Jones it was far more ordered, and you always had to be on full alert. You could never relax because every second line, statement, comment or throwaway quote could be the one to propel your story to the top of the back page or even the front. Jones never held back.

Jones worked the rugby network. It had already propelled him from near obscurity to becoming the Wallaby coach, and it was now how he protected his barricaded kingdom from the marauders. With Jones, you were either with him or against him; divisions were inevitable. Inner sanctums dominated his world, and those who entered it often left wondering what exactly they had just experienced.

Jones' steps from school coach to national coach were swift and momentous, and he swept many along with him on his voyage to the top. He had been an English teacher, a prime ministerial speech writer, an accomplished junior tennis player and a rugby dabbler, moving from the periphery of the game to the centre when in 1974 he coached the King's School's first XV to the Sydney GPS premiership. At this illustrious school he earned a reputation for getting the best out of willing young students but also for causing divisions.

It was as a political aspirant in a failed bid for a Liberal state seat that Jones met Ross Turnbull, who at the time was a member of the Liberal Party executive. Turnbull was immediately taken by the bluff and bluster, the showmanship and the intense, broad but scattergun intellect of Jones. They became close, with Jones looking to Turnbull, who was also the New South Wales Rugby Union chairman, as a way of moving further up the rugby food chain. Soon Turnbull became a key Jones backer.

In 1981 Jones was appointed a country representative on the New South Wales Rugby Union executive, a particularly powerful position considering that this often disorganised bushie faction then held a ridiculously strong sway on what occurred in Sydney football. A year later Jones had pushed himself even closer to the epicentre when appointed New South Wales team manager. What he now needed was a Sydney club to show that he was also a master coach. Sydney University wasn't interested but the Manly club was receptive, with the King's School connection proving crucial as several former students had been in its first grade team. They helped convince Manly that Jones was its man.

In 1983 Manly provided Jones with an open stage by making him its senior coach, and he immediately went about transforming the Sydney rugby scene with some sensational theatrical appearances.

Suddenly Manly Corso was alive with strange rumblings of an out-there coach who was convincing this sleepy old club that it was time to get into the modern age by providing detailed game plans and using video cameras, psychology and advanced training and fitness methods. He was also making it clear to the players it was his way and no other way. Jones thrived on the kinship of those who became devoted to him, so players had to be his disciples otherwise they were encouraged to walk.

Adding to all the excitement were the suggestions that Jones was getting a bit too close to some of his players. Even if a great deal of the scuttlebutt was exactly that, the rumours were soon being whispered in every premiership club in the city. This also meant that when Jones was in charge, Manly Oval home games became a sledger's paradise—with the unusual twist that most of the barbs from visiting players were directed not at their opponents, but at the coach sitting up in the stand.

Jones was so incensed at what he perceived to be a smear campaign that as Chris Masters explained in *Jonestown,* 'some Manly players believe he hired a private inquiry agent to identify the source of the gossip'. He was concerned that his confirmed bachelor status would derail his campaign to coach a representative side. A Manly premiership in 1983 helped, but more importantly Turnbull was pulling the votes in Jones' favour. Turnbull had told Jones that if Manly defeated Randwick, Dwyer's club side, in the grand final he would support him in ousting Dwyer as Wallaby coach.

With Turnbull wielding enormous influence within the New South Wales Rugby Union, a body that held almost half the votes in determining who would become coach, and with Dwyer at odds with Queensland, Jones' Manly Shute Shield triumph gave him the numbers for an overthrow. A devastated Dwyer was ousted. To this day Mark Ella believes he cost Dwyer his position because of his missed field goal that would have given Randwick the premiership.

There was great angst over the decision to appoint Jones. The erudite *Sydney Morning Herald* rugby commentator Evan Whitton wrote: 'To say that this decision is a disgrace will seem to many supporters of the game to elaborate the obvious.' With those words Whitton joined an ever-growing list of media commentators who were to be snubbed or sledged by an often puffed up Jones over the next few years.

During his controversial, often bizarre but never boring four-year reign Jones certainly knew how to wield his power, especially when wrestling with the press. He also unconsciously succeeded in exposing the impostors and brown-nosers of the media of that era. And there were a few. But he was also the master self-promoter, helping those who could help him achieve his aims. Anyone who opposed him or was no longer of any use to him he would coolly cut off. He did not want any disbelievers in the ranks, whether they were players, administrators, sideline hangers on or media.

It didn't take long for Jones to make enemies in the press even if for some he was a lazy journalists' dream, offering quote after quote to fill a fruity story. He repeatedly argued that he was the saviour of the truth and once proclaimed: 'I answer questions honestly—ask me anything and you'll get an answer, not the platitudinous tripe some others dish up.'

The *Courier Mail*'s pugnacious Frank O'Callaghan was one of those who soon fell out with Jones and had the courage to stand up to him, once accusing him of toying with the truth. Jones had attacked O'Callaghan following a story criticising the selection process, and O'Callaghan responded by telling him what he thought.

Most members of the Australian rugby writing fraternity had been targeted by some well-directed Jones bile. Jones laughed off a critical column by the *Sydney Morning Herald*'s Spiro Zavos with the words: 'That fellow with a name like a Russian wrestler? We don't take any notice of people like him.' Another Sydney writer was accused of being a 'lickspittle', while yet another experienced the cold shoulder treatment when Jones accidentally brushed into him at a function and then carried on as if he had just touched poison ivy. One scribe who knew Jones during his school teaching days had to face the indignity of walking into a press conference late and having the Australian coach play up to the large media pack by saying, 'What's that bad smell that has just wafted into the room?' Virtually everyone in that room laughed uproariously at that comment.

This reaction had a lot to do with the fact that Jones was willing to assist those who had played his game and ignore those whom he perceived as not being loyal to him. He was hardly the first coach to use this tactic, but he took it to extremes. Whenever a case had to be put or a cause pushed invitations would suddenly arrive asking selected journalists and their wives to lunch at his large Newtown warehouse residence. The reception would be lavish, and Jones would be the ultimate host. But by mid-afternoon the mood would change, when one of his henchmen would appear and announce: 'Gentlemen, would you care to come inside, as Alan would like a few quiet words with you.' The wives and girlfriends would be left outside while in the living room Jones would deliver his sermon, obviously intended for the next day's papers. He immediately found himself unpopular with the women, who thought that this boy's own meeting was the height of rudeness.

An interesting sidelight of any visit to Jones' household was to take a close look at his large bulletin board, which was near the front entrance and was dominated by photographs of himself and friends. For players, it was a chance to see where they stood in the Jones pecking order. On my first visit to Newtown there were several photographs of Manly and Wallaby forward Peter FitzSimons. On my second visit there were none. In the between time, FitzSimons had publicly voiced his concerns about the Jones push towards taking the Wallabies to South Africa.

•

Jones could be exasperating, difficult and moody, but he had the skills to influence and convince players that he could take them to the top. At first, they could only be impressed by his overflow of ideas, his enthusiasm and his commitment to the cause. His speeches, when heard for the first time, were inspirational. And at a time when Australian rugby was meandering, a strong-willed leader with a silky tongue worked. But it was always going to be short-term inspiration. There is only so much haranguing any one person can take, and when the players saw through Jones' facade the end result was bound to be disastrous.

His assistant coach Alex Evans provided a telling insight into the Jones phenomenon, which began with triumph but then fell apart during and after the 1987 World Cup. Evans explained to a British newspaper that Jones always 'regarded himself as the leader of the family. There comes a time when boys mature into men and need space, and so it was with his squad. They broke away from him.' That took some time, however, and before it happened Jones had outright command, demanding respect from his players and coaching team and even striking fear in some but still having the uncanny ability to inspire the best from all.

Jones also knew exactly where the Wallabies had to improve. Sure, you can talk about running rugby, exciting rugby, but there has to be substance behind it. Jones realised that the cornerstone was the pack. If the Wallabies were to suddenly be a world power they had to show might up front. They needed props, bulk and mongrel. Australia had ever-reliable, honest props such as Andy McIntyre, but it required several other anchors who would terrorise opponents. Jones looked around and wasn't satisfied with what was on offer in Sydney, Brisbane and Canberra and so lured the Argentinean front-rower Enrique 'Topo' Rodriguez across the Pacific. Jones also knew it was imperative that the Wallabies win the other crucial set piece—the lineout—and encouraged Steve Cutler, a giant thought soft by some but who blossomed under Jones' tutelage.

Just as crucial was bringing Alex Evans into the fold. A renowned hard man during his playing days with Queensland, Evans developed into a formidable coach who was an expert in forward technique and planning. He was the man in charge of moulding the Wallabies pack. With Jones taking on the role of motivator, Evans was prepared to do the grinding work and happy to stay out of the limelight. In that glare there was only room for one, and Jones happily filled that space.

Even though there was immediate conflict between Mark Ella and Jones, which was exacerbated by the Australian selectors making Andrew Slack the Test captain, the coach did encourage the five-eighth and allowed him his way—with Ella's mid-field direction so important in Australia achieving one of its greatest triumphs, the 1984 Grand Slam through England, Ireland, Wales and Scotland. Ella's transformation was crucial, because in the lead up to the Grand Slam tour he had lost so much of his enthusiasm for rugby. He was tired of playing, and was sick of the training and the regimen and the apparent belief of some officials that he had a poor attitude towards the game. The last thing he needed was a disciplinarian like Jones to take over the ranks. If Ella was to maintain his passion, a softly softly approach was preferable to being beaten over the head with theories and plans.

Jones has often been accused of dropping Ella as Australian captain, but the truth is that there was greater opposition from the other two selectors—Bob Templeton and John Bain. Jones maintains he wanted Ella as his skipper but Templeton, a master wheeler and dealer especially at the selection table, was concerned about Mark's lack of drive and direction. If discipline needed to be returned to Australian rugby, Ella may not have been the right leader. Bain was similarly concerned about Ella's recent loss of form.

No one could surpass Ella for natural rugby skill, but he was forever tainted by the perception he was a lazy trainer. Stories abounded about Mark and Glen's eagerness to find short cuts at training. At Randwick, Mark once fronted club stalwart and one-Test Wallaby Jeff Sayle, explaining they should finish training early and instead go back to the club because they had done enough. Sayle agreed. Ella left, telling Sayle he would meet him in the main bar with all of the players for a team bonding session. When Sayle arrived at the front door of the club, he was stopped by a small man who presented him with a large bill.

'What's this for?'

'All these pizzas,' pointing to a stack of steaming boxes.

'What pizzas?'

'For all those pizzas you ordered for your team. Mark Ella walked into my shop and said that Mr Sayle would pay for all the pizzas for the team.'

Sayle parted with his money.

At a Sydney representative training session Mark arrived wearing a raincoat, concerned as he was about the inclement weather. Sydney coach Peter Crittle asked Sayle, who was the team manager, to get Ella to take the raincoat off. If he didn't, Crittle would drop him from the team. Mark reluctantly agreed, but spent the rest of the night training with the raincoat tied around his waist.

In spite of Jones' defence of his position as captain, Ella was forever suspicious of him. He was secure under Dwyer, as they were kindred spirits. But with Jones Ella was uncertain whether he had a future. He thought that following the demise of Dwyer he would be the next to go, especially as he had been such a strong supporter of his long-time Randwick colleague. Ella knew that those who opposed Jones, even if indirectly, had a limited future. He thought that if Jones sincerely wanted him as captain, he would have pushed far harder. As he was head coach, the domineering Jones could have easily stood over the selectors and demanded Ella rather than the popular and reliable Andrew Slack as skipper.

This just added to Ella's reluctance to continue playing, especially as there was another factor that may have played a role in the decision. It was suggested by some that for a high-profile tour of the United Kingdom the time wasn't right for an Aboriginal to lead the troops to an area of the rugby world where pomp, ceremony, speeches and dinners were an important part of the captain's role.

While Jones may not have possessed the same level of rugby knowledge as Dwyer or Templeton, he made up for it by focusing on crucial areas of the Wallaby game that had been allowed to let slip. He had a great eye for talent. He had schemes and theories that would intrigue the troops. His avalanche of new ideas could be blinding. And he had the intense work ethic that would impress all those around him. He also concentrated on the basics. At training sessions he was obsessive about players getting everything right, constantly shouting, whistling, cajoling and arguing. It was like a night at the circus, where he was coach, ring master and the centre of attention. However, a lot of this appeared to be for show. It wasn't surprising that the players groaned when the media pack arrived at training because Jones would up the theatrics, which meant extra drills, extra torture.

His original theory was the basic KISS game plan—Keep It Simple, Stupid. He also offered his famous line: 'I take the Gucci view about hard work on the practice field—long after you've paid the price, the quality remains!' But it was Jones' belief in the importance of studying the opposition that had the most impact. He provided game plans. He hassled the players into watching match videos, and stressed to them the importance of analysis. The change was immediate.

He also made a point of turning the squad into *his* squad so much so that he became somewhat of a mother hen. When the team arrived in Suva for a one-off Test in 1984, he complained about the standard of the team accommodation and demanded a move to better digs. The Fijians were unimpressed, but the new leader got his way.

Despite his big, intoxicating statements and his vitality Jones' power plays made him at times an intimidating figure. The Wallaby squad to Fiji soon encountered the pit of quicksand that was waiting if they made the mistake of crossing or upsetting Jones. FitzSimons was one of the first to experience the other side of Jones' character after celebrating the team's success against Fiji in the hotel room he shared with back-up halfback Nick Farr-Jones. The following morning FitzSimons and Farr-Jones were the last to clamber onto the team bus, to be bailed up by a stern Jones: 'I want to see you and you.'

Outside the bus Jones began screaming: 'Hear me and hear me well . . . The room you two have been "living" in is a pig-sty, a shambles, a shocker, a disgrace. It might be good enough when you're living at Wesley or Andrews College, but it's not good enough when you're representing Australia.' He continued the harangue for three minutes, telling the Sydney University pair that if they ever wanted to play for Australia they had better lift their game.

For FitzSimons, who was on the way out, Jones hardly looked at him again. The enigmatic, gregarious Farr-Jones survived, however, and became an integral part of the Jones Grand Slam plan. Other players too were soon to be stunned by the Jones steamroller approach.

A few weeks after bailing out FitzSimons and Farr-Jones, Jones caused enormous ructions within the New South Wales rugby ranks when he demanded that his key Wallabies stand down from the Sydney representative team that was to play New Zealand in the middle of a three-Test series. Jones' argument was that the players were jaded and carried injuries after winning the first Test. The real reason, however, was that Jones was concerned that after Steve Cutler had succeeded in winning so many lineouts in the first Test win, the All Blacks would target him and thump him to oblivion the following week in the less important Sydney–New Zealand match.

Seven key New South Wales Test players including Cutler were withdrawn, which caused real confusion at the Sydney training session as nobody knew who was and who wasn't allowed to play. The Sydney coach Peter 'Fab' Fenton stood at the dressing room door at T.G. Millner Field that night with his arms raised in disbelief, not knowing if he would have enough bodies to conduct a training session. Over at the old Millner bowling club, the then Sydney Rugby Union president and one-time hard-nosed Sydney police detective George Marshall was nearly apoplectic, vowing revenge on Jones, whom he believed had deliberately undermined his union. The All Blacks also believed they had been snubbed.

Several of the players who were told not to play were uneasy with the decision but knew the dangers of standing up to Jones, especially when he telephoned each and every one of them to say that the decision had been made for the sake of team harmony. A few thought they had been deliberately isolated by Jones.

When Sydney lost by 25 points, *The Australian*'s Phil Wilkins described it as 'the day the game died of shame'. Jones duly noted that comment, and for a time sent Wilkins to coventry.

This didn't stop the All Blacks from having their usual way in the second Test. Jones' excuse for the Wallaby loss was most unusual. It was all because the players had gone to the movies the night before the game and had been spooked by *Indiana Jones and the Temple of Doom*. Jones moaned he had 'never seen such rubbish in my life . . . people eating maggots and whatever'. According to Jones, centre Michael Hawker was terrified by the snakes he saw on screen and was awake all night due to recurring nightmares.

When Australia lost the third Test by one point, which saw the Bledisloe Cup again head east, it was all referee Irishman David Burnett's fault—even if the All Blacks had been caned in the penalty count 20–9. Interestingly, Australia was out-kicked that day by the New Zealand fullback Robbie Deans, who would re-emerge more than two decades later to be the Wallabies first full-time foreign coach.

Despite getting so close to the All Blacks some Wallabies, Mark Ella in particular, were distressed by how the team had performed. Despite being given relative freedom by Jones to express themselves they too often clammed up, refusing to stretch their play past the centres, and had become too obsessed with the set pieces. Ella was so exasperated that he went to Jones' room following the loss to stress that the team had to be more flexible or he had no interest in being part of it. Jones agreed, giving Ella greater authority in how the Australian backline would conduct itself on the upcoming Great Britain and Ireland tour. There was even a suggestion that Ella may again become Test captain, but the other selectors weren't as interested as Jones in the idea.

Jones' approval for Ella to call the plays was crucial in ensuring the 1984 tour became a defining moment in Wallaby history—luring many new fans to what was once a very bewildering game. That success was due to the power and the mastery of one man.

8

THE GRAND SLAM AND THE BIG CUP

When the Wallabies arrived at Heathrow Airport in October 1984 for the start of their Grand Slam tour, Alan Jones gave them strict instructions. 'When you're marking your arrival cards and they say purpose of visit, I want you to write "business" because that's what we're here on.' Some laughed, but Jones was serious. The team soon learnt they were indeed there for business, and that Jones' over-riding ambition was to be the coach who led the first Wallaby touring side to win all four of the Home Union Test matches.

The players had grown used to surprises. Before their departure Jones had organised for them to have professional singing lessons. They knew it was going to be a tour with a difference, especially with Alex Evans in charge of the forwards, Mark Ella calling the backline plays, Andrew Slack bringing it all together on the field and Jones the off-field vocal overseer.

Some players revelled in this charged atmosphere. Others, like Queensland prop Stan Pilecki, were left agog that the squad was so easily taken in by Jones' verbiage. Pilecki also had little time for Jones' strict training regime. Standing up to Jones in Wales following endless minutes of being screamed at, Pilecki walked past him, blew a few smoke rings and growled: 'I hope you are hoarse, you @#$%, because I am fucking deaf.'

Having Jones around, however, didn't stop Pilecki from drinking, smoking, snoring and being the life of the touring party. His fellow revellers were Ella and Farr-Jones. Farr-Jones was soon a member of a card-playing fraternity that included Wallabies and members of the media pack. Ella, on the other hand, formed the Black and Jack Club, which met every Friday for the open bar in his room—the drink of choice being Jack Daniels and Coke. Over a few quiet drinks Ella's fellow Wallabies could talk about their frustrations, relax and get away from the tour pressures. The Black and Jack Club became a most effective pressure release valve.

Jones kept a close eye on his players, to the extent that Farr-Jones was again summoned to the coach's room early on the tour to explain why he had been out drinking. This time it was a twenty-minute tirade. Farr-Jones just let his coach run out of breath and departed.

Jones may have been overly protective, but at least he made the right decision in having Ella and Farr-Jones, two kindred spirits, rooming together before the first of the four Tests. Most novices are a gibbering mess before their initial Test appearance, but the ever-laconic Ella succeeded in having Farr-Jones in a similarly relaxed mood before the England international. Farr-Jones was keen to know what his five-eighth wanted from him. Instead of the long list of demands he expected, Ella simply said: 'Mate, whether it's good ball or bad ball just chuck it to me. Fling it over your shoulder and I'll be there.' Farr-Jones was immediately at ease.

That level of confidence in each other's ability soon showed at Twickenham. After a stodgy start against a lacklustre England opposition, the Wallabies sorted themselves out in the second half when Farr-Jones threw a direct, flat pass to Ella. It was time to try an oft-practised rugby league move called 'Froggy', which involved a run-around with Ella's centre Michael Lynagh while fullback Roger Gould on the burst took the inside pass. However, in the middle of the execution Ella discovered that Gould had been checked by an opponent and so he instead went for the opening, changing pace and sneaking through the smallest of openings. This was the first Ella try on the Grand Slam tour, and the Wallabies were away with a 16-point triumph.

Within days of that first win Farr-Jones discovered the shenanigans that were then part of Wallaby touring. Teammates Steve Tuynman and Phillip Cox took delight in chopping away at Farr-Jones' hair, and so appalling was the job they did the ever-lubricated Sydney journalist Howard Northey was beckoned to finish it off using a hand-held razor.

Inviting Northey was dangerous. This skinny giant was without doubt the most 'out there' character in the rank of Sydney's sports writers. He loved his illegal substances. He loved his gambling. He loved his movies. He loved taking life to the edge. He was renowned for covering a Sheffield Shield cricket match wearing just his underpants, and at another game wandering out to the centre of the wicket during the luncheon break to smoke a joint. His hotel room was a haven for lonely and bored players and members of the media. All that was required was a hotel towel wedged tightly at the bottom of the door so that the sweet-smelling smoke did not waft out into the corridors. Northery became the soulmate of so many Wallabies. Some years later when he died, many Wallabies from that tour attended his funeral.

It didn't take long for the ever-observant Jones to see that his star halfback had been given a working over. He blamed the genial second-rower Steve Cutler. 'Look at what you've gone and made Farr-Jones do to himself. It's all that rubbish lineout ball you gave him against Munster. You've finally made him snap.' Cutler was aghast, wondering what his coach was going on about but smart enough to know there was no point arguing.

With shaved eyebrows Farr-Jones may have looked a bit odd in the Test against Ireland, but his willingness to follow the Ella line of 'throw it and I'll catch it' worked at Lansdowne Road. Once again Ella succeeded in getting the Wallabies out of a spot of bother.

With just five minutes to go the scores were level when Ella took over proceedings, following up several field goals with a try he considered as probably the most important in his career. Cutler won the lineout, and Ella opted to hurtle straight at his opposite Paul Dean. Noticing that the Irish inside centre had drifted, Michael Lynagh stayed close and took a tight inside pass from Ella. Lynagh then linked with winger Matt Burke, who put Campese away. As usual Ella hovered near Campese, and as he was being swamped by the Irish opposition offloaded to make it two out of the two for the Wallaby five-eighth.

That night the Wallabies celebrated in a Dublin pub. Ella was swamped by well-wishers, including countless amiable Irishmen. One asked if the star Wallaby was eligible for Ireland. Ella looked gobsmacked, prompting his inquisitor to announce: 'That's no problem. We'll call you Ella Fitzgerald.'

Meanwhile, Jones continued performing one of his favourite roles, that of being the last defender of his players. He relished treating the team as his flock, and if anyone upset them or attempted to undermine them he would immediately go on the attack. He was soon tussling with administrators following a fight in one match, announcing: 'I told them to get stuffed. I'm answerable to the Australian Rugby Union, not the IRB. Many of these people are anchored in the past.'

The 1984 Wallabies were also succeeding in using tactics that the British thought they were masters of. For so long the Australian scrum was regarded as second rate, with their northern counterparts believing the Wallabies had focused too much on flashy attacking football rather than hard-up forward-based play. Often Wallaby packs found themselves described as cream puffs.

That all changed after the Wales Test at Cardiff Arms Park on 24 November. The Wallabies quickly dominated this international, and were often perched in the Welsh quarter. Midway during the second half, a Wallabies scrum was set just five metres from the Welsh try line. The Wallabies forwards puffed up their chests, and decided it was time to prove their real worth. The 'Samson' call was given, the signal that the pack would apply an eight-man shove. To attempt this on Cardiff Arms Park was near sacrilegious, as the Welsh pit miners and tough men from the valleys had for decades prided themselves on having the biggest and best international forward pack. But centimetre by centimetre the Australian pack pushed back its opponents, until Tuynman at No. 8 was able to drop onto the ball to complete one of the Wallabies' most celebrated tries. The Welsh were humiliated. Ella took advantage of their despair by 'meandering across the field' and accepting an intercept pass to make it three out of three.

A Grand Slam now beckoned at Murrayfield against Scotland. The group had been away a long time, and as usual some players were getting on the nerves of others. As the pressure intensified friction was inevitable, especially in a group led by such an unpredictable, emotional character in Alan Jones. There were also concerns among some players that Jones was pushing them too hard on the training paddock.

It all erupted in Southport, following a marathon bus trip. An irritable Jones demanded another training session and a planned short practice turned into a slog. When he finally brought it to an end he called on Farr-Jones, Peter Grigg, Ross Reynolds and three other players to continue training. An exhausted Farr-Jones objected. 'Alan, I'm not going to do this.'

Jones looked at the group, told the other five players to do some sprints, and confronted his Test halfback. Farr-Jones knew he was in trouble. Jones' eyes were bulging. He began to screech: 'How dare you talk to me like that! I'll be the judge of what work you can and can't do! I am the coach and my function is to decide such things, otherwise the whole structure of our team endeavour would fall to the ground. Don't you ever speak to me like that.'

As ever Farr-Jones stood his ground. Unlike so many of his teammates, he wasn't going to let the coach get away with that abuse. He told Jones where to go and stormed off the ground. Pilecki tried to settle the situation by fronting Jones and offering to play halfback if Farr-Jones didn't want to do it. Jones didn't see the funny side.

Eventually Farr-Jones calmed down, and decided it would be wise to apologise to the coach. He knocked on Jones' hotel room door. He could hear water running so there was clearly someone in the room, but Jones did not come to the door. Jones was playing his usual games and Farr-Jones knew he was beaten, eventually writing a letter of apology which he slipped under the door.

On the morning of the Scotland Test Jones hopped onto the soapbox, delivering the usual Churchillian speech. Even the most easily bored of the Wallabies were stirred including Ella, who often chose these times to drift off. 'There are four things that don't come back. The spoken word, time, the spent arrow and missed opportunities,' said Jones.

Uncharacteristically Ella's first touch of the ball in the Scotland Test saw him fumble it. The crowd and his fellow Wallabies were in disbelief. This just did not happen. But then his radar kicked in, and a triumph over the Scots was a breeze. The classic moment of that game came in the second half when fullback Roger Gould had the ball, dummied to Campese but instead threw an inside pass to Ella. There was no one in front of him and soon Ella was celebrating an exceptional feat—a try in each of the four Test matches.

And his immediate reaction? 'I just couldn't stop giggling, because for quite a while I couldn't believe it had happened. There I was in the most important game in Australian rugby history, and I was laughing like a hyena.' But the omen of his success was there the night before. Staying in room 358, he realised he had scored three tries and was a five-eighth. As he ran onto Murrayfield, roommate Roger Gould grabbed him by the jersey and said: 'Don't worry, mate. I'll give you the try you need.'

And so the Wallabies joined an elite group—the 1912–13, 1931–32 and 1951–52 Springboks and the 1978 All Blacks as the only teams to win a Grand Slam. More crucially, the twelve tries were the most scored against the Home Countries.

In Australia, the Grand Slam tour had an overwhelming effect on the game. With each Test broadcast live by the ABC, rugby union attracted a new audience, one that was immediately entranced by Ella, Campese and the rest of the strange mob called the Wallabies. Even decades on, the Grand Slam Wallabies are approached by supporters who say it was because of them that they first became interested in the game. Jones too often opted for the hyperbole, but this time he was right. The Grand Slam 'changed the face of Australian rugby. We're now a feared force in the game whenever the game is played in the world.'

Ella had always said he was going to give it away when he was twenty-five, but no one really believed him. A man true to his word, he chose to retire at the end of the Grand Slam—finishing while at the top of his sport, and unlike so many others who leave when they are well past it and punch drunk. He also could no longer handle the stifling control and the antics of Alan Jones. 'You can only handle him in small doses,' Ella explained. 'Too much of AJ is far too much . . . Alan Jones made it easier . . . [to retire].'

Following the last game of the tour, Ella threw his boots into the toilet and attempted to flush them away. Twenty years later Alex Evans presented Ella with those boots, which he had painted gold. Ella also pledged that he would provide the exclusive of his retirement to his close mate Howard Northey. The correspondent for Australian Associated Press filed his story when the team was on the flight home to Australia, ensuring Ella relative peace as he disappeared on a European holiday.

•

With Ella now gone, Jones began preparing for his next conquest—beating the All Blacks on their home turf for the first time since 1949. He really put the pressure on his players by claiming they would do it without recording a Test loss.

So, just over a year after the Grand Slam triumph, in mid-1986 Jones led his troubadours through the rustic wilds of the South and North Islands. He was at his preposterous best. Arriving at the team hotel in Wellington he was appalled by the accommodation, believing it was all part of a New Zealand conspiracy to upset the Wallabies. 'Those cats which are still alive in our hotel have not been swung in my room or they would have received a resounding crack to the skull on several occasions,' Jones whined. 'You feel like a visiting Girl Guide or Boy Scout picnic. I simply have the view that in this amateur game, which makes a lot of money, we should treat people as we treat visiting businessmen. These people are putting money through the turnstiles and playing just for the enjoyment of the game. What they are entitled to is a decent room, a decent feed, and a decent game.'

He remained in full throat following the Wallabies win in Wellington. The Test, played at Athletic Park, one of the most dilapidated, inhospitable grounds in international rugby, was made even more unappetising by the inevitable howling gale that whipped across the ground direct from the Antarctic. Predictably no room had been set aside for a press conference, so the scribes congregated in an old, unused, dingy shower recess to await the Australian coach.

The press gathering was huge, particularly as the New Zealand media quickly discovered that many pages could be filled by just putting a tape recorder under Jones' nose. Jones arrived, turning said nose up at the room and sniffing loudly into the malodorous air, which saw one of the Kiwi writers back off and fall into the urinal. Jones downplayed the Australian effort and made some subtly caustic remarks about his fullback, Campese, who had given away a try late in the second half with a rash pass into no-man's land resulting in an All Black try to Mark Brooke-Cowden. This was the first hint that a serious altercation between Jones and Campese was about to occur.

From Wellington the team headed to the wild west coast of New Zealand, where Jones organised an entertainment night in Westport. He set a demanding standard. He was the first to arrive in the team room and provided a thoroughly convincing Al Jolson impersonation, greasepaint and all. Here was the other side of Jones, enchanting the team with renditions of 'Mammy'. The players responded and Steve Cutler, in one of the last acts of the night, asked the ultimate trivia question: 'Who scored a try for both teams in the last New Zealand–Australian rugby international? Answer: David Campese.' To say that Campese was unimpressed was an understatement. It edged him one step closer to a severe bout of depression.

Even though the Wallabies had won the first Test, there was a strange gloom hanging over this tour party. In the final weeks the team came close to falling apart. The infection began to appear shortly before the second Test in Dunedin when Jones lost his composure at a training session after a New Zealand television crew cheekily filmed the team practising secret backline moves. The crew, which included former All Black Graham Thorne, had been told that the session would be private but decided to see how far they could push Jones, whose superior manner had already irritated the locals. The ever-suspicious Jones went into a rage when he saw them secretly filming from the top of a sandhill. Thorne and the crew eventually left, but the former All Black would get his revenge.

Jones' mood was not improved several days later when, in the second Test, the Wallabies missed the chance of winning the Bledisloe Cup series early through a dreadful decision from Welsh referee Derek Bevan. The All Blacks led 13–9 with seven minutes to go when from an Australian scrum win only metres from the line Farr-Jones passed inside to Steve Tuynman, who with Jeff Miller pushed over the line. Tuynman, tackled by two All Blacks, grounded the ball correctly but Bevan ruled against the try. Tuynman, usually the most laconic of characters, flung the ball in disgust, later declaring he had scored fairly as his momentum had taken him over the line. But Bevan ruled that Tuynman had been held up, and that there were too many hands on the ball. The All Blacks enjoyed the reprieve to square the series after their 13–12 win.

In the Australian dressing room underneath the main grandstand, Jones fumed over the Tuynman decision but also vented his anger at Campese's performance. For the second Test running Campese had had a lacklustre game, dropping several crucial high kicks, which helped New Zealand regain their momentum. While Campese was having a shower, Jones growled to his teammates: 'Anyway, don't worry men; you've played without a fullback today.' Jones has denied making that remark, but too many Wallabies heard it for it to be passed off as a rugby urban myth. Jones also made his displeasure known to the Australian press, stating that Campese's second Test mistakes 'stuck out like a lighthouse in a lily pond', adding, 'I have a very high estimation of David Campese. I hope I don't have to do any revision.'

Several days later Jones and Campese had an argument at the team hotel where Campese was informed by his coach, 'I told the press you were the Bradman of rugby—now you've let me down.' Campese responded that night by getting drunk, an extremely rare occurrence. An occasional Malibu and Coke was his limit.

It took Campese several weeks to regain his composure, and his sense of gloom affected other squad members. He became even more frustrated when he discovered that Michael Lynagh had been picked at fullback ahead of him for the next match against Southland in Invercargill. Campese was instead selected on the wing. When he pulled a sciatic nerve in his leg during the match, he seriously contemplated giving up and going home. The strain was plain to see the following week when the Wallabies played Bay of Plenty in Rotorua. While his teammates celebrated a lopsided win Campese sat dejected in a corner of the room, head bowed, sadly shuffling his feet, trying to avoid the clatter by listening to his Walkman. It was only just before the third Test that he re-emerged from his depression.

There was a revealing aftermath that showed how far coaches can go to retain power and assert authority over their players. During the 1987 World Cup Graham Thorne claimed on New Zealand television that Jones was crucifying Campese and had harshly criticised him during the New Zealand tour the previous year. Jones quickly attempted to defuse the report by inviting Campese on to his radio program, where the Wallaby said there had been no argument nor had he been 'savaged verbally' by the coach.

Later that day Jones and Campese fronted the press at an Australian training session. Campese knew it was a set-up, and so did the press. Standing next to Jones was an extremely nervous, even jumpy Campese. 'At no time have I ever singled a player out individually in front of the rest of the team, at a Test, during a Test or at any other time,' claimed the coach. Campese later wrote in his autobiography that 'tamely and regrettably I went along with the charade because I had no choice'. He thought he would never play for Australia again if he publicly rebuked Jones.

The team gradually regained its composure during the final weeks of the New Zealand tour but Jones was still getting distracted by the locals, who had turned antagonising the Wallabies coach into a national pastime. Anti-Australian jokes dominated New Zealand radio. Newspaper pages were full of anti-Wallaby advertisements—the best being for a well-known New Zealand potato chip that was 'as thick as an Aussie forward'. Most of the gags, however, were directed at Jones.

Jones gradually worked his way around this hatred. He also found the ideal issue to convince the Wallabies they were being persecuted by the locals. Just before the final Test in Auckland the Australians were to play a mid-week game in Thames—an out-of-the-way town on the North Island. Again Jones made his disgust with the team's accommodation loudly known. He did have a point. Some players were forced to climb through windows to get into their hotel rooms (and then couldn't get out again as the window had jammed). Others discovered that when they stretched out on their beds most of their body hung over the edge. The gargantuan Bill Campbell commented that one night his legs would be able to sleep, the next night his head and shoulders. There was also only one toilet block and a handful of showers.

Jones called a team meeting, and it was soon decided that they would leave town immediately in search of better accommodation. The only problem was that the team's official bus driver had had a few too many drinks at a function organised by the Australian press pack and was unable to take control of the vehicle.

The next morning the team fled Thames as quickly as possible, much to the anger of the local folk. A newspaper headlined its front-page story: 'Prima donnas walk out.' But the game went ahead, and the Wallabies quickly discovered that the local team, made up of bushmen, farmers and quarrymen, were out to seek revenge. The general mood of the town was made clear by a sign that hung on the fence at the ground: 'No room is big enough for your mouth, Mr Jones.'

Then followed eighty minutes of mayhem when the Thames Valley players went out to kick, maim and destroy the Wallabies. Peter Grigg was kicked and rucked. Brett Papworth had his nose broken. Michael Cook was kneed in the face, and Brian Smith received threats that he would be lynched if he came over the fence.

Jones was beside himself in the dressing rooms. 'Hear what these mongrels shouted at Brian. Just listen to what they said to him. How dare they . . . I cannot believe this. Why do we have to put up with this garbage? Why do my players, my Australian players, have to be subjected to this?'

Jones was now very close to brainwashing his players into believing that New Zealand was a country of dumb potato farmers with whom they should not fraternise. It was Us versus Them at its worst. That's why when Farr-Jones and Simon Poidevin were caught drinking with good friend but now All Blacks coach Brian Lochore they discovered the full force of Jones' wrath.

Despite these distractions the Wallabies succeeded in getting it all together a few days later when, at Eden Park, they won the series. This time the dressing room mood was upbeat and chaotic as the 1986 Wallabies joined the 1937 Springboks, 1949 Wallabies and 1971 British Lions as the only touring team to defeat the All Blacks at home. The now-naked players, who had decided to follow their own defensive strategy rather than the coach's flawed pre-match directions, stood in line to get the rare opportunity of drinking champagne out of the one-metre tall Bledisloe Cup. Nearby, Jones proclaimed: 'This is bigger than *Quo Vadis* . . . bigger than anything.' Even the chisel face of Simon Poidevin had softened. 'Now I can live in peace,' he exclaimed.

But the school master Jones was still there. He made it known to Andrew Slack he wasn't impressed that the skipper had swapped jerseys and was wearing the Silver Fern when he accepted the Bledisloe Cup. And he later gave the Australian Rugby Union a swipe: 'We beat New Zealand in New Zealand and didn't even get a lunch.'

The 1908 Australian team arrives in England for the start of the first Wallaby tour. (Author's collection)

The 1908 Wallabies were unimpressed when they had to perform a war dance. (Author's collection)

Cyril Towers leading the Randwick team onto the field. (Author's collection)

Wild Bill Cerutti on the burst. (Author's collection)

Left: Rex Mossop showing off his longboard surfing prowess. (Author's collection)
Right: Rex Mossop jumps for the ball at training with Bill Cerutti (right) watching intently. (Author's collection)

It was a tough, miserable tour, but at least the 1957–58 Wallabies captain Bob Davidson enjoyed being chaired off the field after Australia lost the last match against the Barbarians 11–6. (Author's collection)

Bob Davidson and Tony 'Slaggy' Miller scramble for the ball during the 1957 Sydney Test against the All Blacks. (Author's collection)

The 1963 Australian selectors—Dudley Soane, Joe French, Bjarne Halvorsen, Terry MacBride and Bill McLaughlin—observe the action from the sideline. (Author's collection)

They look like a bunch of losers, but are actually winners. Skipper John Thornett leads the 1965 Australian team off the field after defeating South Africa in Sydney. (Author's collection)

Left: Four of the Wallabies greatest players—(left to right) John Thornett, Peter Johnson, Jon White and Ken Catchpole—ham it up for photographers before the 1965 Test against the Springboks. (Author's collection) *Right*: Tony 'Slaggy' Miller hassles an All Black opponent during a Sydney Test. (Author's collection)

Sydney Lord Mayor Harry Jensen hosted a civic reception for the 1963 Wallabies after they won two Tests against the Springboks on South African soil. Skipper John Thornett addresses the crowd on the Town Hall steps. (Author's collection)

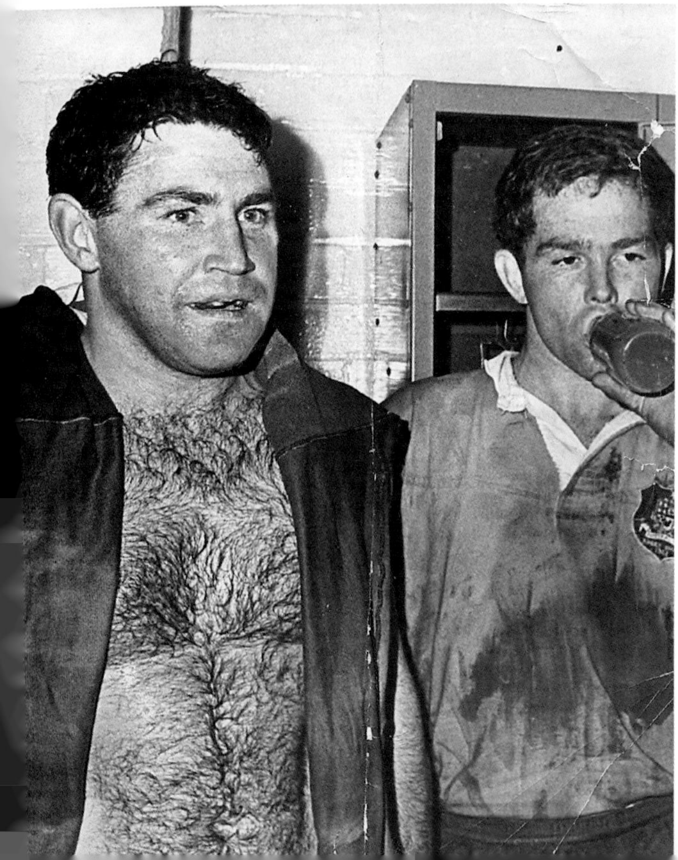

Peter Johnson (right) and John Ballesty (left) enjoy the Wallabies Test triumph over France in Sydney in 1968. (Author's collection)

David Brockhoff (second from right and next to Greg Davis) prepares the NSW team before the Scotland match in 1970. (Author's collection)

An ecstatic Wallabies coach David Brockhoff congratulates his captain John Hipwell after a 1975 Test triumph. (Author's collection)

Tony Shaw shows off the scavenging skills that marked him as one of the Wallabies great forwards. (Author's collection)

Tony Shaw (left) and Paul McLean (right) celebrate a Test victory. At far left is the *Courier Mail*'s rugby writer Frank O'Callaghan. (Author's collection)

Left: Greg Cornelson, of four tries against the All Blacks fame, shows off his tenpin bowling skills. (Author's collection) *Right*: Stan Pilecki. (Author's collection)

Wallabies coach Bob Dwyer puts in the hard yards at training in 1983. (Author's collection)

Top left: Hamming it up at training. Wallabies team manager Chilla Wilson attempts to distract Glen Ella during a photo session. (Author's collection) *Right*: Steve Cutler and Mark Ella offer each other strange sideways glances during training. (Author's collection) *Bottom left*: The 1984 Wallabies learning how to sing 'Advance Australia Fair' and 'Waltzing Matilda' before heading to Great Britain. (Author's collection)

Mark Ella in relaxed mode after retiring from the Wallabies. (Author's collection)

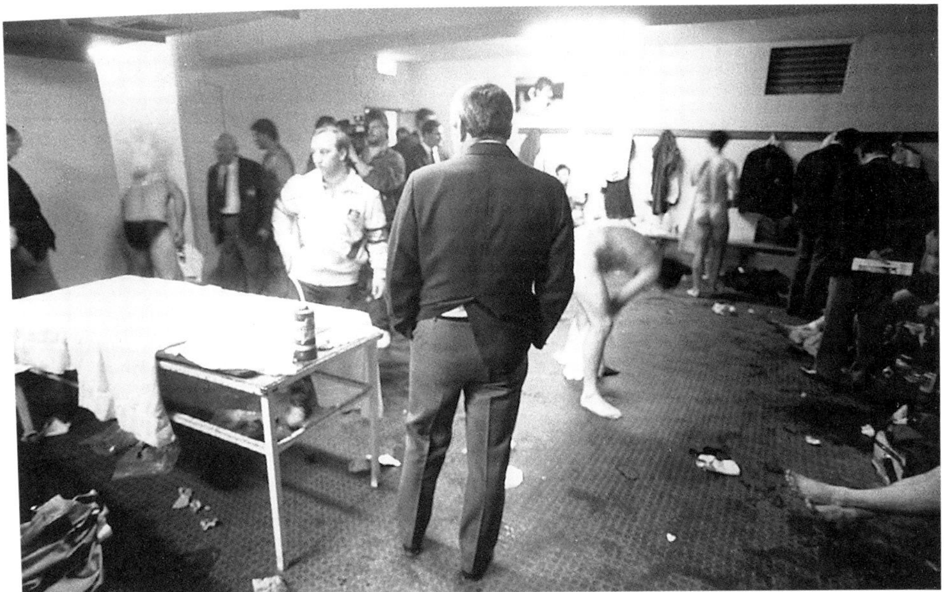

Wallabies coach Alan Jones surveys an eerily quiet dressing room at Concord Oval a few minutes after Australia was beaten in the 1987 World Cup semi-final by France. (Author's collection)

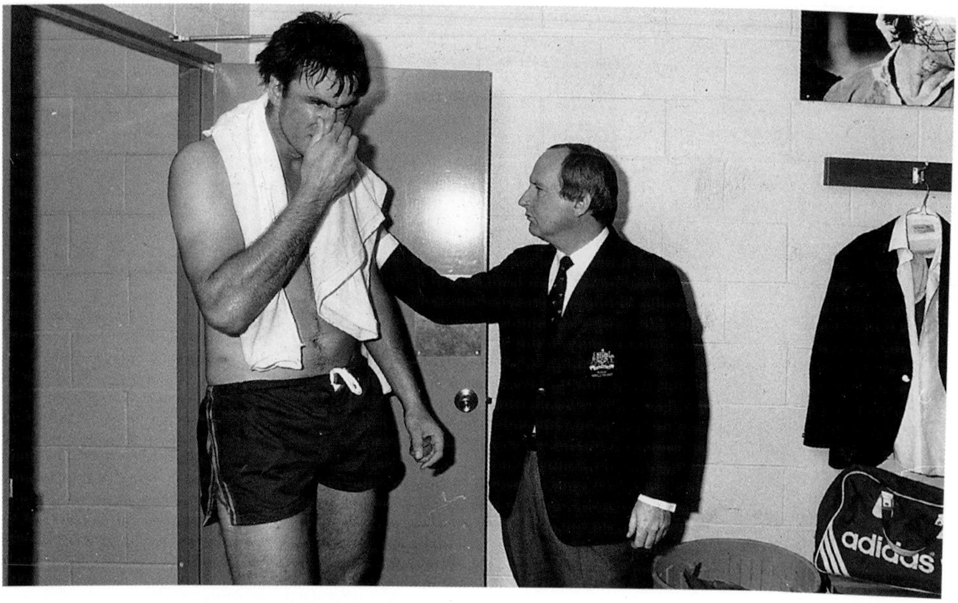

Alan Jones pats his premier second rower Steve Cutler on the back after a Concord Oval Test. (Author's collection)

Mayhem is just seconds away. British and Irish Lions winger Ieuan Evans scores after David Campese's pass lands in no-man's land in 1989. (Author's collection)

Wallabies coach Bob Dwyer and captain Nick Farr-Jones have a quiet word at Australian Rugby Union headquarters during a function before the 1991 World Cup. (Author's collection, Tim Clayton)

Simon Poidevin, Nick Farr-Jones and Steve Cutler enjoy the rewards of success after the Wallabies suddenly became major sponsorship material. (Author's collection)

Nick Farr-Jones introducing himself to the referee. (Author's collection)

Michael Lynagh and Nick Farr-Jones show off the World Cup to the thousands along Sydney's George Street during the 1991 ticker-tape parade. (Author's collection)

War of the wingers. South Africa's James Small and David Campese clash in the 1993 Test. (Author's collection, Golding)

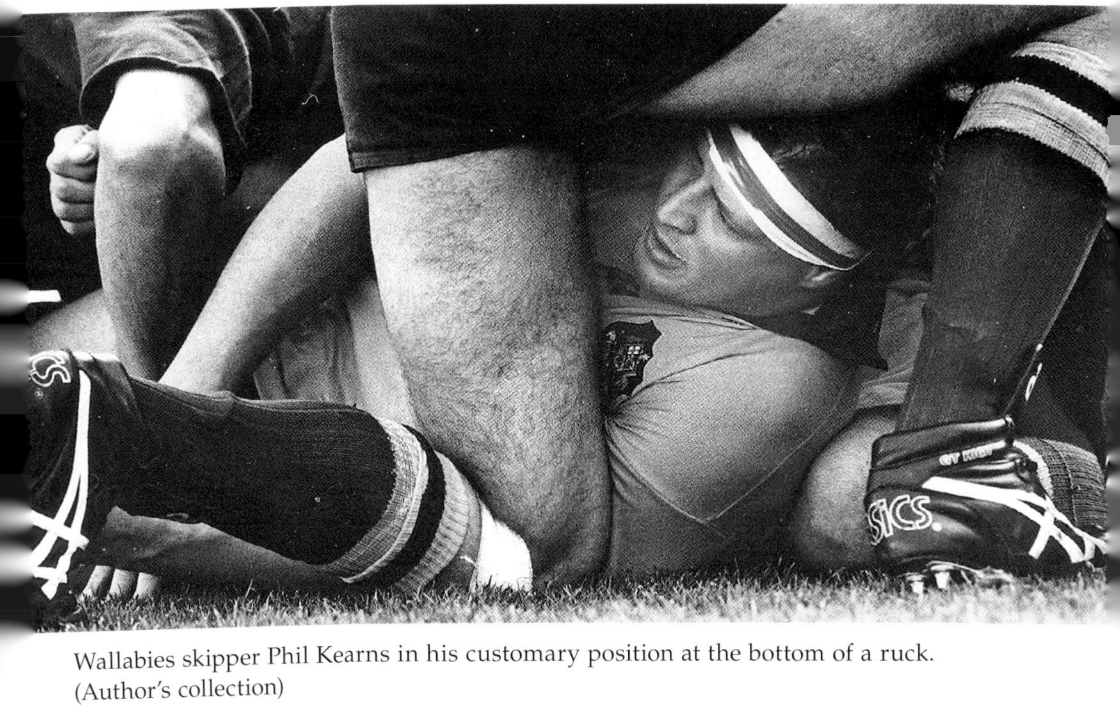

Wallabies skipper Phil Kearns in his customary position at the bottom of a ruck. (Author's collection)

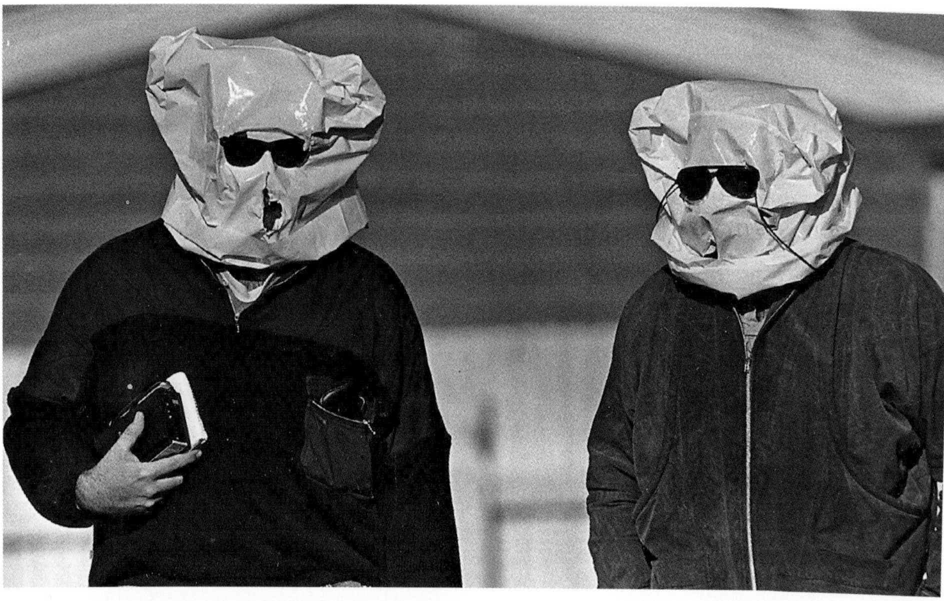

The author (left) and one-time rugby writer for *The Australian*, Greg Campbell, trying not to be noticed at a training session in New Zealand after they had criticised the team. (Author's collection)

Eddie Jones, who later became a Wallabies coach, showed why he was known as Beaver during his playing days with Randwick. Next to him is renowned Wallabies prop Ewen McKenzie. (Author's collection)

9

DECAY AND RECOVERY

The decline and fall of Alan Belford Jones did not take long. Not surprisingly, considering his character, it was painful and dramatic. Wounds festered as many of the Wallabies tired of Jones' behaviour and eventually lost their respect for him. When that happens a coach has no alternative but to move on.

In 1987 Australia failed dismally in the inaugural World Cup, lost the Bledisloe Cup to New Zealand and then went on a dreadful tour of Argentina, where Jones' favouritism towards several players caused dissension among the troops. Leading players grew so agitated by his haphazard leadership that some chose to look for new frontiers and financial rewards, primarily in South Africa.

Rugby union was also losing many of its hard core of supporters, who opposed the move of all major Test matches from the Sydney Cricket Ground to the backyard paddock of Concord—a characterless ground set alongside the busiest, ugliest road in Sydney. The fans were suspicious of the motives behind the move, believing a number of New South Wales Rugby Union officials were chasing the elusive dollar ahead of the wishes of players and supporters. The slump in Australian playing standards also made the drive to the Sydney's west even less appealing.

The seeds of dissent first appeared during the 1987 World Cup. Australia was regarded as equal tournament favourites with New Zealand, and when the Wallabies eventually finished fourth it was heart-breaking for Jones and gave warning his time was up. He was rabid in his desire to prove he was God's gift to rugby by winning the World Cup, but he made a major blunder: he allowed himself to be distracted. He had simply become too big for the role of coach.

Jones' radio career with 2UE was beginning to flourish. This saw him leave the Wallabies stranded at their hotel for most of the morning while he prepared for his talkback show. On occasions he would also disappear for a few more hours to fulfil lunchtime public speaking engagements. Many players resented being cooped up in camp all day with nothing to occupy them until the afternoon training session. They also were privately disgusted that, unlike them, Jones was not giving his undivided attention to the task of winning the World Cup and they saw him as being hypocritical because they had been told not to mix working and playing during the tournament.

Farr-Jones again found himself in trouble when he snuck in one morning to work in his law offices. When Jones found out he phoned his Test halfback from his 2UE offices to castigate him. That did nothing to improve an already tense relationship between the coach and one of his key players. Many of Farr-Jones' teammates were also unimpressed by Jones' response.

For five weeks the Australian players were trapped in their team hotels, as Campese explained, 'not knowing what to do with ourselves for hours and hours'. The situation was not helped by Jones arriving at training looking haggard and sometimes taking his frustrations out on the players. At one training session at Trinity Grammar School a teacher demanded that Jones tone down his language because it was being heard in the classrooms.

Roger Gould, the most individual of fullbacks, eventually grew tired of Jones' tirades and ban on alcohol. He told his coach that this had been the most unhappy experience of his life, and that he was not going to go to New Zealand with the team. He was instead leaving for Brisbane in half an hour. 'This team was very, very happy in 1984 and now it is very unhappy because of you, and I just can't stand to be around it. I'm going home,' he said. Gould walked off and departed the Wallaby camp.

Despite all the off-field dramas, the Wallabies did play to their potential at times and the World Cup semi-final at Concord remains one of the great rugby internationals. But Jones didn't see it that way at the time. He could not comprehend that their World Cup campaign was finished because they had lost to France. He blamed everyone except himself. As winger Peter Grigg recalled: 'I think he blamed Tom Lawton at one stage. I think he blamed Campese, I think he blamed everybody . . . and we blamed him.'

After that loss Jones' behaviour became even more erratic, leading to one of the most controversial moments of the tournament. Jones, deeply depressed by the loss, could not see the point of playing the third-placed play-off. He did not attend one of the lead-up training sessions in Rotorua, with Alex Evans instead taking charge. Jones' contemptuousness at being in Rotorua was not helped when back-rower David Codey was sent off early in the match for stomping. With Australia down to fourteen men they lost by one point. Jones was then reported to the New Zealand Rugby Union for calling one of its senior officials, Dick Littlejohn, an 'obstructive turd' after Littlejohn had refused to tender details of Codey's judiciary hearing.

The fuss eventually subsided, but Codey would provide Jones with further dilemmas shortly after when he and Slack secretly travelled to South Africa to investigate the possibility of a rebel tour of the Republic. A group of Australian players had for some time been eager to ignore the federal government's ban on sporting links with South Africa to instead enjoy the financial benefits of being involved in a rebel tour. There was also the lure of playing the Springboks, who had been out of international competition since the early 1970s.

The players had been openly encouraged by Jones, who made known his support for opening up sporting ties with South Africa. However, ever mindful of his public persona and political aspirations, he claimed interest in becoming involved in such a tour only if it had the official blessing from either the federal government or the Australian Rugby Union. The players were not so patient and this led to bickering, with several players believing Jones was instrumental in the eventual collapse of the rebel tour. Jones had been alerted by his close ARU ally, Ross Turnbull, that the ARU was about to ban for life participants of any rebel tour. Jones back-pedalled, and the players were resentful.

Farr-Jones continued to have his problems with Jones, who had preferred the Queensland back-rower Codey as his new Test captain. Jones had told the new New South Wales coach Paul Dalton, who wanted Farr-Jones as his state captain, that Farr-Jones was only his 'thirteenth choice as captain'. But Codey, who had been used primarily as a reserve in Jones' era, was tiring of the stifling atmosphere in the Wallaby camp and telephoned chairman of selectors John Bain to say he was not available for an upcoming All Blacks Test. He was talked out of his resignation, but with the proviso that he would be involved in the running of the team and that Jones could not be a complete dictator.

Then, shortly before the Wallabies left for Argentina at the end of 1987, twenty-one players admitted they had signed letters of intent to tour South Africa. They also called for the lifting of a one-year suspension imposed on Slack and Codey for their involvement in the organisation of the proposed rebel tour. The ban was eventually lifted, but it was hardly a settled group of players who left for Argentina. Division was deep, especially among the players who thought Jones had thwarted them in their desire to go to South Africa. Players were also angered by Jones' favouritism towards certain individuals on that tour, including the back-up halfback Brian Smith. Jones appeared obsessed in getting Smith into the Test team, and this was suddenly made possible when Farr-Jones strained his medial ligament early in the tour.

Although Farr-Jones' condition improved rapidly Jones was set on Smith as his No. 9, telling the team physiotherapist Greg Craig that

Farr-Jones would be taking 'no further part in the tour'. Craig was astounded, and told Jones that Farr-Jones would be back to normal in a few weeks, that he would declare him medically fit and that he would tell the truth if asked by the travelling media. Craig's protest counted for nothing. Smith was selected for the first Test, and Farr-Jones found himself on the reserves bench. Standards immediately slipped. Many players went straight into partying mode. It also didn't help that the Wallabies struggled to a 19-all draw in the first Test.

Farr-Jones was returned to the starting line-up for the next mid-week game, but the Wallabies knew that Jones had come close to losing the plot when in the dressing room after the match he eulogised Smith's performance at fullback.

Pressure then came from home. Jones was told by his ARU allies that if he didn't drop Smith for the next Test there would be a riot. Farr-Jones was back in the team. But Jones was still eager to select another of his favourites—the injured Queensland back-rower Troy Coker. Craig again objected, but in the end Coker broke down at training and did not play in the second Test.

Australia lost this time and Jones knew he was in trouble. He no longer had the support of most of his players and some of the voting delegates, who were about to decide if he would remain coach, as well as much of the Australian rugby public. When he returned from Argentina Jones put up a brave front, and said he was prepared to 'handle the daggers . . . It is a fairly imposing international record we have amassed over the past four years and if I don't say that no one else will. The best judges of all this is the players—and you should ask them.' One newspaper did. Only ten out of thirty-one Australian players approached said they would support Jones, the man who had coached Australia to twenty-one Test wins from thirty.

The ARU delegates' vote was nowhere near as decisive when they recalled Bob Dwyer to the coaching job in February 1988. Dwyer snuck in by two votes much to the surprise of Turnbull and Co., who believed they had the numbers to retain Jones. Dwyer, on the other hand, had the support of Queensland and several minor states. One

New South Wales delegate defied Turnbull and in the secret ballot voted for Dwyer. This was enough to change the balance of power.

The meeting was also notable in that Queensland's Joe French won the ARU presidency ahead of Turnbull. This effectively ended the Jones–Turnbull era in Australian rugby, and it didn't lead to a torrent of tears.

Jones looked for scapegoats. He blamed Campese, whom he accused of making telephone calls to influential people. Campese argued that Jones had lost the confidence of the players and that he probably would have retired if Jones had remained as coach. 'In the end, the South African tour was aborted, and many players, I believe, blame me for that,' Jones declared, 'and perhaps in the decision that was taken about who should coach Australia, I've paid the price.' Nothing could be closer to the truth.

•

Dwyer decided against taking a softly softly approach. At the start of his second stint as head coach he made the controversial decision to change the captaincy, offering the job to Nick Farr-Jones ahead of Simon Poidevin, who had skippered the team to Argentina. The change had its merits. Farr-Jones had a strong rapport with his fellow players whereas Poidevin was a harder character, preferring to lead by example. But Dwyer, who sometimes struggled in one-on-one relationships, handled the situation poorly.

Unlike Jones he could be aloof towards his players, not explaining the reasons behind decisions to include or sack them from teams. And he believed players didn't need molly-coddling. This standoffish attitude bothered some Wallabies, who preferred to know exactly where they stood in the pecking order. Some even complained that on tour Dwyer purposely kept contact with them to a minimum.

The national selectors then followed Dwyer's uppercut with a low blow by leaving Poidevin out of the team to play a World XV. Poidevin telephoned Dwyer from Monte Carlo, where he was playing in a Sevens tournament, to find out if he had to return for the match only to be candidly told that he was not in the team. Farr-Jones was the new Australian captain. Several hours later, however, Poidevin discovered he was back in the side and was vice-captain. Jones made public the selection confusion after he had been telephoned by a distressed Poidevin. He knew he still had the power to cause trouble, and did.

On the flight back to Australia from Europe Poidevin decided to retire, and after playing in the World XV game officially announced he had played his last Test for Australia. The retirement lasted just forty-two days. He was in the first Test team to play New Zealand after being approached by Dwyer when several back-row candidates became unavailable through injury. A most patriotic Wallaby, Poidevin could not resist another wrestle with the best.

But he could not stop New Zealand from winning the series with the All Blacks rallying after a poor start. The All Black turnaround was reputed to have its beginning after an infamous drinks session at the Eastwood rugby club in Sydney following an early tour loss. As back-rower Mike Brewer recalled: 'There were twelve-ounce glasses lined up in a circle and we basically kept going until we fell over. I remember a thumping fight in the bus as the players up front attacked those on the back seats. I don't recall crashing, but I do remember waking up in the hotel in Gosford the next morning still in the footy jersey and long trousers.'

Poidevin, who opted for a more sober approach than the All Blacks, was unable to be part of the 1988 Wallaby tour of England and Scotland because of work commitments. Michael Lynagh was also a late withdrawal. Arguing he wanted a rest, Lynagh had been unhappy with his form but he also appeared not entirely comfortable with Dwyer. The Queensland five-eighth was not convinced of the effectiveness of his coach's attacking plans, but due to the number of injuries to squad members Lynagh arrived mid-tour to play in both Tests.

There were some dreadful performances during the tour, including a disorganised effort in the England Test at Twickenham where the Wallabies were beaten by an average home team and Dwyer realised he had given his players too much leeway. Players had taken advantage of a far more relaxed atmosphere and training sessions were no longer as regimented as they were during the Jones era.

With Jones having a field day on Sydney radio, throwing unrelenting barbs at Dwyer, the Australian coach decided to take action. He announced that he had 'kicked some of them up the arse . . . It must have something to do with Australians. If you don't get up them like a rat up a drainpipe they fall into bad habits,' Dwyer commented.

The squad's performance picked up when it headed to Scotland, where the Wallabies were accommodated in the enchanting Borders district and enjoyed the delights of midnight fishing, hunting expeditions, the great golf courses of the area and occasional flirting on the football field. There were also many memorable functions, none more so than the Scottish Rugby Writers annual dinner held in Edinburgh. The last speech of the evening was given by a retired newspaper editor who had clearly spent too much time soaking his typewriter in various alcoholic substances. He may have been struck down by the poisonous filth, but his mind and mouth were in perfect sync as he warned: 'Gentlemen, never underestimate the press. Never. Dealing with the press is like making love to a porcupine. You are just one prick up against a thousand.'

At the Scottish Test dinner, the finale to a special day, the Wallabies put on their kilts to celebrate a conclusive victory at Murrayfield, which helped to soften the pain of the miserable England leg. Wallaby prop Andy McIntyre proudly showed off his sporran, which was full of ice and had a can of Australian beer nestled in the middle. The Scots reciprocated the respect with a bagpiper piping in the haggis and then piping in the players. The two teams then stood on their chairs, arm in arm, to sing 'Auld Lang Syne'.

There was, however, one further final tour highlight when Cardiff Arms Park stood as one to show its approval of an overseas player. Moments earlier, in the final minutes of the last game of the tour against the Barbarians, David Campese scored a most astonishing try. Combining all his finest attributes—the zigzagging speed, the unpredictability, the deft change of pace, the uncertainty of what would happen next, the juggling of the leather from arm to arm—Campese proved that sometimes his brain did know what his legs were doing. He went one way, that way again, teasing everyone then anchoring himself and springing the other way to ruin whatever defensive pattern had been organised. There were steps, swivels and swerves and an eerie sense of suspense as everyone wondered 'what next?' and he found his way around Gavin Hastings, Jonathan Davies and others to score on his twelfth such run of the Wallaby tour.

With the ball tenderly tucked under his arm Campese returned to centre-field to his team, led by centre Michael Cook who had thrown the last pass, standing to attention clapping him back to his spot. High above in the terraces the fans stood up in a thunderous tribute. A bemused Campese looked up and clapped back in appreciation at this fine gesture, the most rousing since the Cardiff crowd sang 'For He's a Jolly Good Fellow' to All Black captain and prop Wilson Whineray at the end of the 1964 Barbarians match.

After the game four spectators ran onto the ground with a sign that proclaimed: 'Dave Campese Walks on Water'. No one could argue against that. At last Campese had left behind the horrors of 1986. But the British and Irish Lions would soon clip his wings.

10
WORLD CHAMPIONS

It was a rude initiation, but Australian rugby grew up in 1989. Its soft centre was brutally exposed. Its reliance on flashy but often impotent forwards was shown as a considerable weakness. And the overriding message was that if the Wallabies didn't harden up, Australian rugby would be left far behind. The catalyst for change was a nasty, unsavoury group of travellers, the high and mighty British and Irish Lions.

The Lions came to Australia believing good old roughhouse aggression, rather than any appreciable footballing skill, could bring down an opposition. While the Lions pathetically cried innocent all tour, Bob Dwyer was right on the mark when he claimed they were at times the dirtiest side he had ever seen in international rugby. But in the end the tour transformed the Wallabies, and in some ways ensured that Australia headed to the next World Cup with enough belligerence up front to at last establish themselves as world champions.

Several officials in the Lions touring party had long memories. The assistant coach Roger Uttley had been on the field in 1975 when the Australia–England Test in Brisbane degenerated into the Battle of Ballymore. Lions manager Clive Rowlands could also be excused for wanting to get square with the Wallabies after branding the Australians as thugs during the 1978 Australia–Wales series. And although head coach Ian McGeechan liked putting on the airs of quiet intelligence, he and Uttley had been members of the 1974 Lions team that toured South Africa, a side that had admitted to using the number 99 as a signal for an *all*-in brawl. It was a clever ploy, as the referee was unlikely to send off the whole team.

Several Australian players claimed that in 1989 the Lions revived the tactic by calling out 'all-in' just before the first scrum erupted in violence during the second Test. After losing the first Test in 1989 the Lions realised that they could use aggression to distract the Australians, who had their fair share of inexperienced players, including several who were hardly pugilists. Consequently the second Test was a bloody affair. The Lions, led by their captain Finlay Calder, belted everyone in their way. At one time Calder jumped over the referee to swing punches at Nick Farr-Jones, who was on the ground scuffling with his opposite Robert Jones. The grisly tactics worked; Australia lost its way.

One of Australia's most respected journalists, Evan Whitton, vented the feelings of many Wallabies supporters when in his *Sydney Morning Herald* column he wrote of the Lions that 'the scum always rise'. Wallaby hooker Tom Lawton simply described the Lions as 'hooligans'.

However, it was during the third Test at the Sydney Football Stadium that rugby fans became more interested in the general demeanour of that great rugby chameleon, David Campese, than the issue of violence when Campese found himself cast as the ultimate villain after a blunder changed the course of the match. Australia was leading 12–9 when Campese caught on the full a Rob Andrew field goal attempt that had sailed to the right of the posts. Logic demanded that the ball should be grounded, kicked into touch or run back into play by Campese, joining up with his teammates in mid-field. Campese instead decided to run it towards the left wing and then threw a wild pass to fullback Greg Martin, catching him on the shoulder. Lions winger Ieuan Evans gleefully leaped on the fumbled ball for the softest of tries.

As Evans rose from the turf defiantly shaking his fists, Campese and Martin tried to comprehend what had gone wrong. The look of horror on both players' faces confirmed that Campese's illogical decision had helped the Lions to a one-point victory and a series triumph. One Australian back-rower abused Campese behind the goal posts, calling him a collection of unsavoury names. This was a gentle introduction to the barrage of criticism he would encounter over the next few days.

Campese was shattered and close to tears after the match. A disconsolate figure was seen leaving the dressing room about fifteen minutes after the game, walking down the players' tunnel towards the ground exit. His teammates had ignored him in the dressing room, turning their backs on him as if to say it was all his fault they had lost the series. The public was similarly vicious and maintained a long memory. Some years after Campese retired a Sydney horse racing syndicate decided to name its three-year-old gelding Can't Tackle. It was the offspring of Mr C and Goosestep. After many months of soul searching, Campese eventually got over his gloom. Some years later Martin revealed he had repeatedly called for the pass.

The ferocity of the Lions monster during that Test series convinced Dwyer that his forward pack had to be completely rebuilt or it would continue to wither. It gave him the excuse to demand of his fellow Australian selectors that some new hard-heads were required and that experimentation was crucial. Many of the changes he introduced came from left field but they all worked, including the selection of Phil Kearns, who was the Randwick reserve grade hooker, prop Tony Daly, who had no senior representative experience but had played for the Australian under-21s, and eighteen-year-old centre Tim Horan, who was only in the Queensland B team in that year's Test against New Zealand.

The meeting at which all three were selected was memorable. Dwyer expected that Horan and Daly wouldn't pose problems, but he was unsure of how the selectors would react to Kearns' name, especially because of the Randwick links. The conversation as Dwyer recalls went as follows:

Dwyer: 'The bloke I think who has an enormous potential is Phil Kearns.'

Bob Templeton: 'Who's that?'

Dwyer: 'Phil Kearns, he's currently playing second grade.'

John Bain: 'If you think he's the best, then why don't you propose him?'

Dwyer: 'Okay . . . I propose Phil Kearns.'

Bain and Templeton (together): 'Right, done.'

Kearns was in the Test team.

Australia lost that one-off Test in 1989 by twelve points, but the groundwork had been set for future successes.

Several Queenslanders were unimpressed that Kearns had been selected ahead of Mark McBain, who had spent countless Tests perched on the reserves bench as Tom Lawton's understudy. Called 'Lightning' because his lineout throws never hit the same target twice, and castigated by Steve Cutler, Bill Campbell and Farr-Jones every time he made a mistake at training, Kearns received his initiation into the Wallabies club when he tried to find refuge in the hotel room he was sharing with Poidevin. 'Poido was sitting in the room talking to a priest,' Kearns recalled. 'I thought this was going to be a rough encounter, because Poido's getting the last rites even before the Test started.' He didn't find out until later that the priest was a family friend.

Kearns survived, the Wallabies held up against the All Blacks and an end-of-season tour of France beckoned. Before heading to Paris, Dwyer decided to talk to his young squad about the dangers of imbibing too much alcohol. While having a drink was a terrific way to relax and helped with digestion, binge drinking was dangerous, he said. If the players needed to get inebriated then they should let the coach know, and he would get them to see a psychiatrist to work out the problem.

The following morning there was a frantic banging on Dwyer's hotel room door. It was the Wallabies team physiotherapist Greg Craig, looking deeply concerned. When asked what was wrong, Craig replied: 'Let's just say we need sixteen psychiatrists.'

The highlight or lowlight of any French tour is an itinerary stacked with mid-week encounters against French Selection teams. The aim of the French Selection sides is basically to soften the opposition by being as aggressive as possible. The 1989 tourists had many such games against dodgy teams that looked as if they had come straight off the set of *Papillon*. The most notorious were the bunch of thugs the Wallabies encountered in Toulon.

From the grandstand the Wallabies match against the Cote D'Azur Selection seemed fairly innocuous, with fine flashes of play and the Australians winning by twelve points. However, it was a different matter in the Australian dressing room. Every player had his own tale of thuggery to tell. Five of the Wallabies claimed they had been eye gouged, head butted or blatantly kneed in back play. Peter FitzSimons complained that he had been eye gouged by the notoriously dirty French Test breakaway Eric Champ, before providing the quote of the tour: 'It's the first time in my life that my eyes have been twisted so much that I have seen my own brain . . . and it is big.'

FitzSimons, the master of self-promotion and a self-confessed media whore, was at the height of his game during this tour, earning Test selection with several excellent mid-week tournaments. Having played French club rugby, he was one of the few who could speak the language so he also became a tour leader of sorts. But he still had to learn what it really meant to be a Wallaby.

Before making his Test debut that year, FitzSimons remarked to Test veteran Tom Lawton, the grandson of the masterful Wallaby forward of the same name, how moved he had been in a tour match when the players stood arm in arm and sang the Australian national anthem for the first time on foreign soil. Lawton's eyes bulged, before he snorted: 'I'll tell you what "moving" is. Moving will be if you play a Test match in France . . . and they play the Australian national anthem and the fifteen of you can only just hear the tune from the band against the voices of the 70,000 froggies that are screaming for your blood, but you all belt it out anyway . . . and you line up to receive the kick off, and you can see this little sliver of white coming straight at you end over end and like it's in slow motion and you take it, and get belted by four of them, but your mates close ranks to protect you and knock them backwards and you form the first scrum with our blood just trickling down your nose onto your lip and your eyebrow's swelling up and you can see the grass about three inches from your eyeballs and you feel this massive heave coming from behind you . . . and that . . . that is what "moving" is mate.'

Fitzsimons got the general idea.

He also became the 'go-to man' of the tour. Before the first Test in Strasbourg no one was giving the Wallabies any chance of winning because their lead-up work had been dreadful and more than a dozen leading players had made themselves unavailable to tour. Still, FitzSimons declared Australia would win. 'The French team believe, in the words of Charles de Gaulle, that they have a rendezvous with destiny, but my own guess is that they have an appointment with disappointment.' Who would have thought his hero was Muhammad Ali.

Despite FitzSimons' optimism a win for Australia appeared too big a task, especially as the Wallabies were going in with four new Test caps—FitzSimons, Brendan Nasser, Rod McCall and Jason Little. So inexperienced was the team that McCall was named vice-captain. Yet these young bucks proved everyone except FitzSimons wrong, matching the far more experienced French pack to enjoy one of Australia's most important overseas Test triumphs. The most crucial discovery in Strasbourg was that Australia again had a first-class backline, and that at last it had a centre combination it could rely on. After countless changes during the previous eighteen months, Little and Horan played their first Tests together in Strasbourg to establish one of Australian rugby's most successful mid-field partnerships.

The final try of that Test has long been forgotten, but it gave a hint of what was to come. Midway during the second half Campese threw one of his 'Hail Mary' passes, hoping that someone was in the right spot to catch it. Horan was, and leaped in Australian rules fashion to pluck the ball from nowhere and score. At last Campese had found another soulmate who knew what he was up to on a football field. It had been a slow five years since Mark Ella stopped playing.

This try was the finale of an extraordinary game where Australia beat France on French soil for the first time in eighteen years. The home nation suffered its biggest defeat in nine years and its heaviest loss on home soil since 1952. Later that night the French Rugby Federation president, Albert Ferrasse, told the Wallabies: 'You have humiliated us.' Dwyer was overwhelmed. 'It is all beyond belief. If you ever said that Australia would beat France by four tries to nil, they'd all say you're having yourself on.'

In the Strasbourg dressing rooms Farr-Jones and FitzSimons were found in the bath, arm in arm, frolicking like babies. Raising a bottle of beer above his head, FitzSimons announced to the media: 'This is a preview of the 1991 World Cup final night at Twickenham.'

Like FitzSimons, Tim Horan also had a sharp wit. Sitting next to FitzSimons at a restaurant while on tour, an exasperated Horan could not understand a word on the French menu. 'I don't want to eat any of this crap,' he announced.

FitzSimons tried to help. 'I can recommend the soup de jour.'

'Nah,' Horan moaned, 'I had that yesterday and it was terrible.'

Apart from being among Australia's most dynamic centre pairings, Horan and Little were also one of the most mischievous. Their friendship went back to their schooldays in the Queensland bush, and for years their prime aim in life was to catch the other out. One morning Little discovered a carpet snake at his sister's house. After triple checking it was dead, he hid it in his car and took it to the game. While the rest of his Souths Club team ran onto the field, Little placed the snake at the bottom of Horan's kitbag. After the game, in a dressing room packed with well-wishers, Horan discovered the snake under his towel. Little made a quick exit.

While Horan was a schemer, Little was the dreamer. A new term, 'Jasonism', started to be used by the Wallabies for the 'most ridiculous comment, suggestion or action by any member of a touring party'. This term found its way into Australia's rugby vocabulary when Little asked Queensland physiotherapist Col O'Brien to strap his injured wrist. Shortly after the job was completed Little returned to O'Brien seeking further attention.

'Can you do this again, Col?' Little asked.

'Why, is it too tight?'

'No, it's on the wrong hand.'

Another celebrated Little story involved an incident at Tokyo airport when he noticed a black labrador sniffing bags on the luggage belt. Little is purported to have said: 'Look at that guide dog, up here looking for the blind man's luggage.'

With the Horan and Little pairing secure the rejuvenated Australians left for Lille and the second Test, believing they now had a rendezvous with destiny. But that old Australian weakness of relaxing when the job is only half done again gripped the Wallabies. Communication was poor. Inexperience saw the team lose its way in the second half, when it squandered a lead and allowed the French to tally fifteen points in almost as many minutes. And so another drawn series, and anguish that an inherent weakness was still troubling the core of this team.

Alan Jones was waiting to criticise the Wallabies on their arrival home, using his radio show to needle Dwyer. Taking the second Test loss as a sign that Australian rugby was going nowhere, Jones ranted about how it was a tragedy that the talent of so many had been squandered by a few. 'Will Mr Dwyer now admit that his second stint as Australian coach has been even worse than his first?'

Shortly after Dwyer was voted back as coach, beating Jones' former assistant coach Alex Evans. Not that Dwyer could afford to relax. As the team prepared to head to New Zealand in 1990, speculation of a boycott by Queensland players intensified. The complaints were the same. They didn't like being coached by a New South Welshman whom they believed was biased towards players from his Randwick club.

This dissatisfaction led to a meeting between players and the Queensland Rugby Union management committee four days after a highly publicised argument between Dwyer and Queensland assistant coach John Brass at the after-match function following the traditional state game. The stand-off was such that the Queenslanders even pushed for Farr-Jones to take over as captain-coach. The Queensland Us versus Them mentality was again rampant but thankfully this time the QRU, hardly a Dwyer ally, persuaded the disgruntled players not to boycott.

•

On the eve of his second New Zealand tour, Dwyer could have easily thought it was 1982 again. But the pressure this time was even greater, because he could not use the excuse that he had been left with a bunch of novices. Within weeks he was looking for *any* excuse when the team lost its way in the first Test, with the 21–6 defeat prompting volatile headlines of 'Woeful Wallabies' back home.

Dramatic changes were made for the second Test, including the dumping of Peter FitzSimons. 'I'm very upset as I imagine everyone else is,' FitzSimons explained on the night of his knifing. 'Let me just say this though, I would appeal to all my supporters who I know will be marching down George Street tomorrow, to only protest with peaceful means. No bloodshed please, at least not yet. And rest assured, I have also alerted all the selectors where the closest optometrist is located.'

FitzSimons' Test career was over, but it was long enough for him to know first hand what it was like to encounter the All Blacks. 'There you are minding your own business during the Test, trying to keep out of everyone's way, when, just for the pure hell of it, you decide to dive on a loose ball. Next thing you know a maul has formed over you and you have to watch helplessly as a couple of men dressed in black use their steel-studded leather boots to write their initials all over your lily-white legs. There is also your back to worry about. In All Black games it is also fairly standard procedure for your own scrum to collapse while theirs does not and then you will swear, I mean you will positively swear that a giant black centipede has just danced a jig on your back.'

The changes did little, and couldn't stop the All Blacks from stampeding to their fiftieth straight win and twenty-third Test victory in a row when they won the second Test at Eden Park. This time the Australians could not be condemned or ridiculed by the headline writers because they produced a courageous effort. This time it was, as Dwyer put it, a stark contrast in levels of performance. New Zealand would have beaten anyone that day, and the Bledisloe Cup was gone.

By the time they arrived in Wellington for the final Test the Wallabies were an irritable, distracted bunch. But the clown prince of the team, Sam Scott-Young, put them back on track. A throwback to the mad dog Queenslanders who dominated the Australian teams in the 1960s and 70s, Scott-Young was a big kid in a big man who had a way of letting his emotions get the better of him. His pre-match routine involved standing on his head in the corner of a room. Slammin' Sam once arrived at a Queensland training session in a New South Wales jersey and thought it was a great prank until he was kicked by his teammates every time he was found at the bottom of a ruck.

On the eve of the Wellington Test word got out to the travelling Australian media that Scott-Young had 'blacked out'. After getting the all-clear from the team doctor we were soon knocking on his hotel door. After a few seconds silence a feeble voice croaked, 'Who's there?'

'Err, Sam, it's the Aussie press. Sorry to disturb you, but we are just checking to see how you are.'

'Come in, boys . . . come in,' came the reply.

We opened the door, still uncertain if this was a good idea. The room was in darkness, there was an overwhelming smell of vomit and clothes and football equipment were strewn everywhere. We couldn't even make out Slammin' Sam in the gloom. Gradually our eyes grew accustomed to the darkness and we saw a head with light curls peeking out of the bed sheets.

'C'mon in, boys.'

Now surrounded by tape recorders and flashing pens, Scott-Young pulled himself up and slumped his shoulders. He explained that he was in a bad way. 'I threw up standing at the sink. I blacked out and hit the bathroom floor. I was out and slowly, slowly came to. Somebody was saying to me: "Wake up, wake up" and it was me. It was very scary. I didn't want to die in a hotel room like this.' The next day he was in the Australian team, ready to take on the All Blacks.

The first sign of his defiance came shortly after the teams ran onto the field. A few days earlier an All Black had told the Wallabies they were an inferior team because they could not look the New Zealanders in the eyes during the haka. Disgusted at the slur, the Wallabies assembled in front of the All Blacks and eyeballed them as they performed their war dance. Scott-Young was the most combative.

This was only the beginning, however. The Wallaby forwards were seething with anger that the Sydney press had been at them, while the New Zealand press had questioned whether they should even be in the same arena as their almighty All Blacks. And now the All Black front-rowers were whining away, aiming to get under the skin of their young, inexperienced opponents. Sean Fitzpatrick and Richard Loe were up to their old tactics, sledging Phil Kearns, Ewen McKenzie and Tony Daly.

'Look at those fat boys in the front row,' 'Get off the field, little boys,' 'What are you doing here?', 'You're not good enough . . . you're not good enough,' 'You don't deserve to be here,' 'You're out of your depth,' 'You're a reserve grader.' It was childish stuff, but it was working. The Australian front row was getting testy.

Then shortly after half-time a lineout was forced a few metres from the New Zealand line. Fitzpatrick had the throw. Kearns had positioned himself near Daly at the front of the line, ready to seize on a misdirected ball. The throw was short. The All Black jumper Gary Whetton did all he could and tapped the ball down perfectly, except that halfback Graeme Bachop was out of position. The ball was bobbing in no-man's land.

Kearns seized the moment. He pounced through a gap in the lineout, grabbed the ricochet, buried the ball into his chest, bounded over the line and bashed it down. Australia was now ahead. As Kearns rose to his feet he saw Fitzpatrick trying to hide. He angrily thrust his fist towards the All Blacks captain, shaking it in his face. Then, looking directly at Fitzpatrick, he pointed his fingers in the air as if to indicate 'up yours' and growled: 'Stick that up your arse . . . Have a nice day, boys.'

That try, and the hand signal, was the first indication that Australia was on the ascendancy. A half hour later it was all over. Australia had won 21–9, the first team in twenty-four Tests to defeat the all-conquering All Blacks.

It took some time to find the Australian dressing room amid the maze of corridors under the Athletic Park main grandstand. The bowels of Athletic Park hadn't changed much—they still resembled a men's urinal—but there they were, the celebrating Wallabies. Few wins over the past decade had been met with such joy.

Dwyer rose to the occasion. With his arm around Farr-Jones, his bristling moustache almost disappearing behind his gargantuan smile, he bellowed at the Australian media: 'Not so woeful Wallabies now, eh, boys.' They could only nod in agreement. It was now the turn of Wales to wear the woeful mantle.

•

Wales' southern hemisphere tour in 1991 was a debacle. The players were disorganised and the training sessions a shambles, as evidenced when five-eighth Adrian Davies nearly knocked himself out by running into a goal post. There were enormous rifts within the team, prompting a memorable brawl among the players during the after-match function following the Brisbane Test. In the words of their captain Paul Thorburn, the players were a 'bunch of whingers and drinkers'. Their coach, Ron Waldron, had completely lost control. When asked by the *Daily Telegraph*'s Peter Jenkins what he would do if Wales won the first Test, Waldron replied: 'I'll kiss your arse.'

It didn't happen; Wales lost 63–6.

The Australian players took note of how a team can lose its way if it is not unified and later that year, with far more difficult opponents to confront and bigger prizes to chase, the Wallabies went about making certain they were the complete opposite of the Welsh. If they were to win the 1991 World Cup tournament they had to be united.

Preparations began in meticulous fashion. The Australian Rugby Union started by getting the warring New South Wales and Queensland factions in line, ensuring there were representatives from both states with major roles in the running of the team. It also provided the necessary back-up staff by including in the touring party three selectors, two assistant coaches, a physiotherapist, a dietician, a sports psychologist, a media manager and several Australian Institute of Sport representatives, who spent the campaign watching and analysing the other teams and referees.

Presiding over it all was the Australian Rugby Union president Smokin' Joe French, who with years of hands-on experience had seen it all, especially during the days when the Wallabies were mere scrappers. Forever dragging hard on a roll-your-own cigarette, French had been manager of the 1964 Wallabies tour of New Zealand, the equally disastrous 1971 French tour and the infamous 'woeful Wallabies' tour of New Zealand in 1972.

As French, then in his seventies, watched the Wallabies train at the London Irish ground, he talked about then and now: 'In those days, we never had a physiotherapist, doctor, dietician or physical education instructor when we went on tour. It would just be the manager and the coach trying to sort it all out. There was nothing scientific about the preparation. If someone was injured, we couldn't call on the doctor straight away. No matter how serious the injury, we had to ring for a taxi and get the player to a hospital, where we hoped he could be fixed up quickly.'

On one tour the Wallabies were housed in a mental asylum in Strasbourg until French 'blew up'. He was also the official wine taster at each Test dinner on that tour. After one Test the waiters offered the Wallabies manager the best wine in the house. French sniffed it, gulped it, shook his head and complained: 'No . . . too ropey.' The waiters had to remove every bottle from the table and replace them with something more to his liking.

French was a lot less conciliatory during one Queensland tour of New Zealand when a match in Rotorua was under threat of not starting on time because the team bus had been stopped by a locked back gate at the ground and an officious Maori gatekeeper refused to open it. Although the gatekeeper shadowed over French, he soon moved when Smokin' Joe growled: 'Open the fucking gate.'

He was similarly blunt when he sat next to Princess Di some years later at a Cardiff Test. After the game, the team wanted to know what it was like to be close to one of the world's most glamorous women. 'She knows fuck all about rugby.'

French was naturally proud that professional support was at last being provided to the still theoretically amateur Wallabies. In 1991 this meant taking a lot of the pressure off Dwyer and the players, who were left to focus on the more important matters like actually winning the trophy and courting the media. The Wallabies arrived in London conscious they had to be approachable and receptive and that there was no point getting the British media offside, because if provoked it could turn into a dangerous enemy.

Here the expertise of the team's media manager, Greg Campbell, formerly of *The Australian* newspaper, came into play. Campbell's tuition of the players and management was mirrored by the positive press the team received on tour. The Australians were easily the most publicised visiting side of the tournament, not surprisingly considering they held a major press conference every day. Campbell provided the blueprint for every rugby media manager who followed, but no one did it better. In contrast, several other teams including England and New Zealand just remained mute and treated the media like rubbish. They were burnt by this approach.

As important for the Wallabies' success was that they based themselves in Dublin, where their quarter-final and semi-final games were to be played. It certainly settled the team, even if their first afternoon in Ireland was a hair-raising affair.

Normally the trip from Dublin airport to the centre of town takes around thirty-five minutes. In a scene reminiscent of the Keystone Cops the Australian team did it in just over ten minutes, thanks to a crazed bus driver and two motorcycle escorts who took great delight in pushing away interfering cars with their boots. Traffic went in every direction to get out of the way. When the bus blared its way down Dublin's famous pedestrian mall in Grafton Street an Australian player asked: 'Do they have to get the bus back by midday?'

But the Australians soon discovered their heart beat was in tune with their surroundings. They quickly related to the Dubliners and their impish wit. Deepening the bond was the common dislike of the British.

Training sessions were conducted at Trinity College, the impressive university situated in the middle of Dublin. On the short walk to Trinity through the centre of town the Australians were followed by hundreds of locals, many of whom involved themselves in deep and meaningful conversations with the visitors—undoubtedly trying to find a long-lost Irish relation among them. The locals were lucky. The Australian team had a sturdy Irish base, with such names as Crowley, Dwyer, Slattery, Daly and Horan. But even more exciting for the Irish was the discovery that the Australian team manager, John Breen, was related to Irish freedom fighter Dan Breen.

Nonetheless, Dwyer remained a little uneasy about all this local hospitality. Was it a big Irish put on? As Australia was facing Ireland in the quarter-final, Dwyer was worried that the locals had begun talking about a Wallaby victory before it happened. The Irish even began pleading for the Wallabies to be kind to them. It was in the final minutes of the quarter-final that the genuineness of the Irish affection towards the Wallabies became clear.

With five minutes to go Australia had been unable to draw away from the lesser Ireland side when suddenly the Irish flanker Gordon Hamilton was off. As he went over the line to score hundreds of Irish spectators jumped the Lansdowne Road fence, and it seemed the Wallabies were about to make a premature departure from the tournament. The country went into a wild jig—Australia could not win from here. Four minutes to go, and Ireland was three points ahead.

One of the few who believed Australia still had a chance was acting captain Michael Lynagh. He assembled the troops near the goal posts and gave them what would become one of the most celebrated speeches in Australian sport. 'It was all so clear what had to be done,' Lynagh later explained. 'As soon as Ireland had scored, I approached the referee to ask how long to go. He replied about four minutes. So I called the guys together and said: "We just got to keep calm. Just get us down their end and we will score, I promise. And if you are in any doubt, hold on to the ball and always run towards the goal line."'

After some misdirected kicking from both sides, a lineout was set inside the Irish 22-metre line. 'Campo came back inside, and was caught,' Lynagh remembered. 'Campo held on to the ball and stayed in the ruck, always going towards the opposition goal line. So for once Campo was listening. He held on to possession, we got the drive forward, we won the feed to the scrum, so we now had the opportunity to organise the backline move. We had done this move four or five times before, including earlier in the game and I had always finished in the same spot, but never received the ball for various reasons.'

The move involved a cut-out pass from Tim Horan to Marty Roebuck, with Jason Little looping around and darting in next to Roebuck's right shoulder before offloading to Campese. It was assumed that Campese would score, but he was tackled. His task was made even more difficult as Little had been obstructed. Somehow Campese tossed the ball up in the tackle to Lynagh, who found space amid the confusion of legs and arms to score just inside the corner flag.

The final whistle came a few seconds later. In such tense circumstances the Irish crowd could have almost been excused for rioting and looting the premises. Instead there was an outpouring of affection. The Irish players immediately embraced their Australian cousins, offering them genuine congratulations, demanding that they win the cup for the Irish community as much as for Australia. For the spectators, the Wallabies were *their* team for the rest of the tournament.

When an Irish official approached Dwyer and said, 'Congratulations, Bob. You were far the better team,' the Australian coach turned to Templeton and remarked: 'Did you hear what he said? I couldn't have said that. Even if I had thought it, I wouldn't have been able to get the words out.'

But that was the Irish, and the respect was genuine. The *Irish Times* proclaimed: 'Here's to another advance by Australia Fair against the All Blacks next week. All Ireland will be behind you.' From then on the Irish newspapers described the Wallabies as 'our boys'. It did help of course that the Australian captain had appeared on the front page of an afternoon paper with his mitts around a pint of Guinness.

This feeling of being at home helped in the lead up to the New Zealand semi-final, particularly as the local media focused on how rude and unco-operative the All Blacks had been. Not for the first time, the All Blacks had fallen in the trap of taking themselves too seriously.

Relative calm up against agitation worked in Australia's favour, enabling the Wallabies to enjoy what Sir Nicholas Shehadie, one of the original movers behind the World Cup concept, described as the most significant victory in the history of Australian rugby. In fact it was its greatest performance. Most matches eventually become a blur, but even now there are so many moments from that semi-final that are as vivid today as they were then. And most revolved around Campese.

First that run. That audacious run. In the first half Campese completely bamboozled the New Zealand defence when he ignored the first command of backline play of running straight, by speeding across the field at a perilous 45 degree angle. It was a taunt that worked. Although Campese had a wall of New Zealand defenders in front of him, none were sure what to do. Should they pounce on him and be exposed by a scissors pass or a cut back inside? Instead they held off with the ultimate embarrassment of Campese, still on the same 45-degree run, beating John Kirwan to score.

Then that pass. That audacious pass. Just before half-time Lynagh chipped the ball behind the winger, giving Campese just enough room to retrieve it in front of fullback Kieran Crowley. Campese was off, darting this way and that, before he was expected to be blotted out by the cover defence. Then came a moment of sophisticated mental telepathy. Tim Horan was on his left, but decided to curl around him. Campese had only a faint idea of where Horan was, and at the perfect moment hurled the ball over his right shoulder straight into the arms of his centre, who crossed for the try. The second half was almost as good and the Wallabies were on their way to the final.

That triumph also brought about an important change to the psyche of the Wallabies. For so many decades they had treated victory as an added bonus. They had entered countless Tests just hoping to do well. Mediocrity was enthusiastically promoted. That they were amateur part-timers up against the big boys such as the All Blacks was often the feeble excuse used for another dreadful drubbing. This all changed when Australia was convinced it would defeat New Zealand in the semi-final. Many Wallabies sides have claimed since that they were the first not to be intimidated by the All Blacks. They weren't. The first was the 1991 World Cup team. They just kept it to themselves.

Despite having to leave Dublin, the Wallabies were in the right frame of mind to do something special in the final. They headed to another perfect location—the luxurious surrounds of the King Henry VIII hunting lodge in Weybridge, Surrey. Fax machines, specially installed to allow fans back in Australia to send messages of goodwill to the team, worked non-stop as supporters from the far reaches of the country let the Wallabies know that they had been enraptured by their performance and were already expecting World Cup final joy. The front page of the Melbourne *Sun* newspaper said it all with the announcement that a baby girl had just been named Harriet Elizabeth Nicola Farr-Jones Davina Campese Wallaby Geddes.

On the day of the final the Wallabies were calm and confident, but without being complacent. They only had to overcome one last irritation to take their place as world champions—a traffic jam in front of their Twickenham dressing room caused by the arrival of Queen Elizabeth II and her entourage.

In their rooms at last, the Australian team management decided against a fire and brimstone speech to stir up the players. Instead Bob Templeton went for the heartstrings. He produced from his pocket a crumpled copy of Peter Fenton's poem 'The Spirit of the Wallabies' and recited it:

> There's a spirit in the Wallabies,
> Mere words cannot describe.
> It's as if they had descended
> From some legendary tribe
> There's a kinship, a tradition,
> As in days so long since past,
> Of crusades, of knights in armour,
> And of men before the mast . . .

By the time Templeton had read the four verses, a number of Australian players were wiping away tears. The others just wanted to get out there to show that the 1991 Wallabies were a legendary tribe. Two hours later, they did just that.

The final was a scatty affair, despite the English making a strange about-face. After having played so negatively all tournament they attempted an attacking game: a reasonable tactic had they prepared that way, but ridiculous when they did not have the resources. The Wallabies absorbed it all. The only try of the match was the result of a lineout, a charge and a collapse of bodies that saw props Ewen McKenzie and Tony Daly fall on the ball over the England line. Such was McKenzie's gentlemanly nature that he allowed Daly to take glory for the try.

The Wallabies won 12–6 and then savoured the most important moment in Australian rugby history. And standing in pride of place in the famous photograph of Farr-Jones and Campese raising the World Cup to the Twickenham crowd was Smokin' Joe French.

Bob Dwyer, too, made his own very expressive mark on that final. Perched in front of the Royal Box just below Queen Elizabeth were Dwyer, his assistant coach Bob Templeton, selector John Connolly, assistant coach Jake Howard and manager John Breen. In the excitement of the game Dwyer's mouth got the better of him, particularly when David Campese and Michael Lynagh opted for a backline move that appeared doomed for failure. As Lynagh drew away from Campese and was about to be swamped by the England defence, Dwyer leapt to his feet and screamed: 'Kick it to the bloody shithouse!' It was only then that Dwyer remembered where he was, put his head in his hands and sheepishly sat down. As Dwyer later explained: 'Amid the din, there was no way any of the Wallabies could hear me, but those within immediate range—including Her Majesty—certainly could. A hundred faces turned and stared in astonishment. One didn't. Her Majesty was too engrossed in the game.'

This was one of the few errors Dwyer made in that tense World Cup period. He was at the height of his powers as a coach. The Wallabies' first World Cup triumph still remains Australian rugby's most significant moment. Dwyer's role was critical, and for that he rates as Australian rugby's most important coach.

11

POLITICAL PAWNS

There was a downside to becoming world champions. For the first time every other international side became obsessed with bringing down the Wallabies—on and off the field. Their ideas were copied and used against them. But first, the Wallabies had to learn a new role—that of being champions.

They returned home to a ticker-tape parade down Sydney's George Street, followed by a Lord Mayor's reception in the Town Hall. Most of the players honestly thought they were being set up. They were concerned that no one would turn up and the parade would be a resounding flop. Some players even had to be convinced to attend. Instead the crowds queued ten deep down George Street. It was the moment when Australian rugby came of age, when it at last became a mainstream sport.

With such success some players began to wonder whether it was time to say goodbye. David Campese thought about it. After the 1984 Grand Slam success, the 1986 Bledisloe Cup triumph and then the World Cup, he pondered whether there was anything else to achieve. He approached Bob Dwyer, who was blunt as usual.

'Campo, you're mad,' Dwyer said. 'In my opinion there is only one important game.'

'What's that?'

'The next one.'

'I knew you'd say something stupid like that.'

Campese stayed on. But he was soon wondering if he had made the right decision. Shortly after, those mongrel All Blacks arrived in Australia to put the Wallabies back in their box before an historic tour to South Africa. Neither series was pleasant, and both were tarnished by controversy and anger.

After New Zealand's failure in the World Cup there was the inevitable purge. Alex Wyllie was replaced by the sour and paranoid Laurie Mains. Mains had become known as Lugubrious Laurie for his lack of warmth and social skills, while the All Blacks players even called him 'Old Lemon Face' behind his back.

With Mains in charge, the All Blacks embarked on one of its most unpleasant tours of Australia. There were several disgraceful incidents of foul play. And in the middle of it was Mains. Following the All Blacks–New South Wales game he made it known he was incensed that the *Sydney Morning Herald* had run a front-page photograph of bloodied and distressed New South Wales fullback Marty Roebuck with the headline: 'All Blacks beat NSW, not many dead.'

Soon Australian teams were accusing the All Blacks of being dirty and arrogant. After the first Test Sam Scott-Young required fifteen stitches to a large wound behind his right ear, the result of lying on the wrong side of a ruck. He later said that 'an All Black used my head as a trampoline, and jumped on it'. The All Blacks were asked by the ARU to investigate the Scott-Young incident. They refused.

Relations between the teams degenerated even further during the next Test when All Black prop Richard Loe rabbit-chopped Wallaby winger Paul Carozza across the nose with his forearm, supposedly in a bid to stop the winger grounding the ball for the try. The action was unnecessary and unforgivable, with Dwyer describing it as 'disgraceful' and 'cowardly'. The All Black management and the NZRU ruled that it was not satisfied the injury received by Carozza had resulted from foul play. They even mischievously argued it

John Eales thanking the Sydney crowd after his last Test. (Tim Clayton)

Wallaby jubilation. (Steve Christo)

Matthew Burke practising his kicking at training. (Steve Christo)

All Black fans give their thoughts on a Wallaby try. (Tim Clayton)

Ben Tune beats his Irish opponent Brian O'Driscoll to score a Dublin try. (Tim Clayton)

George Gregan displays the ecstasy and pain of scoring. (Tim Clayton)

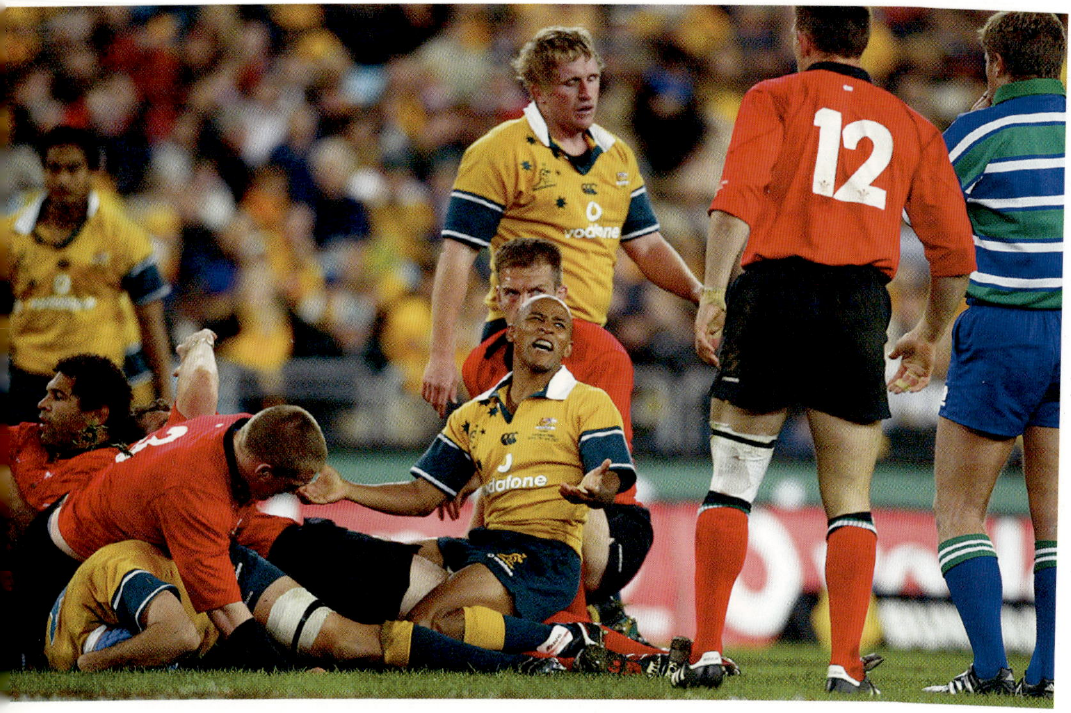

George Gregan asking for mercy from the referee. (Steve Christo)

George Smith and those locks. (Steve Christo)

Stephen Larkham kicks before being pounced upon by Jonny Wilkinson. (Steve Christo)

Shadows and light. Lote Tuqiri at a Wallabies training camp at Victoria Barracks, Sydney. (Steve Christo)

The national anthem. (Tim Clayton)

George Gregan in Marseille, 2007. (Tim Clayton)

Stirling Mortlock attempting to get Australia back into the 2007 World Cup quarter-final against England. (Tim Clayton)

Matt Giteau displays the despair of disappearing early from the 2007 World Cup. (Tim Clayton)

The future: Robbie Deans. (Steve Christo)

The future: Will Genia. (Steve Christo)

was all an Australian media beat up aimed at upsetting the New Zealand team.

Later Mains, who was clearly going gaga, argued that Carozza's nose was not even broken and that Dwyer was only whingeing because Loe was a good scrummager, and if the Wallabies could get him rubbed out then they were a chance of winning the set pieces. But the controversy around the All Blacks was nothing compared to what the Wallabies were about to confront next. For the first time in two decades they were on their way to South Africa, where they would meet the real Doctor Gaga.

•

For many years Australian rugby officials had been among the supporters of South Africa's return to the international sporting scene, even though virtually no progress had been made to break down apartheid. But as the ARU was so dependent on federal government funding it reluctantly had to toe the official line, which involved widespread sanctions against South Africa. That meant staying put, but angrily mumbling under its breath despite the constant reports of unrest in the townships.

Gradually the political momentum changed in South Africa and Nelson Mandela's release from Robben Island in 1991 provided hope for the country's first free election. Ever so slowly the white minority recognised the power of the blacks. The old white hard-heads of South African rugby, Dr Danie Craven and Louis Luyt, met with the ANC, which pledged to help them get South Africa back on the international rugby circuit but only on the proviso that a non-racial body be created to control South African rugby. It was on this basis that Australia made its way to the Republic for the first time since 1969.

Wallabies' captain Nick Farr-Jones was uncomfortable about the proposed tour, realising that the team could easily become a political puppet. He was also uneasy that the team would be surrounded by bodyguards during the trip and that it would be arriving on the eve of a national strike called by the ANC to protest against more black deaths in the township. 'I have intense concerns, particularly when you are told that you should go out in groups and not on your own when we are in South Africa. This is not like your normal rugby tour,' Farr-Jones said.

It was a nervous Wallaby party that headed to the Republic, and they became even more confused when they arrived in Johannesburg. Even before customs they were met by Dr Danie Craven, who had tears rolling down his cheeks. This was the moment the eighty-two-year-old autocratic president of the SARB/SARFU had been waiting for decades.

Like all the players and team management, I too was greeted like a long-lost friend and reminded of 'the last time we had been together' when I stayed at Craven's place in Stellenbosch. This was a complete surprise; I had never met Dr Danie before.

A few days later Craven's mind turned to other matters. At a welcoming function he announced that: 'I would urge you not to have anything to do with women journalists. They cannot be trusted. We all know what they are after.' An embarrassed Arrie Oberholzer, the SARFU's chief administrator, tried to retrieve the moment, grabbing the microphone: 'Some people say you are going senile. Perhaps they're right.'

That night Dr Danie was renamed Dr Gaga. Perhaps he should have been called that years earlier. During his playing days he preached to his teammates that masturbation sapped them of all their energy and went so far as to tightly wrap bath towels around his private parts before going to bed. Then, as Springboks coach, he would hand each of his players a football and tell them to stare at it for thirty minutes to improve their concentration.

Never the diplomat, Campese was the first to break in the harsh South African landscape. It never took much to trigger him, and he fumed at an advertisement in the national newspaper, the *Sunday Times*, that showed a No. 11 Australian jumper strung out on a rack with the words, 'Watch a Wallaby get skinned alive on television'.

A press conference was organised, and Campese dumped a bucket of bile on South Africa. Some of his more inflammatory remarks included that South African captain Naas Botha hadn't made a tackle in four years, that the South African public were 'arrogant', that South Africa should have toured Australia first before being given a Test at home and that even if they defeated Australia in Cape Town the South Africans could not call themselves world champions. Quite a few other Wallabies began to question why they were in South Africa as the tour progressed on its crazy way.

Farr-Jones was the next to earn the ire of the South Africans. On the way to training one morning he peered out of the team bus and was aghast to read a newsagent's billboard, which screamed: 'All of South Africa arrogant—Aussie captain.' The *Pretoria News* headlined its front page report: 'Aussies call us arrogant.' The report said: 'That's what Wallaby captain Nick Farr-Jones, along with his teammate David Campese, has accused South Africans of. But whereas the outspoken Campese's statement is limited to the rugby field, Farr-Jones reckons all South Africans are arrogant—that is what he told the *Sydney Morning Herald*.'

Farr-Jones was distressed by this report. Several months before he had addressed the National Press Club in Canberra and expressed the view that in cricket and rugby, South African arrogance had the country believing itself to be the best even after decades of isolation. It was this comment that was turned into a front-page beat up.

While one player described Pretoria as 'Canberra circa 1978', the Wallabies' first game at Potchefstroom was played on a dusty, dry pitch that could have easily been mistaken for a back of Bourke rodeo ring circa 1952. So glary was the light that the referee in the curtain raiser wore sunglasses.

The game was followed by one of the most bizarre rugby functions the Wallabies had ever attended—a barbecue in a gold mine 226 metres beneath Johannesburg. What made it unique was that South African President F.W. de Klerk, ANC sports spokesman Steve Tshwete and Chief Mangosuthu Buthelezi of the Inkatha Freedom Party had also been invited together with the New Zealand and South African teams. Democracy talks had broken down some months earlier, and the ANC and Inkatha had been blaming each other for township massacres while criticising de Klerk's government for creating most of the original sins.

Having these three bitter enemies all together down a gold mine was a security nightmare, but the three teams intermingled and were entertained by a risqué can can and the rhythm of the African tribal drummers. Smoke filled every cavity except for the cave known as the Diggers Inn, which had the distinction of being the deepest pub in the world. It was here that the Australian media bluffed its way next to De Klerk, Buthelezi and Tshwete.

De Klerk was happy to talk. When asked why he had never visited Australia he replied: 'I have never been invited.' Australian Rugby Union board member, the late George Pippos, was less diplomatic, asking de Klerk: 'How many whitefellas?' When told the republic's white population was around five million, he continued: 'How many blackfellas?' Around twenty-eight million. 'Geez, you're fucked,' came the reply.

Chief Buthelezi wandered past wearing an All Black tie. When asked why: 'Well, I am an All Black, after all.' With a little wink, he opened his left hand to show an Australia tie.

The mood in the cave was so relaxed that Farr-Jones approached de Klerk to ask if he had a 'ciggy'. Fossicking around, the South African president found one and lit it for the Wallaby captain.

But reality soon hit when the guests returned to ground level where de Klerk's car was parked. Fitted out like an armoured tank, there were machine-guns on all doors, a bazooka in the boot and thick bulletproof glass on every window. De Klerk himself carried a compact machine-gun under his coat.

The deep political undertone of this tour continued a few days later when several Australian players and officials were invited to an audience with the ANC leader Nelson Mandela. Images of Mandela sitting at the press conference with a small Wallaby cap on his head, a gift from Farr-Jones, were beamed all over the world. However, the relative peace of the tour couldn't last forever. This was South Africa after all.

The Wallabies had been invited to attend the historic return Test between New Zealand and South Africa at Ellis Park. They were shuttled into the ground, which was lucky as the atmosphere outside the arena was frightening. After having been excluded from the international rugby community for so long, South African emotions and frustrations quickly showed. The Afrikaners' aggression towards Australian and New Zealand supporters was extreme—they screamed abuse, gave wrong directions and were physically intimidating.

It was apparent that for many of the Afrikaners in the crowd this was not the day to celebrate a step closer to democracy. It was their moment to show they were still the dominant race and that the world had come crawling back to them.

Inside the stadium the atmosphere was marginally more restrained. At regular intervals some lunatic would run across the field brandishing the South African flag, aggressively taunting the security guards in the hope of being tackled. The plea that no national symbols be displayed at the ground had fallen on deaf ears.

SARFU, which was relying on the ANC's support for the tours to continue, had agreed to the ANC's request that 'Die Stem', the white's national anthem, would not be sung at the Tests, that there would be a minute's silence for 'all victims of violence in the country' and that the South African flag would not be flown. Instead these demands acted as an incitement to those who believed that rugby had no reason to pander to liberal South Africans. Louis Luyt, the boorish boss of Transvaal Rugby, put his dreadful stamp on the day by allowing 'Die Stem' to be played. The crowd took up the challenge. There was no peace and love echoing around Ellis Park that afternoon, and the rest of the world saw that South Africa had progressed nowhere.

The ANC was so disgusted by what happened at Ellis Park that it was prepared to take action by withdrawing its support for the Wallaby tour. It was not going to back down, which meant the Australian players' safety could no longer be guaranteed. There appeared no alternative but to return home. At around 2 am in their Port Elizabeth hotel, coach Bob Dwyer, Farr-Jones, team manager John Breen and ARU executive director John Fordham were summonsed to the room of ARU president Joe French. He told them that if player safety could not be guaranteed they would catch the first flight from Johannesburg, via London, to get home. Shortly afterwards the Australian media contingent was awoken and asked to go to French's room. Smokin' Joe, who cut a sartorical figure with pyjamas askew and a cigarette jutting out of the side of his mouth, explained the situation.

Conspicuous by their absence during this tense period were South African officials, who not for the first time had gone to ground at the slightest whiff of trouble even though South Africa had the most to lose if the Test was aborted. In the end it was left up to French, the Australian Ambassador in South Africa Colin McDonald and Steve Tshwete to work through the problem.

McDonald and French did eventually receive a private undertaking from the ANC that the Cape Town Test would proceed, but they were sworn to secrecy. There was, however, one important rider: if the same conditions that were laid down for the Ellis Park Test were not adhered to, no further rugby tours of the Republic would occur. As the next World Cup was scheduled for South Africa, the country was on notice to behave itself or risk losing the biggest prize of all. The ANC wanted the South African officials to stew for a few more days, but the Wallabies could confidently continue their tour.

In Cape Town the Wallabies were met by about thirty members of the South African Council of Sport, who held signs telling the Australians what they really thought of them. 'Disgusting Aussies', 'Go Home Aussies', 'Australians have no conscience', 'You have a vote, we don't'. The Australian management had told the players that if they were confronted by demonstrators the tour would be called off. This did not happen. The ARU gave in to the local officials, immediately downplaying the demonstration and arguing that it was nothing special, just local citizens exercising their democratic rights. This was outright rubbish. French and company clearly wanted to appease the local rugby administrators.

Several Australian players, the captain included, were angry that they were seen as supposedly supporting the white South African regime. Farr-Jones even contemplated going back to the airport to explain to the protesters that the Wallabies had come to South Africa in good faith and wanted to push the black cause. He eventually decided not to return to the airport, but said sternly that night, 'I want to play this Test and then go home.'

The Wallabies were still extremely uneasy. They had been confronted all over town by rude locals and told they were second rate and that they could not call themselves world champions until they had beaten the Boks. It was just the needle the Wallabies needed. They went on to put the Springboks in their place with a record twenty-three point win, the biggest defeat on South African soil since the Republic first began playing international rugby in 1891.

One moment in particular stood out. In wet, miserable conditions Tim Horan showed that he was the complete footballer. He broke the line. He chip-kicked through. He tackled. He regathered. He offloaded. He watched Campese score. He then revelled in one of Australia's most vibrant rugby moments.

After most Test matches the atmosphere in the Australian dressing room can be somewhat sombre. But this afternoon the build-up, tension and the frustrations of this most demanding and un-rugby of rugby tours were released. Michael Lynagh, generally the most diplomatic of players, was especially animated. 'We didn't have to look for any extra motivation than the South African supporters . . . they were our biggest motivation. All the guys have been pretty pissed off with the arrogant attitude of the South Africans, as we have really been battered from pillar to post here. It has been relentless, with them showing a total disregard for privacy and manners.' They were all relieved that they were finally going home.

•

After that eventful tour the next few years were somewhat of an anti-climax for the Wallabies, who continued to assert themselves as a considerable rugby power. Oppositions still took delight in baiting them, including in late 1992 when on an end of season tour the gnarly men from the hard, tough Welsh mining town of Neath delighted in playing their own special brand of roughhouse rugby. The stories from that game still bring tears of pain to the eyes of players. They claimed they were grabbed by the testicles, spat on, had their eyes gouged and were stomped on by Neath players. Jason Little was even kicked while signing autographs. Dwyer was so livid he described Neath as the 'bag-snatching capital of Wales'.

A year later the Wallabies toured Canada and France, where no-frills Queensland second-rower Garrick Morgan became the Australians' biggest asset. Morgan was ribbed by his teammates for his uncomplicated outlook on life, and he soon provided the Wallabies with another word to add to their touring vocabulary: a Morganism, which was used to describe crazy occurrences.

Morganism had its origins when Horan and Morgan were watching the television news together and the Russian president Mikhail Gorbachev suddenly appeared on the screen. The conversation went something like this:

Morgan: 'Who's that?'

Horan: 'Mikhail Gorbachev.'

Morgan: 'Who's he?'

Horan: 'He is the head of the Russian nation.'

Morgan: 'What's that thing on his head?'

Horan: 'That's a birth mark.'

Morgan: 'How long has he had that?'

Strange, but true. However, not all was well with the team despite its continuing success. Dwyer was under constant threat of losing his job to Queensland's head coach, the ever-scheming John Connolly. The noise from the Maroon stirrers was incessant, with claims continuing that Dwyer seemed to prefer New South Welshmen to those up north. Dwyer succeeded in keeping the Queensland faction at bay, including in 1993 when the players saved his skin by winning 24–3 against France. It was the first time the Wallabies had won in Paris for the first time since 1928.

While this win was a defining moment in Australian rugby, it also involved one of the stranger sights in an Australia–France international. As the final whistle went, Wallabies fullback Marty Roebuck sprinted towards one of the Parc des Prince corner flags, getting down on his hands and knees and pawing frantically at the ground. He stood up and proudly showed off a small, shiny object to his teammates before being named man of the match.

So who or what was behind this strange routine? None other than Tim Horan, with whom Roebuck had bet a million francs that he wouldn't be able to find the ten-franc coin he'd buried in the ground for good luck.

With about five minutes to go and a French scrum set a few metres from the Australian try line Horan decided to try one on his teammate. Sidling up to Roebuck just as French halfback Aubin Hueber was about to put the ball into the scrum, Horan produced a ten-franc piece from his shorts and exclaimed: 'I've found it. I've won the bet, Marty. You have to pay me the million.' Roebuck was horrified. How could Horan possibly have found the tiny coin in between all the French charges on the Australian try line? But being the ever-careful punter, as soon as full time was blown Roebuck sped to the corner spot to check whether he was the victim of a Horan sting. He had, of course, been duped. Horan had carried a ten-franc coin in his shorts for the whole match, waiting for just the right moment to startle Roebuck. All good fun, but it didn't take long for life in the Wallabies to became ultra serious. The All Blacks were hovering.

12

INNOCENCE LOST

On 16 August 1994 Wallabies captain Phil Kearns led with his chin. He told the *Sydney Morning Herald* that the Wallabies were no longer in fear of the All Blacks. 'I've never had any fear about playing against them,' said Wallaby coach Bob Dwyer. Generations of former Wallabies wobbled at the knees when they heard these extraordinary remarks. Too many had experienced the carnage at the hands of the All Blacks. But the words of Kearns and Dwyer were an inspiration and the prelude to one of the greatest tackles in Australian rugby's history—*that* tackle, the Gregan tackle.

George Gregan achieved many highs in his long and controversial career, but he will always be best remembered for that tackle in the final stages of a rare mid-week Bledisloe Cup Test in Sydney. In the eyes of many rugby fans, those few seconds of ingenuity remain his greatest moment.

With just minutes to go at the Sydney Football Stadium, Australia appeared doomed when the All Blacks looked as if they were about to score and take the lead. All Black winger Jeff Wilson had found open space, and after dodging around four Wallaby defenders was on his way to the corner and in the clear for the line. But from nowhere emerged a frantic Gregan, who had already been involved in two of the game's best tackles when he flipped two of the biggest men on-field—All Blacks prop Richard Loe and second-rower Mark Cooksley—even though both were forty kilograms heavier than him. Wilson leapt for the line. Gregan leapt for Wilson's ribs. Gregan connected. The ball spat out of Wilson's hands and over the sideline.

Five minutes later and after nearly sixty seconds of chaos following the final bell when New Zealand again attacked from everywhere in one last valiant but failed attempt, the Australian players were able to claim victory and salute their smallest but mightiest member.

In the Australian dressing rooms Dave Brockhoff strode up to Gregan, shook his hand almost out of the socket and proclaimed: 'That was it, my boy . . . the Bledisloe Cup tackle.' Gregan just put it down to a lot of luck.

Success was great while it lasted, but it didn't last that long. The following year the Wallabies, the victims of poor management, bad selections and outright greed, suffered an uninspired, fractured and most irritating World Cup campaign. Four years after their greatest triumph, the team that went into the World Cup in South Africa seeded as the outright favourites was a mess.

And their demise had a lot to do with a report that appeared on the front page of the *Sydney Morning Herald* six weeks before the start of the tournament: 'Australian rugby union officials made the most stunning announcement in the 170 year history of the code last night: it is now a professional game.' On 12 April 1995 the New South Wales and Queensland Rugby Unions, concerned that they were about to lose their best players to News Limited's Super League competition, passed resolutions recognising that rugby was no longer an amateur sport.

The officials were, however, playing with the truth, because for quite a long time key players had been receiving payments under the table or were paid massive sums to play in the northern hemisphere. All they had to do was keep their mouths shut. Countless Australian players admitted privately they were 'shamateurs', a state of affairs privately condoned by Australian officials.

Super League needed players and had lots of money, and rugby union was its perfect stalking ground. Some weeks before the Wallabies headed to the World Cup the ARU was bracing itself for the possibility of losing at least a dozen Wallabies to Super League. This prospect even saw ARU officials going to News Limited headquarters in Sydney for secret meetings in the hope of devising a new professional rugby competition aimed at the worldwide pay TV market.

Also hovering in the background was a group of rugby entrepreneurs who had grandiose plans for the game. Eventually emerging as the World Rugby Corporation (WRC) the group was headed by former Wallaby player and manager Ross Turnbull, who wanted to take over the game. Although they did not reveal themselves until after the World Cup, the group's existence was known of by a number of players and several people close to the Wallabies during the tournament. One of those was Dwyer, who was alerted by a friend that 'a group was setting up a project to help rugby withstand the league onslaught. He wanted to know if I'd be interested in having a chat. I said I would.'

The WRC proposal, as explained to Dwyer, was devised around keeping the Wallaby centres Tim Horan and Jason Little in rugby union following solid information that both would switch codes the following season. Dwyer was also told on the eve of the World Cup that a Super League agent was heading for South Africa 'to use the tournament as a one-stop shop for new recruits to the league revolution . . . The bomb was ticking.'

A rugby war was looming and the Wallabies were bound to be early casualties, but they did not help themselves in their approach to the World Cup. They made the mistake of carrying too many senior players who were either past it or were hiding serious injuries. The mood was all wrong. Players were standoffish with the media, and seemed to believe they were better than they actually were. Former All Black captain Sean Fitzpatrick later remarked that he knew Australia had no chance when he saw them hop off a bus in Cape Town all wearing state of the art sunglasses.

They were also not prepared for the South African ambush. Their training sessions were uninspiring, with Dwyer later conceding that 'perhaps we were too over the top in our intensity'. Two days before their first game, their 'focus fell away'. Phil Kearns wasn't one hundred per cent fit. Horan was still recovering from a knee reconstruction and Campese's presence was fading. And Campese and Lynagh, now the captain, had been bickering.

Lynagh and Campese were certainly different characters. Lynagh was a contradiction, a self-absorbed character, a thinker and an introvert who struggled when criticised. Campese talked then thought. They were bound to clash. Lynagh explained in his biography, published shortly before the World Cup, how irritated he became when 'anyone within the team publicly criticises the way individuals might have played a particular game . . . After some Australian games, Campo has occasionally had a crack at me in the press saying how little he enjoyed those matches because he didn't get all the ball he wanted.'

Lynagh was even more peeved that Campese had castigated him for getting special dispensation from the ARU to play in Italy during the off-season. Healing this rift appeared near impossible, and with two leading members of a World Cup squad deliberately avoiding each other Australia's outright favouritism appeared ridiculous.

For the first match against South Africa several Wallabies went into the game well short of full fitness. And the Springboks had done their homework on the Wallabies' half-pairing of Gregan and Lynagh. According to the South African five-eighth Joel Stransky, they had prepared for a year with this specific match in mind. Headed by the shrewdest of coaches, Kitch Christie, the Springboks had not been bluffed by the Gregan phenomena. Christie and his players fervently believed that if they focused on Gregan and Lynagh, played right in their faces and put them under endless pressure the pair would get distracted.

This approach appeared to be working, with both players clearly having serious communication problems. The Australian captain and his young halfback seemed to be at odds in determining the best mode of play. Gregan also misinterpreted some of Lynagh's calls, opting for back-row moves when the Test skipper instead wanted the ball and vice versa. The Wallabies' attack that day at Newlands was badly disjointed, as Gregan explained: 'Noddy and I just didn't gel as a combination during this World Cup, a fact which was more my fault than his.'

Not surprisingly an early lead was squandered and Australia's World Cup campaign was derailed when the Springboks won by nine points. For the Wallabies this stumble turned into a disaster when they were dismissed in the quarter-final after a field goal by England five-eighth Rob Andrew. The Wallabies, victims of their own complacency, were numb after the defeat. Campese expressed the team's despair: 'Going from first to eighth in only four years is not very nice.'

Campese contemplated retirement, but didn't. Lynagh said he would, and did.

•

Not surprisingly there were casualties—the biggest being Dwyer. His position was always going to be fragile, but he wasn't helped by a number of ARU delegates fervently believing that he and his assistant Bob Templeton had been colluding with the enemy, even acting as agents for WRC.

Under enormous pressure to keep control of the game, the rugby establishment finally had to react. Just before the World Cup final, the Australian, New Zealand and South African unions announced a US$550 million ten-year television rights deal with News Corporation, which would fund player salaries and allow the introduction of a Super 12 provincial series and a Tri Nations tournament.

After the *Sydney Morning Herald* had broken a series of stories on the new professional deal, Peter FitzSimons (now working for the *Herald*) and I were given a tip-off that if one of us went to a dinner with some of the officials who had stitched up the deal we would get the whole story to ourselves. FitzSimons volunteered to attend the private meeting, held in a Johannesburg steak house. Returning to the hotel in the early hours of the morning, a somewhat under-the-weather FitzSimons managed to wake me and for the next few hours we set about writing the story that announced the new era of rugby to the world.

By that time the Wallabies were long gone, and their agony was prolonged with two defeats against the All Blacks. Dwyer now had no chance of holding on to his place, especially as on the night of the Sydney Bledisloe Cup match the All Blacks signed en masse with WRC, joining a number of Wallabies who had also secretly signed up. Phil Kearns, the new Wallabies captain, gave the game away when he announced to the crowd after the match: 'We hope whatever happens in the future, you'll continue to support us.'

Several months of uncertainty and infighting followed. Eventually an unsteady peace was achieved when a number of leading rebels rolled over and returned to the establishment. It was an ugly period. Friendships were affected, and some players were never again trusted by their teammates. WRC inevitably collapsed.

There were, however, a few moments of brightness in this black period of Australian rugby. One involved the up-and-coming halfback Steve Merrick, who had ousted Gregan from the Test team. More interested in playing club rugby with his mates, Merrick was a real knockabout bushie. A phenomenal talent who worked in the coal fields in the Hunter Valley, he had gone to Auckland and played the All Blacks but was seeking a promotion in the coal fields. New South Wales and Australia wanted him to move to Sydney and establish himself as the world's best scrum half. 'I hate Sydney,' Merrick announced. 'I couldn't live here. I want to live in a place where you can play cricket out in the street and get twenty overs in before the first car comes.' They threw big money at him. Forget it, he said. 'I've done everything I've ever dreamed of in the past four weeks. I wouldn't be disappointed if I broke my leg and couldn't play again. I'm off. Hooroo.'

Merrick continued to play rugby for Singleton, wearing the All Blacks shorts he'd swapped with his opponent, Graeme Bachop, after the Auckland Bledisloe Cup Test until they were burned on the barbecue outside the Singleton clubhouse after a long celebratory drink.

The establishment revelled in the defeat of WRC, although it was far from squeaky clean. The game was now professional, but its administration was strictly amateur. The way it ousted Dwyer was farcical and ensured that the weakest candidate became the next Australian coach.

•

Dwyer was on the nose, and his successor was either going to be Queensland coach John Connolly, long-time New South Wales coach Greg Smith or the new Waratahs coach Chris Hawkins. The clear favourite was Connolly, as his record was exemplary. Smith, a complicated character, had achieved little, while Hawkins was only in his first year of representative coaching. However, the bloody mindedness of the ARU board, stacked with New South Wales delegates, ensured that Connolly stood no chance.

In an outdated system New South Wales held the power on the ARU board, with five of the fourteen votes. Queensland only had three, while each other state and territory had a vote each. Those two extra votes gave New South Wales enormous influence. As long as its delegates could get the support of the minor state delegates, New South Wales controlled the board.

That the minor states were even given a vote was ridiculous, especially as many of their delegates were out of their depth, were short on rugby knowledge and were swayed by the lobbying skills of New South Wales or Queensland. Often these delegates had little idea about who or what they were voting for. A former representative coach recalled that the night before the ARU voted on whether Alan Jones should replace Dwyer almost a decade earlier he'd received a telephone call from a southern delegate who said he knew little about Jones and wanted some information about his abilities. The coach was astounded by the delegate's lack of knowledge. And one of the delegates voting this time round made it publicly known that he wasn't aware there were four candidates until two days before the vote, and that he had virtually no idea whom any of them were.

When Dwyer, who was overseas, learnt that Smith had won he went apoplectic. He predicted major dramas ahead. He was right.

John O'Neill, who was about to join the ARU as its new chief executive officer, provided some insights into that infamous meeting in his biography *It's Only A Game*. He had been told before the meeting that Connolly was a 'shoo-in' and that it was a 'done deal', but when it was announced that Smith had won the vote, 'Pandemonium ensued', he wrote. 'Fists hammered on the table; there was a rush of noise; papers flew in the air. QRU chairman Dick McGruther could be heard above the din claiming treachery. His fellow Queensland delegates, John Breen and Norbert Byrne, were finger-pointing and the language was blue. [ARU president] Phil Harry called for order, and the three Queenslanders simply stormed out of the room. They eventually returned, still seething, while NSW delegates sat there with heads down and the hint of a smile playing at the corners of their mouths.'

O'Neill was suspicious that a deal had been done between New South Wales and at least one southern delegate. A few weeks later at an ARU finance committee meeting he was told of a major allocation to the South Australian rugby union. When asked why South Australia had received such a large amount, 'the looks around the table told me it was none of my business'.

The pandemonium of the meeting was nothing compared to the turmoil that was about to hit the Wallabies. Although Smith had for some years been New South Wales coach, he was an odd choice. His success rate at club and representative level was hardly spectacular, and his approach to coaching was decidedly unusual. At club level he was known for being a hard disciplinarian who revelled in playing mind games and endlessly changed his team line-up. When he was with the Eastern Suburbs club it was not uncommon for him to drop up to a dozen players after a loss. He was indecisive at the selection table, and his players never knew where they stood. He was sometimes a bit too clever for his own good.

As a teacher at Randwick Boys High School he developed an unenviable reputation when in charge of its school rugby team, often telling his players to be physical with their opponents. Players from surrounding schools, and that included numerous Wallabies, never forgave Smith for this aggressive approach.

Smith was a complex character. He revelled in being a loner. He was a mimic, a master of the put-down line and he also knew how to use the media to do his dirty work, demeaning players whom he thought out of form and oppositions he thought could be distracted by inflammatory remarks. He would then delight in pointing out the criticisms to the players, especially those he had virtually directed the press to write.

He was always unpredictable. Once in New Zealand, Smith wasn't keen to take his sunglasses off during a television interview. Although he was asked several times by the producers to do so, he refused. 'When we win, I'll take them off. At the moment, I'm in disguise.'

Smith had his players constantly on edge. Matt Burke recalled that during a New South Wales training session Smith took him aside for a 'quick word'. They walked side by side in silence. Eventually the coach said: 'Mate, big game this week.' Burke agreed.

'Yeah, nah, big game,' Smith responded. After another period of silence he added: 'Yes, a big game.' There was another pause before Smith asked his fullback to 'Send your mate over.' Scott Bowen ran across, and was given the same treatment.

On another occasion Smith began his team talk by asking: 'Do you know one in twenty blokes is gay?' While the players laughed, Smith continued: 'And I think it's Matt Burke. Look at his hairstyle.' He then walked out of the room.

From the very first meeting with the Wallabies Smith's stance was aggressive and nasty. He explained that if the players didn't like this approach they could 'just fuck off'. But he did have some idea of how to manoeuvre a football team. A number of players credited him with introducing to the Wallabies 'sequence plays', which treated rugby like a game of snooker rather than an impromptu ball game. Just as importantly he appointed John Eales as the new Wallabies captain. Eales had established himself as the world's premier forward, and through his diplomacy and fine people skills he brought some authority and calm to Smith's chaos.

But Smith also made some ridiculous decisions. The first came in just his fourth Test when, in his first venture to New Zealand in search of the Bledisloe Cup, he told his players not to face the haka. Despite Eales' concerns, in one of the rudest moments in the history of Australian rugby the Wallabies ran to the other end of the field to undergo some skill drills as the All Blacks performed their war dance. This naturally infuriated the New Zealanders. It was nearly as stupid as Smith's decision to take the team out to the match venue—Athletic Park—the day before the Test.

On a wet, miserable day with a gale whipping straight down the ground, the players sat huddled in the main stand as Smith gesticulated wildly and tried to charge them up. It was soon evident that the players were completely spooked by the surroundings. Twenty-four hours later they suffered a record loss to the All Blacks, and Smith had to take much of the blame. It was coaching at its worst.

Gradually the Wallabies picked up their game, but the quality of football was uninspiring. It was heavily structured, grim football. Meanwhile, Smith's behaviour became even more idiosyncratic and anti-social. His common practice when the Wallabies were on tour was to immediately book into the hotel and head straight to his room. He would not eat with the players or officials, instead preferring to sit in his room eating toasted ham, cheese and tomato sandwiches and drinking milkshakes. A 'Do Not Disturb' sign often swung from the doorknob.

The success of the 1996 end-of-season northern hemisphere tour, where Australia defeated Italy, Scotland, Ireland and Wales, was marred by Smith's odd behaviour. Several players, including Jason Little and Tim Horan, have vivid memories of being told before training that one of them would be running with the forwards and the other was suddenly a winger.

Then one afternoon in Dublin several days before the Ireland Test News Limited journalist Peter Jenkins and I were summonsed to Smith's hotel room to be asked by the coach if we would help him select the Test team for that week. We naturally thought it was a joke, but Smith was serious. The coach had clearly hit the wall. An official who was in the room pleaded with us to keep what happened at the meeting to ourselves. We did, because we didn't think anyone would actually believe us. It was so bizarre.

Despite this, the Wallabies still somehow kept winning. It was all about player power, which was fortunate because other officials, not just Smith, were hardly helping. After an early tour match in Italy in which the new Wallabies back-rower Toutai Kefu excelled, a high-ranking ARU official introduced himself to the rising star in the dressing room. Wearing an ARU blazer and waving his arms around to indicate an aeroplane, he said: 'Toutai Kefu. Me big chief of ARU. Me fly a long way to see you play. And you play really well.' Kefu looked up and said in his best Australian accent, 'Geez, thanks, mate.'

The entertainment continued as the team travelled through Europe. Smith even decided to play the team trainer Dirk Williams in one mid-week match, and then gave Tim Gavin a near heart attack when he arrived midway during the tour. While waiting for his flight to Edinburgh, Gavin picked up a newspaper at Heathrow airport to discover that he had been picked to play in the Wallabies match that night. It didn't matter that he had no gear or boots, he had to run out that night in freezing conditions.

By the following season the ARU realised that Smith's tenure was going to be short. He was too erratic at the selection table, too insecure and too often looked for shadows to remain the Wallabies leader. He was also telling the media and the players vastly different stories.

ARU chief John O'Neill attended one training session in Brisbane and soon realised 'the coach was losing the plot' and 'the wheels were coming off this team'. He even called on the senior players, including Eales and Brett Robinson, to take on extra responsibilities, to the extent of basically coaching the team. And Smith wasn't helping himself by continually asking O'Neill: 'Am I safe?'

He wasn't, but O'Neill tried to prop him up. Then in 1997 the Wallabies suffered their greatest ever loss. In the lead up to this match against the Springboks in Pretoria even the players were trying to get the media to help them be rid of Smith. While not prepared to go public, a number of senior players asked journalists to push the case for Rod Macqueen to take over as head coach. Finally the players took the matter into their own hands. Watch a video of the Pretoria Test and you will understand how this happened. In the final stages it was clear that a number of senior players just gave up. Losing by thirty-nine points, this was an unforgivable performance.

If the ARU had been tough, it would have ensured that several of the Wallabies who took to the field that night never played in the green and gold again. Instead of showing pride in the national colours, they allowed their coach to cop all the blame. Smith was gone a few days later, but not before some embarrassingly sad scenes took place. The Sydney newspapers had announced that Smith would be sacked on his return to Australia, and when these articles were faxed to the Test hotel in Pretoria his behaviour became even more erratic than usual. On the team bus heading to Johannesburg Airport he handed around a petition to the players demanding that they support him. O'Neill told Smith this was one of the dumbest things he'd ever seen and to keep the players out of it. It was an ARU board decision, he said. Smith believed it was a conspiracy.

On the flight home Smith went to pieces. While in transit in Perth, a clearly agitated and dishevelled coach wandered around the airport trying to corner players, pleading with them to support him. Many hid from him. A few days later Smith was sacked by the ARU.

Smith later confessed that during his time as Australian coach he was often hit with blinding headaches that lingered for hours, which affected his motivation and 'explained a lot of my very negative behaviour'. Unbeknown to officials, players and the media at the time, his health was deteriorating. These were the first signs of a serious illness that would lead to his death from a brain tumour in 2002.

•

Rod Macqueen took over, and with a completely different coaching style. While Smith was outlandish, at least he wasn't as sensitive as his successor. Macqueen was quiet and calculating, and he certainly knew how to be aloof with those he was suspicious of. And there were many in that category. He opted for the 'one in, all in' policy. If you weren't in, you were treated with suspicion.

Macqueen approached the Wallabies as if they were a small business. Delegation was crucial. Strong back-up staff was imperative. Sharing the workload was important. His planning and organisation were meticulous and were dependant upon a strong off-field team. He took the Wallabies' management system to a higher and often smarter level.

The Macqueen approach had many advantages but there were some down sides, in particular media spin and 'agendas'. Agenda A was basically what was going on. Agenda B was the bland line fed to the media. He also tried to appease the opposition to the extent of playing golf with his Tri Nations coaching foes. Not surprisingly Macqueen and a disenchanted media were soon at odds, especially as the coach clearly believed he was far wiser than those following and chronicling the success and failures of his team.

Macqueen's meticulous approach to coaching had a lot to do with his background which, in 1989, involved at least one confrontation with death. The discovery of a bleeding tumour at the base of his pituitary gland meant that he didn't take too much nonsense. It also turned him into a creature of habit, drinking, eating and going to bed at virtually the same time every day. ARU officials also noticed that he faded considerably in the latter part of the evening, which made night Test matches a sometimes difficult chore for him.

Macqueen also wanted the Wallabies to be a separate entity to the ARU, with him taking the team's chief executive role just as he had done at the Brumbies. He wanted the power to appoint his own people. In Canberra, Macqueen made certain the Brumbies players were involved in every organisational decision, from choosing the team blazer, the team emblem and the team song to having a real say in which moves and which tactics they would adopt on match day. With such a history of player power, the Brumbies believed themselves to be bullet proof. They cared little what anyone else thought. This would eventually have serious ramifications on the national team.

The ARU was wary of the Brumbies experience and Macqueen's demand for control so put in several important stoppers, including appointing its own manager and assistants. Jeff Miller became forwards coach and John McKay team manager. Both these appointments proved to be master strokes, and despite the initial grumbles from Macqueen, Miller and McKay made his job so much easier.

But the early signs that all was not well were there when the Wallabies inexplicably lost their second Test under Macqueen's reign to Argentina in Buenos Aires in November 1997. It was a dreadful 18–16 defeat. Macqueen was astounded by the players lack of intensity. Were they already trying to get rid of another coach? Tim Horan recalled 'sitting in the bus after the game seeing the smoke come out of Macqueen's ears. He was fuming not at the loss, but how the Wallabies acted and reacted after the game. Some of the side watched the Argentineans do a lap of honour and some were in the dressing room. We weren't a unit. He called the senior players together and tore strips off us—not because we lost, but how we handled the loss.'

Just as disconcerting was the concern that the Brumbies culture had now become the Wallabies culture. Was this the cappuccino club mark II—a team within a team? And Macqueen was hardly helping himself by selecting several Brumbies ahead of other better credentialled players.

One selection that did not add up was that of ACT captain Brett Robinson ahead of David Wilson as the open side flanker. Robinson was a fair player, but not in Wilson's class. Wilson's demotion did not make sense. Another concern involved several players approaching Macqueen and ARU officials shortly after the Buenos Aires loss requesting that when they arrived in England for the next stage of the tour they be allowed to stay closer to London and not in the backblocks of Windsor. The Wallabies obviously did not have their minds on the job.

If that was not a big enough problem, Macqueen then took issue with newspaper reports criticising the team and putting the coach on notice for his indecision. He repeatedly changed his mind about when he would announce the team to play England. It meant wasted training sessions because no one seemed to know who would be in the Test team. Macqueen appeared to be struggling to keep control. This prompted a heated moment at one training session when he stood at the other side of the field and refused to head anywhere near the *Daily Telegraph*'s Peter Jenkins and myself. Instead he sent Jeff Miller across to be peace maker. The act only inflamed the situation. When asked why Macqueen didn't have the courage to do his own dirty work, Miller just shrugged his shoulders. Eventually Macqueen, who maintained he was going to retain the team that had succumbed to the Pumas, gave us a list. There were three changes. Macqueen was described in the *Herald* as having performed 'the biggest back flip since Nadia Comaneci'.

There were even bigger rumblings in the background, however. Upset that Jenkins and I had the temerity to suggest he was unprofessional, Macqueen told the ARU he wanted to resign. It took a lot of convincing by O'Neill but Macqueen agreed to stay on as coach. It was clear we were dealing with a fickle character.

Eventually Macqueen distanced himself from the Brumbies culture. His selections improved and his philosophies began to be taken seriously by the players. Most importantly he was persuaded not to drop Eales in favour of Gregan as captain as he'd been threatening. Macqueen had doubts about Eales' leadership capabilities, believing he wasn't forceful enough and too often sided with his teammates. A good captain had to be like a good coach, he claimed, and know when to distance himself from the players.

O'Neill went to Eales to explain Macqueen's concerns, but Eales was adamant he wanted to remain Wallabies skipper. He was, however, willing to adapt his leadership style, and a meeting was organised between captain and coach. Eales explained to Macqueen that a number of Queensland players were concerned that the coach was Brumbies fixated at the selection table. He also believed the coach did not properly support him as skipper.

A crucial partnership was secured with this meeting. Eales remained captain; Macqueen became more confident as coach. The team, which had decided to base itself at Caloundra on the Queensland Sunshine Coast, began to win consistently and took on a far more professional approach to training and playing. A series triumph over New Zealand followed. Macqueen discovered a great new five-eighth in Stephen Larkham, David Wilson was back in the starting line-up and good players were jostling for positions. Under the tutelage of trainer Steve Nance the team's fitness dramatically improved. And another World Cup beckoned.

13

THE BEST OF VINTAGES

Several days before the 1999 World Cup final and with a look of boyish excitement, John Eales admitted he had been 'truly blessed. The planets are still aligned,' he said. He knew everything was going to plan. The Wallabies were just one step away from achieving glory.

Eales has many admirable qualities including his ability to put everything in perspective, to not lose sight of the basics and to remember and cherish those who have helped him along the way. It was less than seventy-two hours until the World Cup final kick off, but Australia's greatest rugby player was as humble as usual.

Five days before the start of the 1999 domestic season, Eales had injured his shoulder so severely that several Queensland officials believed he would never play again. Even he conceded privately his future was in serious doubt and that an appearance at the World Cup was the most remote of possibilities. Too much had to be done in too short a time. But someone, somewhere, was working in his corner. After several months of recuperation he was back, and he was involved in enough representative games before the World Cup to convince the Australian selectors that he was the only man to lead the Wallabies campaign.

'Yes, I have been blessed,' Eales said that day in Cardiff, 'but it was touch and go.' Not so touch and go was the confident stride he made across Cardiff's Millennium Stadium a few days later as he approached Queen Elizabeth to raise the William Webb Ellis trophy above his head.

In the dressing room that night the Australian captain was somewhat subdued. This had a lot to do with the tension of the final, which almost saw Eales walk his team off the field in protest at the French team's grubby tactics. It also had to do with him trying to comprehend why life had provided so many good turns in recent months. The team, however, was joyously relishing its World Cup victory. David Wilson, that tireless, understated beaver of the Wallaby pack, explained the thrill of 'achieving the ultimate goal after being together for two years, some of us four years . . . all the hard work, hours in the gym, weeks away from family, this has certainly made it worthwhile'.

Celebrations began on the field with the players going into a huddle—the cup in the middle of the circle—to sing a lung-bursting rendition of the national anthem followed by the slowest of laps of honours, taking more than thirteen minutes. One fan, wrapped in a green and gold scarf, beanie and jersey, walked just about the whole distance with the players, even though he was turfed over the fence three times by security guards, until even they gave up, realising there is no way to dent the spirit of Australian fans. In the dressing room the trophy, full with French champagne naturally, was passed from player to player with the chant: 'Matthew Burke, world champion; Ben Tune, world champion; Daniel Herbert, world champion . . .'

So why did the Wallabies win? There were plenty of stutters and U-turns along the way, but they were easily the best team at the tournament.

And how did they win? Some of the most telling observations came from the Wales coach Graham Henry, who had moved to Cardiff a year earlier after a successful career with Auckland. The crafty New Zealand headmaster knew something about national pride and how it compared on both sides of the equator. Before the Australia–Wales quarter-final he explained: 'As a Kiwi, and a guy who had coached New Zealand players, I know they take defeat a lot more to heart than people do in this part of the world. I'm not just talking about the Welsh. I'm talking about people in Europe generally. It's not part of their culture. I can't change that. Only generations can because there is a difference in attitude here. They don't take defeat inwardly as the All Blacks do, for example. That's why UK sport underachieves. The best sporting country in the world is Australia. They are hugely determined to do well whatever it is. It is all part of their education system, part of their pride in their country. They value that hugely, more than it is valued here.' Henry's point was made clear some days later. Wales had been beaten relatively comfortably by the Wallabies, but instead of heading immediately to the dressing room as Australia or New Zealand would have done, the Welsh did a lap of honour as if they were the conquerers.

That determination to do well was very much part of the culture of the 1999 Wallabies. It had been a long haul, however. The team had lived together for almost a year, hidden away in their Caloundra cocoon, allowing players to focus on winning the World Cup.

The campaign plan was intricate, long-sighted and painstakingly formulated by Macqueen, who was prepared to take inspiration from anywhere. It was also flexible, especially when opposing teams such as England and Wales began to copy it. Devising new moves became harder, especially with law interpretations at the breakdown restricting Australia's aim of quickly recycling the ball and the introduction of video analysis, which killed many secrets.

This didn't deter Macqueen, who with the help of his assistant coaches Jeff Miller and Tim Lane continued to think of new ways to bewilder the opposition. 'It has to do with options,' Macqueen said. 'You have got to have options off everything you are doing. It's not just having one move . . . you've got to have several options off it. It is always the best way to go, instead of resorting to tricks. A trick works only once.'

The greatest test though was to find ways to overcome cluttered, well-drilled, perfectly aligned defence. Improvements in defensive strategies had made try scoring that much more of a chore. 'A clue to this is to say, "What games have had a flat and structured defensive line for many years?" One of those is rugby league, and they've worked out different angles and different running techniques, including cross-field running, which Andrew and Matthew Johns at Newcastle are so good at. And there are rewards in taking some of the ideas from league.'

With Macqueen looking to rugby league for inspiration, it was no surprise that he sought someone from that code's ranks to improve the Wallabies' defensive strategies. That person was John Muggleton, a former Kangaroo representative.

Muggleton, who had been North Sydney's assistant coach until the club dismissed him, claims he 'was on the scrapheap until Rod came along and picked me up'. For a whole year he worked on ensuring nothing could get through the Australian defensive line. No one, not even the Wallabies, could have comprehended how effective this strategy would end up being, with France in the final becoming the fifth team in the World Cup unable to score a try against the Wallabies. The only player to cross the Australian try line at the 1999 World Cup was the unknown United States centre Jean Grobler, who scored during the pool match in Limerick.

The players were soon talking about keeping their opponents 'nude'—that is, tryless. During the finals week the message was 'Keep France nude', a war cry maintained by Phil Kearns, who had returned home midway during the tournament because of a serious foot injury. Sitting in his Sydney lounge room for a video conference call to Cardiff, a scantily dressed Kearns encouraged his teammates by chanting 'Keep France nude'. And not for the first time another Wallaby ran around the team hotel naked before surprising the coach by charging into his room.

Every coach has detractors within the player ranks and Macqueen was certainly no exception. While he was justifiably praised for his team management, some Wallabies struggled with his habit of sitting in the background. He was for some too standoffish, too rigidly focused and sometimes too sensitive. However, he was smart enough to get capable people to act as his go-betweens. Here Miller, Lane, technical adviser Alex Evans and team manager John McKay excelled.

The job of managing the team was also made a lot easier by the high level of camaraderie and intelligence within this squad. There was none of the usual bickering, and the players were genuine friends. While some in the back-up squad believed they should have been in the World Cup run-on team, they never let those frustrations spill over in public.

Still these Wallabies weren't the easiest team to train. Macqueen soon discovered how hard it was to restrain the 'ratbag, larrikin' element. For several days in a row he made mention of the difficulty of coaching a team that enjoyed 'yahooing and mucking around at training'. He had to interrupt practice several times while the Wallabies were in Ireland to remind them there were times when they actually had to be serious.

Unlike many teams where the forwards and backs train separately, Macqueen made certain that the Wallabies operated as a single unit most of the time. This undoubtedly helped communication and understanding and made for a vastly different team dynamic to the flawed 1995 World Cup campaign. This time around the Wallabies were relaxed, and no player or official was allowed the luxury of being big-headed.

Baggage master Ben Spindler was one of the first to show the team's spirit when three tonnes of gear, including 120 bags, was nearly left behind in Brisbane after the truck that arrived to cart it to the airport was discovered to be too small for the job. So Spindler hijacked a beer truck, instead. 'Mate, do it for your country,' he exhorted. And the truck driver did.

Matt Cockbain and Mark Connors were the next to show that Wallaby spirit following a strange mix-up in the minutes leading up to Australia's first match against Romania in Belfast. Just before kick off Cockbain accidentally stepped on David Wilson's foot and jarred his leg in the process. The team management opted against risking Cockbain, calling in Owen Finegan from the reserves to start the match. Connors, who was on the other side of the ground getting ready to commentate for ABC Radio, was beckoned back to the Australian dressing rooms to get changed to go onto the reserves bench. The only problem was that he had no gear with him. Connors borrowed Cockbain's jerseys, boots and shorts and eventually ran onto the field in the sixty-sixth minute.

Around the same time two streakers hopped the fence, one of them, a woman, performing revealing cartwheels in the middle of the field. With the Wallaby forwards in a huddle so they didn't lose their concentration, Tim Horan announced straight-faced: 'Come on, guys, focus.' He could joke, especially after scoring a try in the opening minute that earnt him a year's supply of Guinness beer, most of which was tipped over his head by teammates at a training session later that week.

Dublin again proved the ideal home away from home for the World Cup travellers. Camped at Portmarnock, a golf resort about fifteen kilometres from the centre of Dublin, the team was almost forgotten. Well away from the media spotlight, they were allowed to enjoy various diversions. As Matthew Burke explained: 'Back home people must be thinking we're on a golfing holiday because all the footage on TV has been of us on the tees.'

The locals soon avidly watched Wallaby training sessions. In return the Irish never ceased to fascinate and entertain the Wallabies. John Eales recalls when the team was staying at Dublin's Burlington Hotel, he had asked for a 9 am wake up call. He was up early and downstairs in the breakfast room with several players the next morning when he heard a frantic voice on the intercom: 'Will a Mr John Eales please report to reception, there is an urgent telephone call?'

At reception Eales told the frazzled attendant who he was. Pointing to the phone in her hand, she screamed to the hotel telephone operator: 'Quick, this is the John Eales, put the urgent telephone call through here.'

'Hello,' said the Wallaby captain into the phone.

'Is that John Eales?'

'Yes.'

'Mr Eales.'

'Yes.'

'It's your early morning wake up call.'

The Wallabies' ability to remain calm was crucial, especially when the atmosphere on the field became tense. The only time they were really threatened was during the semi-final against South Africa at Twickenham—an excruciating game that went into extra time.

On the way to the ground former Springbok captain and now back-up Wallaby back-rower Tiaan Strauss read out a message from Australian cricket captain Steve Waugh: 'There's only one thing better than beating the Springboks in a semi-final. That's tying with them and going through.' All of the players vividly remembered how the Australian cricket team had advanced to and then won the World Cup that year after tying with South Africa in a semi-final. But as surely as it couldn't happen again, it did. Tied 18–18 at full time and tied 21–21 halfway through extra time, the Wallabies finally won and went through to the final.

Conditions were appalling with a swirling wind and teeming rain. No tries were scored but, as the game was dominated by kicking, it was a compelling spectacle that revolved around two special characters—Australian five-eighth Stephen Larkham and centre Tim Horan. Larkham, sometimes a muddled dreamer, stunned the crowd with an amazing bolt from the blue. He knew little about kicking field goals and couldn't recall if he'd ever kicked one before at senior level. Yet there he was, about forty-five metres out, ninety-three minutes of the game gone, the scores level at 21–21, his right leg throbbing because of a cork injury about to do something extraordinary.

In front of him was a sea of South African defenders. He was going to be swamped. But the words from Wallabies assistant coach

Tim Lane as Larkham ran out of the dressing room for extra time came back to him: 'Mate, if you get in the opposition half, don't wait for de Beer to take a field goal—take one yourself.'

Larkham only had a second. He took quick aim, the ball wobbled off his boot and floated away, helped along by a powerful if fickle wind. 'It was a pretty ordinary drop, but it sounded pretty sweet and I just watched it go the whole way over,' Larkham said. As did everyone else with their mouths agape. Larkham's teammates went into hysterics as he tried to keep a straight face and to fathom what exactly had happened.

The previous week South African five-eighth Jannie de Beer had thanked God for kicking his team to victory. This time Larkham said: 'I'm not a churchgoer, but after what happened today I might have to consider it.'

The other Australian hero, Horan, was further out in the backline. After the match Eales compared the ageless centre with Australian Test cricketer Dean Jones, who scored a double century against India in Madras in 1986 despite being close to physical and mental collapse for most of the innings.

Horan's problem started on Friday morning after a severe gastric attack forced him to spend the next twenty-six hours in bed with a raging fever. Probably the toughest player in the World Cup squad, Horan was so sick he considered several times on Friday night withdrawing from the semi-final. Even at 10.30 am on match day team management was still unsure whether he would play.

However, Horan had convinced himself to ride out the pain. He took every precaution, making sure he sat next to the toilet on the team bus during the half-hour trip to the ground. He took a carbohydrate solution before the game and several tablets at half-time to quell abdominal cramps.

In moments of need Australia had always relied on Horan, and he played few better games than this one. Every facet was perfect. The Springbok defence had no counter for him, with his repeated mid-field busts and his ever-straight running seeing him break the advantage line time and again. His impenetrable defence, a hallmark of his seventy-nine Test career, often saw South Africa lose critical possession.

Eventually his legs 'turned to jelly' and Horan was replaced in the seventy-third minute, but by that stage he had done more than enough. How had he kept going?

'Adrenalin, I suppose,' Horan said. 'Before the game I was crook. On the bus I felt crook. But I just tried to forget about it.'

And how was he going to celebrate? 'I'll probably double up and have two pieces of toast tonight.'

Elsewhere, ARU chief executive John O'Neill and Archbishop Desmond Tutu were enjoying more than just a few pieces of toast. In London to give the Springboks a blessing before the game the Archbishop, wearing a Springbok jersey with the number 22 on his back, was in hysterics when O'Neill told him that in Australia a beer had been colloquially named after him. 'In the days of the Tooheys 2.2, when anyone wanted to buy a can of it from the bar they would ask for a "Desmond",' O'Neill explained.

The day after their epic victory against South Africa the Wallabies returned to their Cardiff base to watch France play New Zealand in the second semi-final—a match that surpassed theirs in drama, when the All Blacks suffered one of the most unexpected losses in international rugby history. As they watched the French apply the guillotine to New Zealand, the Australian players whooped, hollered and danced. But then reality hit: 'Hey, we don't know anything about the French.'

For several weeks, and especially the previous twenty-four hours, they had been preparing to face the All Blacks in the final. That was natural, as the All Blacks were the undisputed favourites. They had never contemplated meeting the French, particularly after Les Bleus had finished last in the previous Five Nations tournament. The Wallabies had compiled lengthy videos exposing possible weaknesses in the All Blacks' armour, organised dossiers on each opposing player and spent hours working on strategies to cut off New Zealand's power sources. The team's video analysts and strategists, including the New South Wales coach Ian 'Speed' Kennedy and John Muggleton, had attended virtually every recent All Blacks match to ensure that Australia knew exactly what their expected rivals were up to. They hadn't even thought of attending any French matches.

Video analyst Scott Hamilton had a sleepless night trying to find footage of recent French games while the coaching staff desperately tried to remember how they had prepared for their previous encounter against France less than twelve months earlier. Defeated by the Wallabies 32–21 in Paris, only two members of the 1999 French backline played that day.

Adding to the Australians' concern about their lack of preparation was the French unpredictability. Virtually all international teams have a structure and basic strategies but the French had always relied on free spirit and free expression, which on any day could make them either the most destructive team in world rugby or the most ridiculous.

Australia decided to work on its strengths by not giving the French any room, by intimidating them with a solid defensive structure and by not allowing them any time to go wide in attack. Macqueen's modus operandi throughout his lengthy coaching career relied on an intense defensive strategy. His teams from club, representative to national, were all similar—rigid, tight and cautious outfits. In the previous fifteen months the Australians had been held try-less in a Test four times, which saw Macqueen criticised for his team's lack of adventure and for wasting his two wingers Joe Roff and Ben Tune.

Macqueen was not going to change his approach in finals week. All it required was focus and for his players to remain on the alert, especially after the All Blacks accused the French of biting, head butting, eye gouging and even grabbing their testicles during the World Cup semi-final. The French were widely condemned for their behaviour, but the matter was further inflamed when their tight-head prop Franck Tournaire miraculously escaped suspension after clearly biting the face of All Blacks captain Taine Randell.

In the rooms, a former Wallaby also played an important role. Front-rower and now television commentator Chris Handy was given the job of being Classic Wallaby for the day, handing the Test jersey to the match day captain and then explaining what being a Wallaby meant to him. Macqueen had introduced this ritual shortly after taking over as Australian coach, with illustrious former Wallabies being asked to address the players before they ran onto the Test arena. The emotion of the moment was too much for some, with several well-known former players breaking down in tears when explaining how important the Wallaby jersey had been to them.

Handy arrived with a bottle of 1991 Grange Hermitage under his arm. He handed it over to Eales. 'Nineteen ninety-one was a good year,' he said, 'and we know 1999 will be the same. On behalf of all Australian supporters, please don't leave any gas in the tank.' There was hardly a dry eye in the dressing room.

A few hours later, after Australia had fastidiously worn down the French in a clinical, dour final, beating them 35–12, that 1991 Grange was treated with special reverence. It wasn't tipped into the Webb Ellis Cup as the champagne had been, but was carefully poured into special glasses and shared by the players.

It was at that moment they knew they were special. They had succeeded. And, yes, they had been blessed. It was the best of vintages.

14
FAME AND FAREWELLS

Just down the coast from the centre of Cape Town, along the Camps Bay strip, are countless alluring drinking spots. It was here that several ACT Brumbies players started the 2000 season by being held by South African police following an incident that has never been properly explained and that still has ramifications to this day. It was an incident that threatened the fabric and culture of the Wallabies.

The Brumbies had just beaten the Stormers in a Super 12 tournament match, and to celebrate one of the team's most important victories several players headed to Camps Bay for a quiet drink that turned into a marathon session. At the end of the night five players—Owen Finegan, Rod Kafer, Joe Roff, Peter Ryan and Bill Young—took a cab back to the team hotel. There was an argument over the fare, and one player decided to pull the taxi meter out of its socket. It was soon after that Brumbies manager Phil Thomson got an early morning telephone call from the local media telling him that five of his players had been detained by police on a disorderly conduct charge and for trashing a taxi. The driver, Riedewaan Abrahams, said that he had picked up the players around 1 am and that they were 'raucously drunk'.

Days of chaos followed as the Australian media and the ARU demanded that the Brumbies send the guilty players home immediately. Receiving nothing more than a minor ticking off the Brumbies, who complained that the incident had been dramatically 'overblown' by the Australian media, appeared to have lost touch with reality. The incident also confirmed what most observers knew, that the club was controlled by the players.

While originally apologetic and contrite about their behaviour, soon after the Brumbies orchestrated a well-choreographed campaign to try to apportion the blame elsewhere. When the team arrived back in Australia, it was clear that a number of officials, players and supporters were looking for a fight and that the Sydney rugby media was No. 1 enemy. The entire team believed that everyone was out to get them. This was rubbish, of course, but it worked in psyching them up.

Some years after leaving the Brumbies Eddie Jones, their coach at the time, conceded that they 'sometimes' carried a huge chip on their shoulder. When he could, Jones certainly drove that vehicle with gusto, using it to motivate his players. And they could get away with this behaviour in Canberra because the Brumbies were a protected species. Some of their biggest allies were Canberra radio, television and newspaper journalists who openly displayed their allegiance. Objectivity was often lost in the process.

Sadly this Brumbies' culture quickly manifested itself in the Wallabies. When George Smith made his exceptional Test debut that year in Paris he declined to speak to News Limited journalist Peter Jenkins in the dressing room. The directive appeared to have come from his Brumbies teammates.

As Wallabies coach Macqueen found himself in a difficult position. Having relied on the Brumbies model to get the national coaching job, he now realised its shortfalls. The Wallabies had developed an arrogant streak. And they could get away with this behaviour because they were winning. They were even applauded for defeats, which was the case with the opening Bledisloe Cup Test of 2000 in Sydney—described as the greatest rugby match of all.

Under the headline 'The Night Heaven Came to Earth', the *Sydney Morning Herald* editorialised: 'Once or twice in a lifetime, a sport lives up to its promise—transcending the mere mortal. On Saturday, a world-record crowd—109,874 people—witnessed a contest that will be talked about for as long as any of us live. Put simply, it was the best Test match, not just in the history of the Bledisloe Cup, but in the history of rugby union. Rarely are any of us privileged to watch two champion opponents, at the peak of their powers, slug it out for the finish. Think of Muhammad Ali versus George Foreman in the Rumble in the Jungle. Or Bjorn Borg versus John McEnroe in the last of the Swede's Wimbledon victories. Or Don Bradman batting against Harold Larwood's bowling before the word Bodyline tarnished their rivalry . . . The two best rugby teams on the planet fought out a contest so epic, so unpredictable, and so preposterous, that some people went straight home from the stadium to watch it again on video. Sure, the purists can carp about the defensive errors from both teams, and the wayward kicks which eventually cost Australia the game. But this was the night when the code lived up to its self-appointed title, Heaven's Game.'

This was some game. In the most extraordinary start to any top-level Test match, Australia appeared dead and buried after just five minutes when Tana Umaga, Pita Alatini and Christian Cullen each crossed the try line within three minutes of each other. Even the All Blacks were astounded to be 24–0 up 292 seconds into the game, with their hooker Anton Oliver thinking, 'What's going on? This is ridiculous.'

That the scores were level at 24–24 by the thirtieth minute is testament to the spirit and resolve of the World Cup champions. Every other international team would have probably given up. But the Wallabies again showed why they were the most intelligent team for nearly a decade. As against Ireland at Lansdowne Road in 1991, where they devised a plan that turned despair into World Cup glory, they proved they were the most clinical thinkers under pressure. They didn't get rattled. They didn't rush. They just painstakingly worked themselves back into the game, taking some risks but always trusting themselves.

Chris Latham, Stirling Mortlock and Joe Roff scored the four tries to level the scores. They could have even taken the lead at half-time had the ball not been spilled at the most inopportune time by the forwards following the best pass of the match, a backhand flick from Stephen Larkham to Roff. Finally it all came down to a speculative basketball-like pass by All Black Taine Randell to Lomu over the outstretched arms of Jason Little. The New Zealand winger took off to score and win the Test by four points.

David Campese described it as 'the best game I've seen'. Simon Poidevin thought it was more than just a game of rugby: 'As a sporting contest it was right up there with the best in the world.' The only person who applied the brakes to the enthusiasm was Dave Brockhoff, who groaned: 'I don't go for all that Harlem Globetrotter stuff. What Bledisloe Cups mean to me is winning. It's not football. It's winning ball. We were better for so long, and we lost.'

It was expected that every game after that would be an anti-climax, but the Wallabies continued to produce extraordinary feats that season. Just three weeks later in Wellington another Bledisloe Cup match was anyone's to take. With seconds to go the Wallabies were two points behind when referee Jonathan Kaplan penalised the All Blacks at the breakdown. The result hinged on the final penalty goal kick.

Wallaby captain John Eales assumed that Mortlock would take the shot. There was an eerie silence, until replacement hooker Jeremy Paul sidled up to his skipper and said that Mortlock had been replaced several minutes earlier. 'Stirling's off, John. You're up,' Paul said.

Eales shrugged his shoulders, beckoned for the kicking tee, took aim, and from an acute angle kicked the ball through to the astonishment of all. Then in Durban it happened again—but this time Mortlock kicked the last-minute penalty goal for another triumph.

While his team was playing with great skill and determination, Macqueen was becoming increasingly suspicious of anything he thought would affect their preparation. He was even upset when helicopters hovered near training sessions, believing they may be spying. In Wellington he conducted a madcap secret training session on the afternoon before the match that even saw players checking bushes around the ground in search of intruders before they started their drills.

For the Durban Test, the Wallabies decided to spend the week before the game more than one hundred kilometres down the coast at a plush golf resort. The players loved the space, and Macqueen was in his element. At one stage the Wallabies decided to have a 'bad shirt' golf day. Macqueen joined in, but became increasingly edgy when a Sydney television crew began filming. He didn't want the wrong message to be sent back to Australia. Later that day he approached the crew, making it clear he didn't want the footage to be seen in Sydney. The crew stood its ground, and the footage was sent back to Australia and shown on the major television news bulletins. Everyone except the coach took it in the right vein.

Struggling with a painful back, Macqueen's actual involvement in the Test preparation was limited. On the day of the game he could hardly walk, and then he missed parts of the Test because he was forced to lie on the floor of the coach's box. His assistants Ewen McKenzie and Tim Lane did an excellent job taking over a great deal of the coaching of the team that day.

Celebrations of the win turned riotous when the team took over the main bar at the golf resort. In the early hours of Sunday morning prop Bill Young grabbed one of the pink flamingoes from the pool area and brought it inside, to be joined by a sizeable group of Wallaby-types dancing naked at the bar.

But Macqueen was gradually losing interest in his role, and this became very clear in 2001. Even though the British and Irish Lions were in town, he seemed distracted. As one member of the team management explained: 'The passion had gone. He was wanting out. It was just a case of when. He wasn't really that interested in the Lions tour. He'd had enough.' So much so that it was Ewen McKenzie who gave the final team talk before the second Test because Macqueen had decided to take a phone call.

Macqueen had first begun contemplating retirement following the Durban triumph, telling John O'Neill over lunch that he wanted to give it away after the Lions series. He didn't think he was physically or mentally capable of continuing. O'Neill wanted him to stay on until at least the end of the 2001 Tri Nations series, and Macqueen reluctantly agreed. Macqueen's relationship with several leading Wallabies had also turned sour. Not surprisingly the core of this group were Brumbies, who openly lampooned him.

By the time of the first Test against the Lions Macqueen had made up his mind. He was going at the end of the series, no matter what. It was time to find a successor. That's why Eddie Jones was sighted at the back of the coach's box in Sydney during the first Lions Test sitting near the legendary Australian swimming coach Laurie Lawrence. Lawrence was more than an onlooker, having been Ken Catchpole's halfback back-up on the 1964 Wallabies tour of New Zealand. But no one expected him to take over proceedings in the way he did that night. Many in the box thought that he had convinced himself he was actually the Wallabies coach. He was not invited back.

The real highlight of the British and Irish Lions series revolved around one lineout in the third Test in Sydney. With two minutes to go in a series locked at one-all and Australia leading 29–23, the Lions had taken play into the Wallaby quarter in their last bid for glory. The Lions had the throw about seven metres out. Hooker Keith Wood aimed at his captain Martin Johnson at the front of the lineout and threw a bullet at the second-rower's outstretched hands. The plan for the Lions was to win the lineout, form themselves into a rolling maul and then attempt to steam-roll their way over the Wallaby line. But somehow Justin Harrison, the Australian second-rower playing in his first Test, plucked the ball out of Johnson's grasp, taking it to ground. Australia staved off defeat. The series won, Macqueen was able to finish his career on a high.

Macqueen deserved the widespread praise he received. He was a most meticulous coach, understanding the importance of consensus and teamwork both on and off the field. He understood the role, when to be involved and when to stand back. His great skill was being able to delegate, and ensuring that he was surrounded by talented offsiders. He knew how to build a buffer and how to protect himself. But he was helped in his exceptional seventy-nine per cent success rate of thirty-four wins from forty-three Tests by having so many capable footballers in his team. As renowned Australian cricketer Bill O'Reilly would say: 'A collie dog could have coached that side.'

Whether Macqueen was the ultimate super coach is open to conjecture. His assistant coaches, including Jeff Miller, Tim Lane, Ewen McKenzie, Glen Ella and John Muggleton, all played major roles in helping to prop him up. Macqueen's parting words to a team that still had doubts about him—'You'll definitely find my successor far more interesting and newsworthy than me'—certainly foretold of an interesting new era and the jackhammer, no holds barred approach of Eddie Jones.

•

It was during this time of strength that the ARU decided on an interesting change of direction. For decades the code had lost its best talent to the professional league ranks. Shackled as it was by its amateur status, the lure of huge salaries had been impossible to resist. However, with the game having gone professional and being unencumbered by salary caps, rugby union could now virtually offer whatever it liked, which was certainly far more than league.

Suddenly high-profile league players wanted to be part of the other rugby code, and playing in a truly international game. The contracts were also very attractive, with salaries at least threefold what league offered. For the first time rugby was seen as a real power, and not just the forgotten cousin of league, AFL and soccer.

Crowds were growing at games and public interest had intensified through pay television and the attraction of the Super 12 and Tri Nations competitions. It also helped that the Wallabies were winning.

Rugby league wasn't exactly teetering on the edge of extinction, but it was certainly under threat after the prolonged Super League battle. The ARU had no shame in attacking while league was distracted, with John O'Neill pushing the idea that he wanted rugby union to be the people's game and not the pastime of networking toffs. The planning was intense, with dual international Michael O'Connor employed as a consultant and talent spotter.

Wendell Sailor, one of league's highest profile and showiest players, was the first to be approached. A man full of bravado, he liked what he heard, particularly the opportunity to strut on a far larger international stage. He signed in early February 2001. At his first training session with the Queensland Reds at Ballymore he walked through the turnstiles and proclaimed, 'Dell sells, so watch these babies swing.'

Sailor's signing was a blatant headline grab but it did not end there, with Mat Rogers and Lote Tuqiri soon following. Not surprisingly the signings led to disenchantment among the rugby ranks, including within the Wallabies. Stephen Larkham was among those concerned, later writing in his World Cup diary: 'There was discontent, maybe even some resentment, at the whole concept of importing players from league. For one thing, it rankled with senior players that the league recruits were reportedly on bigger contracts than they were. Somehow it just didn't seem fair that rugby players who had spent most of their lives in the game and worked their way up through the ranks should be leap-frogged—money-wise—by league players who had just arrived on the scene and had yet to prove themselves in rugby.'

Eventually Sailor, Rogers and Tuqiri were accepted by the players because of their sheer talent. But there was a downside—Tuqiri and Sailor's behavioural problems. Both were eventually forced to leave the game, one for dabbling in drugs and the other for a succession of incidents that contravened Wallabies team protocol. Some years later many rugby diehards were still wondering whether the overall investment had actually been worth it.

•

John Eales had decided that the Sydney Tri Nations game against New Zealand would be his last, and with it came an outpouring of emotion. The *Sydney Morning Herald* devoted a four-page liftout to the departure of Australia's greatest rugby player and most successful Wallaby captain.

The public John Eales is very close to the private John Eales, and while he is the last of the nice guys he is no angel. Like everyone else he has a few stories he wishes to remain in the bottom drawer. But as Australian captain he took international rugby diplomacy to its highest level. Unlike the always expressive Farr-Jones, the only other Australian captain to hold a World Cup trophy over his head, Eales was no walking headline. He was smart and didn't treat the media as dills. It is just the way he was.

Eales did enjoy telling stories against himself, however, including one about his first pub crawl with the Brothers club. Meandering his way around some of Brisbane hotels celebrating a triumph with his teammates, he realised he'd left the lunchbox his ever-caring mother had packed somewhere behind in a bar. Knowing his mother would crucify him if he returned home without it, Eales sprinted from one bar to the next to look for it. For years, his Brothers teammates ribbed him about his frantic search.

Then after the 1999 World Cup triumph, while waiting at the checkout with his family, two children walked up to him and asked for his autograph. As he obliged, an elderly man looked him up and down and asked: 'Are you w-w-w-w-w-w with the W-w-w-w-w-w . . . ?'

The ever-polite Eales replied: 'Am I with the Wallabies?'

The pensioner looked aghast. 'No, no, no, are you w-w-w-w-w-w-w-w-w-w-w with the W-w-w-w-w-w-wiggles?'

A few weeks later he read in yet another Brisbane newspaper report that his nickname was 'Nobody'—as in 'Nobody's perfect.' Eales was perplexed. 'Look, nobody calls me Nobody.'

Precisely.

His last match was a fitting finale for the much-liked and much-admired Eales. Just a few weeks after Australia succeeded in winning in Dunedin, following ninety-six years of fruitless trips to the New Zealand South Island city, the Tri Nations revolved around the outcome of the Sydney Test. The match was excruciatingly tight. With just minutes to go the All Blacks led by four points. Australia had been awarded the penalty, and Eales had the choice of going for goal or chancing his arm with a final fling for a try. Pointing to the sideline, he chose the latter option. The Wallabies kept the pressure on in the All Blacks quarter until Toutai Kefu opted for the head down, go straight approach, somehow ploughing his way through a paddock of black soil and then, Inspector Gadget like and under a pile of bodies, extending his body over the try line to score.

An overwhelmed Eales was the first to leap onto Kefu, realising that a potential horror tale had just been transformed into the perfect boy's own story hero ending. Eales' gratitude to Kefu was everlasting. 'I will buy Toutai Kefu a drink any time and anywhere.'

Kefu, known as Tonga's Bob Hope because of his wacky sense of humour, holds Eales to that pledge to this day.

15

FAST EDDIE

Eddie Jones is the ultimate scrapper. He loves confrontation and the intellectual challenges that coaching provides. He is a workaholic, single minded, disciplined, dictatorial and often tricky to handle. Andrew Blades, one of his many assistant coaches, conceded that working with his mother-in-law was easier than working with Fast Eddie. He has sent a long line of assistants one step closer to the funny farm. Jones' grinding 'fingernails scraping across the chalkboard' voice was as grating as his temper tantrums were legendary. One of Jones' assistants was once sighted on a flight reading a book about self-confidence. The reason? 'So I can stand up to Eddie better,' was the reply.

As a footballer Jones played well above his weight. A resourceful hooker who represented New South Wales, he was just too small to go to the next level. But what he lacked in height and weight he made up for in bravado and commitment. Not too many hookers got the better of Fast Eddie. His other nickname—'Beaver'—was also apt, renowned as he was for burrowing in, getting in everyone's way and hovering centimetres away from the action. The ultimate competitor, he was a master sledger who was always in the face of his opponents. His reputation for having one of the nastiest tongues in the first-grade ranks was renowned. Even though he had calmed down considerably since his playing days, when in the mood Jones knew how to use caustic language to great effect. He was guilty at times of belittling his staff, but he could also be wickedly funny.

When Jones replaced Macqueen he explained that his primary interests were rugby and his family and there was virtually no time for anything else. His was a 'fairly obsessive life'. As Brumbies coach, between ten to fourteen hours per day were devoted to coaching, but the pace picked up even more when he began wearing the green and gold tracksuit. He was invariably the first up and the last to bed, poring over videos, working on strategies or dealing with team management and preparation. He was as meticulous on detail as he was with punctuality.

He demanded a lot of himself, and the demands he placed on his support staff were nearly as high. He hated shirkers. And unlike Macqueen, he sometimes struggled to delegate. Macqueen was big picture. Jones was fascinated by the microscopic detail, to the extent that he dug so far down into statistics that they sometimes became misleading. Nonetheless, no one could fault Jones' knowledge of the game; it was encyclopaedic. Few were better than him in comprehending the intricate nature of an often bewildering, ever-changing game. His technical understanding was second to none.

Jones was the first Wallaby coach in recent decades whose predecessor had gladly handed over the reins. But there was an edge—he was taking over one of Australia's most successful ever rugby teams. 'There's no more trophies left to win,' Jones said. 'You go up to the Australian Rugby Union offices, and everything that's silver in world rugby is up there. So the aspiration cannot be to win more trophies. The aspiration must be, how can we play better?' He wanted his team to be as ruthless as the Australian cricket team, who at that time were 'crushing oppositions'.

This was not a surprising comparison because Jones' other sporting passion was cricket, having played as an early order batsman in the Sydney grade ranks. His hero was Australian Test captain

Ian Chappell. While there was a lot of Chappelli in Jones, he soon discovered that getting the team to go that extra step was difficult. He was lumbered with a squad attuned to success and not exactly hungry for more.

In his first week Jones said more than Macqueen had in his whole term as national coach. Whereas a Macqueen press conference was often stage managed and tedious, Jones' media briefings were always interesting, controversial or newsworthy. In his Thursday sermons during Test weeks he took delight in talking up new ideas and rugby philosophies, or just having a good old sledge to test reporters' shorthand. Some of his ideas were crazy, but none were boring. Many of them attracted enormous headlines.

Jones enjoyed tussling with the media. He was fascinated by it, and appeared to read every word written in every newspaper. And he knew how to use the media. If he missed a call from a journalist he would invariably ring back. He was clever enough to know that by using the media he could always get his say. It was a wise and fruitful ploy. He certainly knew how to sell himself.

Keeping in contact with the rugby media also ensured he knew what was happening in the background—important information, especially as Australian rugby politics ranks among the grubbiest in the world with its constantly changing alliances.

In contrast, the captain Jones appointed—George Gregan—appeared to freeze in front of the media. He basically said nothing. This wasn't a deliberate strategy; Gregan appeared genuinely ill at ease at media events. His words were usually painfully bland, making even Macqueen's utterances seem interesting, almost riveting. Gregan's standoffish and occasionally prickly nature just extended the gap between the media and the Wallabies.

Adding to the pressure of life with Jones was that he could be stifling. Like Macqueen he appeared wary of intruders, and delighted in staging closed training sessions. This approach became so loopy that when the Wallabies made Coffs Harbour their base the training ground was surrounded by security guards. Even the boundary fences were covered so that no one could peer in. It was Us versus Them, the Brumbies all over again.

Jones also did not help himself in trying to separate the Wallabies from the ARU head office. Macqueen attempted to do this and then realised it was smarter working closely with the ARU administrators. Instead Jones tried to create a barrier, which led to friction with his employers—who were worried that Brumbie-like player power would now infiltrate and corrupt the Wallabies.

It didn't take long for the ARU to become concerned about Jones' people skills. He was a difficult task master. Stories were whispered about his near-impossible demands and about him driving members of his staff to tears. As O'Neill remarked: 'He was immersed in minutiae rather than taking a big-picture approach.' For players who had been around for awhile, it forced them to change the way they approached the game. Matt Burke, who had played under a number of Australian coaches, made an interesting observation in 2005, explaining that in the 1990s 'we [the Wallabies] had two set moves we used . . . now we walk out of team meetings with pages and pages of moves and tactics and analysis'.

As at the Brumbies, Jones was eager that the senior players had input into his decision-making. But this turned ill on him, especially during the 2003 World Cup when several players appeared to be deliberately leaking team information to the media. Jones was just the latest leader to discover that when you give players too much rope they will use it to strangle you.

The Wallaby training squad became increasingly selfish, and standards gradually dropped. While the ARU staff were being kept at arm's length, Jones was soon struggling to maintain morale. He made it known that his one-time Brumbies captain Brett Robinson, now head of the ARU high-performance unit, was not exactly welcome around the team. The change in their relationship, where Robinson was Jones' boss, appeared to irritate the coach.

And when the Wallabies began to lose on a regular basis, Jones made the error of getting offside with John O'Neill after O'Neill had criticised the Wallabies during their 2003 World Cup campaign. It even got to the stage where some of Jones' underlings openly criticised the ARU chief in front of the players. Team dynamics were very unhealthy.

Unlike Bob Dwyer, who encouraged his players to get out and discover the world, Jones allowed his players to turn into mushrooms. On his first northern hemisphere tour in 2002 before a match in Madrid against a rag-tag Spanish team at a local university ground, Jones saw no point in having the Wallabies take a guided tour of the Real Madrid soccer stadium. Located only a few kilometres away from the Australian team hotel it was an inspirational place, especially Real Madrid's trophy room housing the most important trophies in international football. It would have been a timely reminder of where the Wallabies actually sat in international sport. When this was suggested by the travelling Australian media, who had just attended the ground, Jones replied that while a visit was a good idea he would struggle to get the players interested in going there.

Within a few weeks they would learn exactly where they now stood. Losses to England at Twickenham and to France in Marseille saw the Wallabies slide down the international ladder. Team spirit also slipped. A number of players became angry that in France the team hotel was in a small out-of-the-way village on the French Riviera. They complained about not having anything to do in the magical village of Bandol, where Marlon Brando once came for secret dalliances.

This was not Jones' only problem. Earlier in the year a drug scandal enveloped the Wallabies when it was revealed that winger Ben Tune had taken a banned substance, probenecid, to overcome a knee infection. Although this had occurred when he was playing for the Queensland Reds, the Wallabies and ARU were swept up in the controversy when it became known that it had taken the national body more than a year to hold an enquiry and that it had allowed Tune to travel to South Africa so he could play in a Tri Nations match in Johannesburg.

That was all momentarily forgotten, however, when midway during the season Wallabies fullback Matt Burke joined the Wallabies Master of Suspense Club by becoming the fourth Australian player in two seasons to steal a Tri Nations victory in the final moments of play against the All Blacks. With just thirteen seconds to go and behind by one point, Australia was awarded the penalty. Adding to the drama was that just a few minutes earlier Burke had hit the left upright from virtually the same spot. As he lined up the Test-deciding kick Burke said to himself: 'Knock it over, you're a hero. Miss it, you're a villain.' Wallaby backs coach Glen Ella could not bear to look, forwards coach Ewen McKenzie could not speak and head coach Jones tried to keep his composure as the ball lobbed over the upright and Burke ensured that the Bledisloe Cup was Australia's again.

•

Wallaby success didn't last long, and victory was followed by losses. The team was on a treadmill. It was even described as boring. When the Wallabies lost to England at Twickenham at the end of 2002 the slanging began in earnest between the Australian media and the coach, and between England coach Clive Woodward and Jones. Asked eventually if the tour had been a failure Jones snarled: 'Well, you blokes have already written that. What's a failure, mate?'

While the Wallabies had disappeared in London, things only got worse when they headed to Dublin to face a belligerent Ireland, going down 18–9. As the victorious Irish team did a magical lap of honour around Lansdowne Road to U2's 'Beautiful Day', the Wallabies sat in their dressing room trying to block the music from their ears. They weren't helped by a dreadful pre-match speech from a former Test player whose general theme was that 'my wife thinks you're crap, and so do I'. The players shook their heads in disbelief at what is regarded as by far the worst speech ever made by a Classic Wallaby.

After the match Russell Crowe, who was in Ireland filming, attempted to brighten their spirits when he visited the dressing room. Ignored by the players, he made a hasty exit. Then Bono and Edge walked past the rooms each with a slab of Guinness on their shoulders, singing 'It's a Beautiful Day.' This sent the players into an even deeper despondency.

Team spirits did lift at the end of that tour, however, when the Wallabies spent a wild week in Genoa. On the eve of the Italy Test, a member of the support staff was given a buck's night at a local restaurant. After several hours of solid drinking, the teetering guest of honour decided to get some fresh air. Sitting in the back of a ute and struggling to see straight, he decided to rest for a minute or two. Within seconds he was sound asleep. He didn't wake up until six or seven hours later to find himself still in the back of the ute but now hurtling at full speed down an Italian motorway. Eventually the driver heard the mad banging from the back and stopped. Neither the driver nor the Wallaby official could make sense of one another so the driver, flinging his arms in the air, got back in the car and took off, leaving the official on the side of the road to hitchhike his way back into town. Despite the revelry, the Wallabies finished the tour with an easy win over Italy.

•

As the Wallabies went into 2003, a World Cup year, off-field dramas seemed to be never-ending. And Jones was taking a tough approach to player indiscretions. The gregarious Elton Flatley was suddenly no longer in the training squad after missing a team recovery session, using the excuse that he had slept in following a Test victory. Two seasons earlier Jones had cut Andrew Walker from the squad when he went missing as the rest of his teammates boarded flights for a Test match in Perth. Walker was again suspended several months later when he disappeared from the Coffs Harbour training base.

But it was the quality of play in the lead up to the World Cup that was of real concern. The Wallabies simply weren't up to it. The statistics were numbing. Australia had lost seven of the twelve Tests leading into the tournament, which was to be played in Australia.

The ARU was bracing itself for a public relations disaster. Jones was asked, 'Where do you go from here?' His reply, 'Maybe Mauritius.'

While their problems were everywhere and they were off the pace, the Wallabies didn't allow themselves to be intimidated on the field during an especially disgraceful Test against the South Africans in Brisbane. The Springboks gouged, bit, spat and king hit their way through the game, losing 29–9. A seething Jones took no prisoners at the post-match press conference, explaining that the Springboks had been involved in a deliberate, underhand campaign to distract the Wallabies by playing the man and not the ball. 'It puts a whole slur on the game, and we need to expose them,' Jones said. Shortly after, South African and Australian officials almost came to blows at an after-match function where the visitors made an official complaint about Jones' behaviour.

While Jones remained belligerent, his skipper Gregan came under considerable pressure over his style of play. He found himself accused of playing within his own comfort zone, especially when two days before the Wallabies went down to the All Blacks he told a press conference: 'I don't buy into that whole passion thing. I think it's a load of rubbish really.' Critics emerged from everywhere. Even former Wallaby Peter FitzSimons took aim. 'Maybe it is not such rubbish after all, George,' FitzSimons opined. 'Everything this correspondent knows about backline play could fit on the back of a postage stamp and still have room left over for the Lord's Prayer but the wise heads I speak with on the subject all seem to agree that the Gregan practice of taking a couple of steps before releasing the ball is severely restricting the space the Wallabies backline has to move in.'

FitzSimons was not a lone voice. Even the ARU chief O'Neill chimed in, publicly arguing that the Wallabies had to provide some value for the enormous amount of money that had been poured into their campaign. O'Neill's comment left Jones seething, telling the players that what O'Neill had said was 'out of order'. Gregan was more reserved, explaining that while he thought O'Neill did 'a very good job', he 'could never understand why he seemed so happy to promote confrontation'.

With a World Cup looming, Australian rugby was now in two camps with the administration on one side and the Wallabies on the other. Reconciliation was going to be difficult, especially when the ARU sent staff to Coffs Harbour to keep an eye on those running Camp Wallaby. The Wallabies accused the ARU staff of 'spying'. They also complained that ARU officials were deliberately leaking disparaging information about the team to the media.

But relations soured even more when the ARU and the Australian players union (RUPA) clashed over a bonus payment system and the use of player images in promotional World Cup material. The ARU proposed a one-off incentive payment of around $80,000 per player if they won the World Cup. RUPA wanted to double that. Believing players deserved more because Australia was hosting the World Cup and the ARU was bound to enjoy a financial windfall, RUPA initiated Supreme Court action seeking orders that prevented the ARU from approaching players to sign a World Cup participation agreement. The RUPA submission included an affidavit signed by Gregan. The ARU was astounded that the Wallaby captain it had appointed had now turned, especially as the affidavit included details of a private meeting in Coffs Harbour that O'Neill had spoken at. Betrayal was the word echoing down the ARU corridors.

In his autobiography published in 2008 Gregan said that O'Neill used 'some colourful language' to explain at that meeting that he didn't want RUPA negotiating on the players' behalf, and accused them of 'ratting' on Australian rugby. 'When I put my signature to an affidavit that was part of the RUPA's court submission, in which I stated that O'Neill had placed undue pressure on the team to sign the PA [participation agreement], our relationship was weakened.'

Eventually RUPA dropped the court proceedings, although there was still disagreement over the player payments. The ARU upped its offer to $20,000 if the Wallabies reached the final and an extra $80,000 if they won. If the players didn't sign the World Cup participation agreement they would be replaced in the team. Gregan was the last to sign.

Amidst all this dissent, it was extraordinary that the Wallabies actually made the World Cup final. Their success was due to a mix of bloody-mindedness and luck plus some inspired coaching and team performances.

Before the tournament, the Wallabies had lost the Bledisloe Cup for the first time since 1997. The question was raised: How many Australian players would make the All Blacks line up? The answer: One. George Smith. How many Australian players would make a world XV? Zero. Bob Dwyer got it right more than a decade earlier when he said the best gauge of the quality of an international team was how many in the squad would make a world XV. Of the 1991 World Cup Wallabies at least six or seven Australians, headed by David Campese, would have walked into any world line-up. Ditto the 1999 World Cup team that had such class performers as John Eales, Stephen Larkham and Tim Horan. But four years on there was not a single standout player in a line-up that lacked instinct, especially in attack.

The one element that had been under-estimated was the home ground advantage. It certainly worked for the Wallabies in 2003, allowing them to cruise through the pool matches until they encountered Ireland in Melbourne. How the Wallabies won this game to finish on top of their pool remains one of the great mysteries of Australian rugby's recent decades. The Wallabies were simply the inferior side, and if a field goal attempt by Ireland's David Humphreys' in the seventy-eighth minute had been successful the Wallabies would have been heading down the difficult path of playing France in the quarter-finals rather than a weak Scotland line up.

The dirge continued the following week as the Australians scrambled to win over Scotland, prompting widespread criticism even from the losing team. Scotland believed the Wallabies had been given an unfair leg up by the New Zealand referee Steve Walsh, who had overlooked several dubious rugby league–like attacking moves that saw several decoy runners charging into the opposition defence while the pass was thrown deep behind them to a wider ball receiver. Nobody believed the Wallabies had a chance of beating the All Blacks in the semi-final.

The constant criticism got to Jones. Despite every leading rugby commentator writing for months that due to their easy draw a weak Australia was still destined to be one of the semi-finalists, Jones instead claimed: 'No one expected us to get here. We've been written off from day one in the tournament. People weren't expecting us to get through the pool of death. Well, here we are in a semi-final against New Zealand.' The pool of death? Argentina, Romania, Namibia and Ireland? Hardly!

Even though the Wallabies were rank outsiders to beat the All Blacks, too many had under-estimated New Zealand's tendency to self-destruct at the World Cup. The semi-final revolved around stage fright, despite one moment when initiative overcame stupidity.

The All Blacks' brilliant but often flaky five-eighth Carlos Spencer hated being put under pressure, and when this occurred he would sometimes throw wild passes. The Wallabies focused on targeting Spencer in defence and attack, attempting to commit as many opposing back-rowers as possible to the breakdown area. Spencer relied on his back-rowers to protect him in the defensive line, so when they weren't there he was immediately vulnerable. It wasn't surprising therefore that his opposite Larkham, a far more complete player, ran past him at least six or seven times during the game.

Spencer soon began to look rattled, prompting him to throw a wild cut-out pass near the Australian line that was intercepted by Stirling Mortlock, who ran the length of the field for one of Australia's most crucial World Cup tries. Somehow the Wallabies were through to the final, sending New Zealand into a pall of gloom out of which they've still not yet dragged themselves.

An Australia–England final provided the ideal climax to easily the best run of the six World Cups, and with it came a spectacular final week where an old-fashioned stoush between the colonial upstarts and the fading imperial power was urged on by the local media. Sydneysiders took up the Wallabies' cause, honking their car horns as they drove past England's oceanside hotel even in the middle of the night. However, the long-time warring coaches—Jones and Woodward—strangely called a truce before the final.

England did win the battle, prompting the most euphoric scenes of celebration by an England sporting team since the 1966 World Cup soccer triumph. But the fact that the Wallabies had stretched the game to extra time, until a Jonny Wilkinson field goal ended the 17-all deadlock, was a great tribute to them. They had exceeded all expectations.

The Wallabies' performance against New Zealand was easily the best from any team during the tournament. It was courageous, spectacular and heart-in-the-throat stuff. But most importantly it was free-spirited Australian rugby at its best, something that had not been seen for some years. Then they succeeded in irritating England. On about five occasions during the final England appeared to have the game won, except that each time Australia rallied and threatened. They were also helped by South African Andre Watson's dubious refereeing. England was regularly penalised because of its scrummaging dominance, but the fact was Australia couldn't hold the scrum up and got away with it.

John O'Neill was a fan again: 'The Wallabies played in the final as if they had the heart of Phar Lap. Simply magnificent.' But Eddie Jones had remained a true believer from the beginning. He also showed he was a person of substance. Instead of bragging after the defeat of the All Blacks, he instead acknowledged that the criticism of the team was justified.

This was Eddie Jones' finest moment as Australian coach. His message was be patient, but it all went downhill from there.

16

LOST HIGHWAY

There are many proud periods in the history of Australian rugby, however, 2003–08 is not one of them. It was instead a barren time of treacherous politics, slipping standards and wasted opportunities.

The signs of decay first appeared in 2004 when John O'Neill was forced to resign in an ARU coup. He was replaced by the considerably more low-key Gary Flowers. Flowers had made an extraordinary admission on his first day on the job, explaining that he hadn't been the ARU's first choice and that several other candidates had knocked back the position because the salary wasn't alluring enough. And during a period where the ARU became known as Fort Fumble, Flowers found his administrative skills constantly under question as much as the playing skills of the Wallabies.

While the Wallabies kept winning Tests in the 2004 season, their performance was erratic. Inexplicable losses would follow rousing wins. Player form fluctuated out of control. They couldn't win overseas, and their inability to succeed in South Africa turned into a major predicament. They even resorted to wearing state-of-the-art sunglasses on the long flight to Johannesburg in 2004, believing this would eliminate jet lag. The rock star look didn't work. They lost again on the veldt. The Australian scrum became a laughing stock of the world game, and then the off-field incidents began to mount up.

The first occurred on the 2004 end-of-season tour when Mat Rogers was accused of assaulting an Australian fan outside an Edinburgh nightclub. After a supposedly extensive investigation, the ARU simply slapped Rogers over the wrist and allowed him to continue playing. It didn't help itself when an official defended the ARU's stance by saying that far worse incidents had occurred on Wallabies tours. All this showed was that the ARU must have been very clever in the past in covering up incidents.

Matters worsened in 2005 when Matt Henjak became the first Wallaby sent home from a tour in thirty-nine years following a nightclub incident in Cape Town during which he threw ice in a dispute with teammate Lote Tuqiri. While Henjak left for Sydney in disgrace, Tuqiri and Wendell Sailor, who was also at the nightclub, were each fined $500 and received suspended two-match sentences for being out inappropriately late. Matt Dunning was also fined $500, a piddling figure that at the time was the maximum possible under the Wallabies' disciplinary protocol. Team management attempted to cover up this bad player behaviour until it was exposed by a South African newspaper.

In the middle of all this chaos, a Cape Town newspaper discovered a completed player questionnaire left behind in a restaurant. Despite being a bit of a joke it was highly embarrassing, revealing that the Wallabies wouldn't actually mind eating one another, but especially Dunning, if they were forced to cannibalism after a plane crash. The South Africans made the most of this and the Wallabies became the joke of the Tri Nations.

Not surprisingly, they lost several days later. The Springbok coach Jake White inflamed matters by blaming the rugby league element for the Wallabies losing their way. 'It's not a rugby union thing. We're lucky we don't have that element in South Africa. I mean, you read things about league guys, don't you? Here we have an ethos developed through the school and provincial system which is formative for guys coming into the Boks side. League is very different to union. League guys have a different make-up. Maybe that's why so many former Wallaby players have been so vocal about these incidents . . . on this tour, and saying that more players should have been sent home, because they realise it's not the way rugby union players would act.'

The *Sunday Times* described the Wallabies as 'Buttheads of the Week', breaking 'new grounds of sheer stupidity. The Wallabies take the cake and the whole friggin' bakery for their epic performance in SA the past fortnight. Gosh, where to start? Players fighting, Matt Henjak sent home, the bizarre "cannibalism" episode at a Cape Town restaurant, their snooty attitude towards the local media—take your pick. Frankly, they have been a disgrace. The Boks always did quite well with their laager mentality in recent years, but Eddie Moans and his boys have set new standards with their attitude. The Wobblies chose to switch themselves off from regular media work and the unhappy consequence was the local media gorging on snippets of their drunk-and-disorderly behaviour . . . Thankfully they're all on their way home now. Good riddance.'

Not even New Zealanders could find a nice word for the Wallabies when they flew into Auckland several weeks later. The *New Zealand Herald* ran a mock photograph of the Australians arriving showing an airport conveyer belt with a wheelchair, walking stick and first-aid kit all labelled with Australian team stickers. The chortling got louder a few days later when the Wallabies again lost to the All Blacks 34–24.

With relentless calls for senior players, including Gregan, to be dropped, Jones' position was also under serious question. He knew that he was on shaky ground, especially when the Wallabies suffered seven Test losses in a row, including during the final stages of an end-of-season tour that saw them defeated by France in Marseille and by England in London.

What Jones didn't know, however, was that several high-ranking ARU officials had been secretly receiving private information from a Wallaby team staff member. This was treacherous behaviour, but several other ARU staff members and three assistant coaches were also asked to put in writing their problems with the coach. Three senior Wallabies, the 'gang of three', had convinced the ARU that Jones had to go. Two even threatened to quit Test football if he remained in the position. A fourth high-profile player even intimated that he would switch to rugby league if Jones insisted that the Wallabies spend most of the season at their Coffs Harbour training base. This player was not alone among the squad in being 'sick and tired of being stuck in Coffs Harbour' during the long international season.

Then before the final Test of the tour against Wales in Cardiff the news broke in Australia that Jones was about to be sacked. When Jones heard the story he was taken aback, but maintained his composure: 'If that is the decision the directors are going to make well . . . I am an employee of the Australian Rugby Union, and I've got a contract in place. If they decide I'm no longer the person to coach Australia, well that's the decision they make. I've always said all along that all I do is coach the side, and if that's not good enough, well, then that's their decision. This doesn't surprise me, we've lost games.'

One day later and after another loss, Jones arrived at the media conference at Millennium Stadium agitated and restless. He showed the hallmarks of someone under siege. He knew that his dream job was at an end. And Alan Jones had also been part of the process. His constant calls on radio for the sacking of his namesake had convinced a number of ARU directors that it was time for change.

Shortly after the team returned to Australia Jones was sacked as national coach. He had made the fatal mistake of isolating himself. He was too much of a one-man band, which meant there were few allies he could call upon for help. But the turmoil within the ARU was not finished with Jones' sacking. In the background another interesting power battle was taking place. Gary Flowers was under pressure to keep his job. Having been accused of weak leadership, he used the Jones issue to his advantage by attempting to insert a wedge between the coach and the ARU powerbrokers.

Flowers, whose relationship with Jones began to unravel during the shambolic South Africa tour, observed first hand the softening of team discipline. He was also aware that Wallabies manager Phil Thomson had been placed under enormous pressure and that he had been 'unfairly forced to carry the can' over the Henjak incident. Then in Wales he and ARU president Paul McLean attended Wallaby training sessions that would not have pleased them. They would have seen several of Jones' assistants doing very little and the players pampered by personal assistants and hangers-on. It was not a healthy touring party and it was not a healthy ARU.

Around this time, the ARU initiated a major internal investigation into information being leaked to the media. Staff telephone records were checked, but the investigation only succeeded in embarrassing those who had instigated the purge by showing they were among the best media leakers of all.

•

A change in coach didn't solve all the problems either. John Connolly, who replaced Jones, should have had the job in 1996 and not 2006. In the intervening ten years the fire and brimstone in Connolly's coaching, which made him a major success with the Queensland Reds, had been doused. Although he remained an astute judge of talent and had a fine understanding of the game, his coaching methods had lost their edge. They became predictable. So much revolves around timing, and the feeling was that Connolly's time may have passed.

As expected, Connolly's two years as coach were a wild, madcap ride. He loved nothing better than rugby politics and the distractions that gossip brought. But eventually the pressure became too much.

Connolly boasted the perfect nickname—Knuckles. As his long-time friend Andrew Slack wrote in his biography of Michael Lynagh: 'If you play rugby and are known as "Knuckles" it is a fair chance you are not the type likely to shy away from confrontation. Very few Brisbane club rugby players of the 1970s and 1980s will argue that John Connolly earned this nickname without cause.' Connolly would insist that he had no recollection of how his nickname came to be, but an employment background that included stints driving semi-trailers in the Northern Territory and being a bouncer at Mt Isa, Darwin and Brisbane pubs indicated that he knew how to look after himself.

After periods with Queensland and then overseas clubs, Connolly argued that he had mellowed. Yet his mischievous side was never far from the surface. Rugby anecdotes about Knuckles abound, most of them concerning how he worked himself up before Queensland's favourite day of the year—their seasonal humiliation of New South Wales.

Connolly went a bit strange around this time. He refused to bet on Sydney horse races in the week leading up to the interstate clash and plastered the dressing room walls with anti-Queensland articles he found in the Sydney press. He was also brilliant in getting the best out of his players by reminding them that the rest of Australia saw the Reds as 'poor old struggling Queensland'. In 1997 he promised that if Queensland defeated the Waratahs he would have the Queensland Rugby Union emblem tattooed on his backside. New South Wales was thrashed in Sydney, but no one was willing to confirm whether Connolly kept his tattooist appointment.

When Connolly took over the Wallabies reins the team was surprised by the change in pace, so much so that the players wondered if the coach was completely focused on the job. After having Jones constantly in their face, a mild Connolly never took the whistle out of his pocket and never raised his voice above a whisper. During one of his first sessions he spent most of the time sitting in my car just yarning away. No other Australian coach would have dared do this. But Connolly was his own man. Instead he allowed his assistant coaches—Scott Johnson and Michael Foley—to do the bulk of the duties. He had agreed to a system, recommended by the ARU, where his role was more of an overseer rather than a real hands-on head coach.

Foley, the former Wallabies hooker, soon developed a strong rapport with the Australian forwards, and it wasn't long before the

Test scrum began to pick up its act. Johnson was more of a 'left-field' coach. The former New South Wales representative five-eighth had spent several successful years as an assistant coach to Steve Hansen at Wales, where he was tagged 'Demis Roussos' by the British media for his wild shock of long hair.

Johnson was also renowned for developing strong relationships with his players and preferred the unconventional approach to get the best out of his squad. He was especially adept in inspiring battlers. He succeeded in upsetting all of New Zealand when he said before one Wales–All Blacks Test: 'We are not calling them the All Blacks this week. They are New Zealand. New Zealand is a poxy little island in the South Pacific.' He apologised the next day, explaining: 'Poxy island in the Pacific—sorry, two poxy islands.'

Connolly may have started mildly, but he soon began his famous mind games. Wallabies prop Al Baxter was one of the first to be targeted. One morning he was told by Connolly that he would be a chance to make the Test front-row by playing for New South Wales against the New Zealand Maori in Sydney that night, but before he left Coffs Harbour for Sydney he would have to survive a marathon scrummaging session. He was also told that his flight had been moved back three hours to 4 pm. Baxter was aghast. Hours of scrummaging before a match sounded crazy. Training began mid-morning. A few scrums were set, and then nothing. Baxter had been had. He was allowed to leave for Sydney at lunchtime.

Nathan Sharpe was another to be put through the Connolly wringer. A few days before the preliminary training squad was to be announced, Connolly rang Sharpe. 'Sharpie, where have you been? I've been trying to get you for hours. You on holiday?'

The Test second-rower replied: 'What do you mean?'

'Well, what I mean is that today I have to telephone all the players who have missed out on the squad.' There was a long pause. Sharpe began to splutter before Connolly continued, 'And I wanted to tell you that you're not one of them.'

Connolly loved playing squad members off against each other. Some players relished this environment, others hated it, and it was not unusual for them to ask journalists for some background about their coach because they didn't quite know what he was on about. They were usually told that if Connolly was playing games with them to be happy; it meant they were in the inner sanctum. If they were being ignored, then they were in trouble.

During Connolly's long reign as Queensland coach his players grew used to such antics, but it took some times for the Wallabies to comprehend them. One Wallabies team official advised the players: 'Look, Knuckles is really a skinny man. His ample physique revolves around a very, very thick skin.' A Reds members of the squad explained: 'If Knuckles tells you it's raining, go outside and check.'

It was quite sunny in those early days but rain squalls soon appeared in the form of fluctuating tour results, with some good performances interspersed with less impressive moments. Connolly's plan was somewhat confusing, especially as he began to intimate privately that he was interested in playing someone else other than Gregan at halfback. It seemed he wanted the media to do the dirty work in calling for Gregan's sacking.

There were also conflicting views at the selection table. Scott Johnson, who doubled as a Test selector, was willing to try new players but was often thwarted by Connolly's conservative streak. Connolly appeared ill at ease with Johnson's extroverted behaviour. He squirmed noticeably when Johnson appeared at a press conference before a Brisbane Bledisloe Cup match dressed in army combat gear after being accused of spying at All Blacks training sessions.

Johnson was not the only extravagant off-field member of the Wallabies at that time. Eccentric kicking coach Ben Perkins was an avid punter and raconteur who was a close ally to many players. The avowed AFL follower carried a business card that said he was, among other things, a speed reading teacher, part-time palm reader and eventual TV presenter. Perkins was also renowned for his pre-match rev ups. Several players repeatedly called on him to give them a 'psyche-up' session before big games. These sessions usually involved the players sitting in a room to receive a brutal old school harangue, with the aim to improve player performance. As vicious as they were the tirades were also hilarious.

While Perkins was kept away from the general public, Johnson soon began generating attention and headlines that made Connolly even more restless. Their differences in style began to have an impact during Test matches. Johnson was eager for the Wallabies to play with width and freedom, but Connolly's fear of losing saw the Wallabies often play the most restrictive rugby imaginable.

The Connolly approach saw its low point during the 2006 Springbok international in Sydney. Not even a Wallabies victory could camouflage the fact that Connolly's team was playing uninspiring rudderless football, based on incessant kicking. It was such an appalling game cluttered with stoppages that many spectators vowed they would never attend a Test match again, especially those played at Homebush in Sydney's west.

At half-time Johnson suggested to Connolly that they change tactics from the kick-orientated games, but Connolly decided not to. Even the players appeared surprised by Connolly's approach. Gregan wrote in his biography that at half-time Connolly 'seemed happy with the way things were going, but his strategy for the second half was stunningly simple: kick it, kick it, kick it. It was a really conservative approach at a time when I thought we needed to get more aggressive, and it went against the nature of an Australian team to constantly boot the ball away. But in the middle of a long season, at half-time in our seventh Test in nine weeks, the coach seemed drained.'

Connolly also fell foul of fans before the Bledisloe Cup match in Brisbane, where he claimed the current All Black version of the haka, which had the players slitting their throats, was irresponsible and sent out the wrong message. His taunt was amplified on match day when the Wallabies brought out the tackle bags following the haka and went through a training drill for the next three minutes. Like Greg Smith and his decision to have the Wallabies turn their backs on the haka a decade earlier this was just a juvenile ploy that provoked the All Blacks, and another Bledisloe Cup match was lost.

•

Connolly did get one area right and that was to turn the Wallabies pack into a viable force. When he took over as coach the Wallabies scrum was regarded as one of the most unimpressive in the international rugby world. However, with the appointment of former Test hooker Michael Foley as forwards coach that was all about to change. Over the course of several years Foley, a close ally of Connolly's, succeeded in transforming the Australian pack from a bunch of nobodies into one of the best in the world. It was hard and exasperating work.

What Foley had working against him was that Australia was one of the few rugby countries where scrummaging was not revered. Attacking players generated the headlines. The forwards were just the unappreciated cattle. Rugby trends go in cycles and when fast, open play is in vogue Australia would run ahead of the pack. But in the more defensive cycle, when the scrum becomes paramount, Australian rugby was often shown up, especially when novices were thrown into the front-row just to make up the numbers. One of Australia's longest-serving rugby scribes, Norman Tasker, described how Reg Smith, a young second-rower, was picked as a prop in the 1971 Australia–South Africa Test in Brisbane.

'I remember getting home from training and my sister had put a note on the bathroom mirror, which said, "Congratulations, you've been picked at prop,"' Smith told Tasker. 'I shat myself. I never played there in my life, and I had to pack against the Springbok captain Hannes Marais, who was as good as they get. The Springboks were dumbfounded at the selection. They thought I was there to go the biff or that it was some sort of ruse. We trained against a school side a couple of days before the game and I found that hard enough. There were a lot of scrums early in the game, and I remember I was bent so low that "Johnno" [Peter Johnson] at hooker had to nudge the ball back with his head. They had picked me to jump in the lineout as well, but after three or four scrums I just couldn't lift my feet. I was absolutely shot.'

South Africa won 14–6.

Several decades on and with Connolly and Foley having spent a number of years coaching in scrum-obsessed European football, improvements up front began to show. Elsewhere, however, unity began to shatter, the first inkling of which came in the middle of 2007 when John O'Neill, who had been in charge of Australian soccer the previous few years, returned to the ARU after Gary Flowers' contract was terminated early.

On the day O'Neill's appointment was officially announced, Connolly was noticeably unsettled. During O'Neill's first term as ARU coach, Connolly, then Queensland coach, had clashed with him on several issues. Their relationship had apparently not improved. When asked for a comment about O'Neill's return, a stern Connolly initially refused. Eventually he was quoted as saying: 'The good thing about John is that he has always been totally supportive of the Wallabies and I look forward to working with him. Australian rugby is in better shape than some people think, and I think John will do a very good job in developing this to another level.'

The comments were made through gritted teeth.

Even though O'Neill attempted to convince Connolly that their past differences were exactly that, the head coach remained unmoved. During Flowers' reign Connolly could do virtually whatever he wanted. They had a tight relationship and looked upon each other as close allies. However, under O'Neill ARU head office demanded greater involvement in the Wallabies program. Connolly felt particularly threatened when O'Neill brought in former player Pat Howard as the new head of the ARU's high-performance unit. Connolly told O'Neill he opposed this appointment, and kept Howard at a distance from the Wallaby organisation. O'Neill also upset Connolly by taking a tough stance over player behaviour.

Connolly was old school and at times was overly relaxed about player behaviour, believing that what happens on tour should stay on tour. It took him a while to realise that times had changed, but by then irreparable damage had been done. O'Neill and Connolly clashed over whether Tuqiri should have been suspended for one or two matches for sleeping in and missing training before the Bledisloe Cup match in Auckland. Connolly pushed for a one-match ban, stressing the importance of Tuqiri playing in the game. But O'Neill was mindful that Tuqiri already had a two-match suspended sentence hanging over his head for previous misdemeanours and imposed a two-match Test ban, further alienating Connolly.

Then shortly afterwards Tuqiri was caught up in another incident, this time with Matt Dunning after an early morning drinking session at the team hotel in Brisbane when a taxi driver was allegedly assaulted. While Tuqiri and Dunning were not involved in the attack, the ARU was forced to hold an enquiry into how those involved in the altercation had been earlier with the two Wallabies in their hotel room.

Connolly maintained the pair had 'done nothing wrong', enraging ARU officials in the weeks leading up to Australia's departure for the 2007 World Cup in France. Midnight curfews were imposed on both Dunning and Tuqiri. Not surprisingly the Wallabies were anything but a united band as they prepared to leave for France. The mood was clear a few weeks earlier at the John Eales medal function when team officials bickered and, in front of astounded onlookers, had heated arguments with ARU officials. And Connolly could no longer rely on the cushy relationship he had enjoyed with the media when he was Queensland coach to avoid scrutiny.

Well before the World Cup O'Neill had made it clear that at the end of the tournament, when Connolly's contract with the ARU would end, his aim was to dramatically improve the Wallabies set-up. He had major issues with how the Wallabies had dropped their standards and wanted to take the radical step of having a New Zealander—the Canterbury Crusaders coach Robbie Deans—take over as coach the following year because 'we need to undertake major cultural change'. This wasn't O'Neill's only concern, however. The ARU's finances had also taken a dramatic hit, being described by one official as 'in a state of decay'. A blow-out in expenditure, a dramatic drop in Sydney Test attendances due to poor matches and second-rate opponents, rising costs the result of a flawed national competition, plus discrepancies involving employee contracts had the ARU looking to at least a $6 million loss in a World Cup year. The heady days of 2003 were long gone.

Matters didn't improve when the Wallabies arrived in France in preparation for the World Cup. Training sessions became like Groundhog Day. The drills were the same, routines were the same, the coaches arrived on the training paddock at the same time and in the same order every day with the assistants appearing first and then Connolly. Even player laughter seemed to be on cue.

The players seemed to compensate for this lack of spontaneity by becoming one of the more popular World Cup teams. They charmed the international media, no one more so than the Wallabies newcomer Berrick Barnes with his wit and Queensland bush honesty. This was one decision Connolly got right, even if his reasoning for including the young Queenslander was bewildering. Barnes had apparently been picked on his performance two seasons earlier. 'We don't think Barnes played particularly well this year. But we think he played well last year,' Connolly explained.

Barnes showed in the early pool matches that he possessed special qualities, combining with Giteau in mid-field and taking over some of the slack when Stephen Larkham was suddenly incapacitated with a major knee injury. He helped the Wallabies cruise through the pool series, but again they fell short with their inability to handle the big moments.

This wasn't helped when O'Neill deliberately baited England before the quarter-final in Marseille with the flippant comment that everyone hated the English. The quip soon turned into a fireball and became a nagging distraction as the Wallabies prepared for the match against their northern hemisphere foes.

Rob Andrew, England's elite rugby director who had spent some time in Australia, fuelled the situation knowing that it would motivate his England team. 'I would not have been surprised if it had come from Campo [David Campese], but coming from the chief executive of a major union was not the sort of thing you'd expect, to be perfectly honest,' Andrew said. 'I don't suppose John Connolly is all that impressed by those comments.'

He wasn't. Nor were several other team officials who thought the comments were a clear indication that the ARU and the team weren't working as one. Several leading Wallabies were also worried by O'Neill's deliberate provocation of the opposition.

Even before the quarter-final kick off England succeeded in distracting the Wallabies. At this World Cup it was normal for the two teams to slowly walk onto the field side by side behind their national flag. However, for this game England broke ranks, running and prancing onto the ground. The Wallabies were clearly bewildered as they continued their slow, deliberate march to what would inevitably be their premature World Cup death.

England completely hoodwinked Australia for the next hour and a half. They showed off the British Bulldog spirit to crush a team that resembled at best a bunch of disoriented chihuahuas. England deserved praise for its purpose and passion, but the task was made so much easier by the Wallabies being out of touch in virtually every area of the game and especially in the forward battles where their inadequacies were again brutally exposed.

With such a shaky foundation up front the Wallabies were always going to struggle, especially when England's loosehead prop Andrew Sheridan—a deserved man of the match—pounded his opponent Guy Shepherdson. And this time Jonny Wilkinson, the king of the 2003 final, couldn't be blamed for the Wallabies' downfall.

Despite some loud speeches in the dressing room at half-time the Australians remained directionless. As now-deposed captain Gregan explained in his autobiography: 'The one thing that nags at me, and it comes back to one of the major lessons I've learned during my football life, was that at the half-time break we should have been more positive and more specific about what we had to do in the next half. So often during my career, I had seen instances where focus and self-belief won the day, where players kept faith with themselves, their teammates and the quality of their preparation, and that confidence took them to victory. I felt that we could have been better at this interval in building the faith and confidence within the group.'

That the Wallabies finished just two points short was a miracle. The defeat hit them hard. Larkham, who wasn't even playing, was in tears, while the young winger Adam Ashley-Cooper was inconsolable. Connolly clambered onto the team bus and sat glumly with eyes cast down. He looked very alone.

The next morning as Marseille Harbour came to life, the Wallabies boarded the team bus to head to the airport. They were grim faced, their bodies turned away from the windows. Ignoring the laughter and jeers from the crowd on the street outside, it was then that they knew they were really going home. And way too early.

The Wallabies' demise was dreadful, but it was nothing compared to what happened to the All Blacks after they lost to France a few hours later in Cardiff. Yet again, the outright favourites had staggered on the big stage. After New Zealand departed the 2003 World Cup, Gregan had taunted his opposition halfback Byron Kelleher: 'Four more years, boys. Four more years.' And for four years the New Zealand public were reassured that the All Blacks had found their way, and had at last overcome their World Cup hoodoo. But they'd blown it again. Anton Oliver, the All Blacks hooker, summed up the feeling in the All Blacks dressing room that night in Cardiff as 'a sort of desolate decay and the smell of death'.

The All Black humiliation did take some pressure off the Wallabies for their failings, but also put the New Zealand Rugby Union into such a tail spin that it handed over their best coach to the Australians. Suddenly life was on the up for the long-suffering Wallabies.

17

FUTURE HOPE

The 2011 World Cup looms and the Australian Rugby Union knows how important it is for the Wallabies to return to glory at that event. Since 1999 their aura of invincibility has slipped dramatically.

When the Wallabies were strong in the 1990s, for a short time rugby union looked like it might threaten the other football codes in terms of popularity. It could brag about the big pay TV broadcasting contracts, the ample funds that were flowing into the Australian game and its ability to lure players from rugby league when that code's salary cap system became a burden.

But with the Wallabies no longer the dominant international force and the provincial and national bodies restricted by financial constraints, fan and commercial support dropped off at an alarming rate. These problems were compounded by a bewildering law book that had turned the referee into the most powerful man on the field. The game soon became too confusing for the supporters.

The AFL and rugby league, on the other hand, have succeeded in establishing a solid and large supporter base by doing all they can to make their codes attractive to spectators. In an age when supporters need a quick fix, these two codes have ensured their games are fast, eventful, dramatic and intoxicating. Not a second appears to be wasted.

Southern hemisphere rugby union governing bodies have attempted some law variations aimed at speeding the game up through the use of free kicks, rather than penalties, for a number of indiscretions. However, outright resistance to these changes from the northern hemisphere unions has seen the game bogged down by endless interruptions and dead spots. The inability of the code's lawmakers to make the breakdown a fair contest has turned rugby into the only ball game where it was often a disadvantage to have possession of the ball. When the pursuit of possession became secondary, the game lost its way.

The heavy weighting of the laws in favour of the defending team and a general fear of taking the ball into the tackle area has consistently led to penalties being awarded against the attacking side, and the ridiculous situation where international rugby often turned into a kick fest with each team waiting for the other to make a mistake. Initiative is not encouraged, and wide sweeping attacking backline moves are seen as too dangerous. Rugby has become a safety-first, defence-ridden game.

The ARU is well aware of the problem, and with its SANZAR partners New Zealand and South Africa used the 2010 Super 14 season to try to provide attacking teams with greater opportunity to attack by advising referees to give them more leeway at the breakdown. The ARU also understands that teams have to be made up of capable, adaptable players and clever coaches who know how to use the laws to their advantage.

Unfortunately, despite having more than one hundred professional players at its disposal, Australian rugby had been consistently incapable of fielding a Test team with any considerable depth. New Zealand and South Africa, on the other hand, have strong back-up because of dramatically less competition from the other football codes. Adding further strain to Australia's back-up pool has been the lure of lucrative contracts on offer in Japan and Europe—to the extent that by the end of 2009 around one hundred Australians were playing for overseas teams.

The drive for more Tests, more revenue and longer and more intense tournaments to lure the pay television dollar has also put enormous pressure on Australia's playing resources in recent years. The resulting spate of injuries has often seen the Wallabies field back-up players well short of international standard. The list of Wallabies who boast just one or two Test appearances before returning to obscurity is many pages long. It has also meant a lot of players know they will never be under serious pressure of losing their spot, so unlike their Tri Nations opponents they can get away with mediocre performances.

At least in the coaching ranks the ARU found someone to take the Wallabies to another level, having stolen Robbie Deans from right under the New Zealand Rugby Union's nose. The former All Blacks fullback has a spectacular coaching record, having taken the Canterbury Crusaders to the Super 12/14 titles in 2000, 2002, 2005, 2006 and 2008. He also served as assistant to All Black coach John Mitchell during the 2003 World Cup. It was not just his success at provincial level that is notable, it is the quality of play he is able to draw from teams, relying on instinct, skill, speed and marvellous interaction between the forwards and backs. Deans is also an innovative mentor, having worked closely with two of New Zealand's finest in Dan Carter and Richie McCaw, both of whom hold him in high regard.

It was an ecstatic O'Neill who, shortly after the New Zealand Rugby Union decided not to replace Graham Henry as All Blacks coach, contacted Deans to say the Wallabies position was open. For O'Neill, this was the perfect solution for the Wallabies' woes. His relationship with his New Zealand counterparts had often been fragile, especially in the lead up to the 2003 World Cup when their co-hosting agreement was disbanded because New Zealand could not guarantee clean stadiums for the tournament. When Australia cut New Zealand out of the running of that World Cup, O'Neill became public enemy number one in the Shaky Isles. While the relationship improved during O'Neill's second stint at the ARU, he still did not mind keeping the New Zealand Rugby Union on edge.

For Deans, it was a tricky situation. He is virtual New Zealand rugby royalty, with younger brother Bruce also representing the All Blacks and his great uncle, Bob Deans, being one of the country's most famous rugby figures. Robbie was well aware of the ramifications if he headed to Australia to give the enemy a helping hand, but the challenge was too irresistible. He wanted to coach at the top level, and knew that if he waited around for Henry and the NZRU the opportunity would be lost.

The complex task of coaching the Wallabies appealed to Deans. A committed athlete whose other interests included cricket and jet boating, he had long been fascinated by Australia's obsession with sport and how the country has achieved international success despite limited resources and a small population. He was also intrigued by the Australian psyche. He loved the country's willingness to be adventurous, its relaxed nature, and how it fought and partied hard. Deans knew it was time to get out of the claustrophobic atmosphere of New Zealand rugby and really chance his arm.

He also had an Australian to thank for becoming a coach. Playing for Canterbury in the mid-1980s, Deans was knocked out against Queensland following a clash with the Wallabies prop Stan Pilecki. After the game, the Queensland coach Bob Templeton went to the Canterbury dressing room to check on Deans' condition. 'He [Templeton] went out of his way to visit me, and it was an act that I never forgot,' Deans said. 'It was the first time I realised how much of an influence you can actually have on people around you. It just made a huge impression on me, and to be frank it was probably when I first started thinking about coaching.'

With this experience came a deep admiration for the Australian character. 'Their resilience is a standout. They are tough, particularly so when under the hammer. They are innovative and creative. They think their way around challenges, and are creative in finding solutions.'

The ARU originally wanted Deans for two years but he baulked at that, arguing that it would probably take that long for an outsider to get acclimatised, discover who and who not to trust and to be at ease in a new and considerably different rugby environment. He knew that several difficult years were required before his plans would start to bear fruit so wanted a four-year term, stretching to the next World Cup. The ARU understood the importance of having a solid base between World Cups, so for the first time ever it appointed an overseas coach to take charge of its national team.

When Deans arrived in May 2008 he was nervous about how Australians would react to him. Would they accept a Kiwi blow-in? His first major appearance at a luncheon in Sydney to celebrate the life and times of David Brockhoff put his concerns at bay. When Deans and his wife Penny walked into the large ballroom, more than six hundred guests stood as one and applauded the couple until they took their seats. It was an incredible, heart-warming welcome.

Deans should not have been surprised by this reaction. Australians adore winners, and for everyone in that room he was seen as the man who would at last resurrect Australian rugby. Helping his cause was that just a few years earlier another foreign coach, also appointed by O'Neill, had taken an Australian team to national glory. When the Socceroos qualified for the 2006 World Cup, Dutchman Guus Hiddink had transformed the team and convinced many Australians that we had to be as ruthless as everyone else in finding the best talent. Hiddink's trail-blazing made it so much easier for Deans.

Not that the transition was without its difficulties. In New Zealand, Deans had the advantage of an enormous playing pool. Rugby was part of the national soul and just about every Kiwi wanted to be an All Black. For a coach, that made the job so much easier. Competition was intense. Rugby was also the working man's game, and that developed a hard, gritty base.

In Australia, the private school system had produced a steady stream of Wallabies who were schooled in the elite nature of the game. But the diversity of sporting choice was starting to take its toll. Prospective rugby players were being lured away by the other codes, particularly the AFL in Sydney, which was making inroads into those schools that had been Wallaby nurseries. AFL and rugby league also dominated Australia's television screens and sporting media.

Deans also discovered that while New Zealand teams rose to a high level and stayed there, Australian teams were guilty of only performing to their potential when the pressure was applied. It was as if the only way the Wallabies would perform was when they were being criticised. As soon as they had 'stuck it up the critics' they would relax. In the Australian vernacular, they could easily be accused of being bludgers. Deans was clearly baffled by this.

Two years into his contract Deans suddenly found himself under pressure. His record was far from impressive with just fifteen wins from his first twenty-eight Tests, giving him a success rate of 53.6 per cent. This was considerably lower than his predecessors—John Connolly (sixteen wins from twenty-five Tests: 64 per cent); Eddie Jones (thirty-three wins from fifty-seven: 57.9 per cent); Rod Macqueen (thirty-four wins from forty-three: 79.1 per cent) and Greg Smith (twelve wins from nineteen: 63.2 per cent)—prompting concerns that Deans was having problems relating to a core of senior Wallabies who were clearly dubious about his 'my way or the highway' outlook.

In his first two seasons Deans introduced seventeen new players to the Test arena. Many of these were complete left-field choices, showing that he was willing to make enormous gambles. The promotion of halfback Will Genia, back-rower David Pocock and utility back James O'Connor were masterstrokes. Deans encouraged his players to show initiative and 'play what's in front of you'. He did not seem to care how young or inexperienced they were so long as they had speed, vision and talent.

The downside of this approach was that a number of established names in the team were squeezed out, and not all of them went quietly. They privately complained about Deans' communication skills and were confused about where they stood in the Wallabies hierarchy, claiming they had been fobbed off when they sought answers.

The far stricter off-field requirements also irked some players. Breath testing was introduced, as was the hard and fast rule that no strangers were allowed in the players' hotel rooms. Lote Tuqiri's contract was torn up in early 2009 after he again broke team protocols and was involved in an incident in his hotel room. His departure did not have any great effect on the team's on field performance as Tuqiri's form had been in a slump for some time. But off-field it clearly affected several of his former teammates. For legal reasons, neither the ARU nor Tuqiri would discuss what had led to his contract termination, leaving some Wallabies feeling isolated and concerned that they too could be at the centre of strict disciplinary action.

Such Wallaby off-field sagas emphasised just how dramatically the game had changed. In the amateur era being a Wallaby had many fringe benefits, including sex and drinking, which were condoned so long as match performance and the team's public reputation was not affected. 'What happens on tour stays on tour' was accepted because of the personal and professional sacrifices players made just to be available.

The professional era changed that. Touring became a more rigid, serious affair, with most players realising that if they didn't perform their spot might be taken by someone else and their hip pocket would be hurt. They soon discovered they could not drink and expect to perform or train to their full potential. This was fine in the short term, but it also lowered the players' resistance to alcohol. Many forgot, or didn't even know, how to drink sensibly.

Touring also became more tedious and schedules cluttered. The days when teams spent months discovering the heart and rhythm of a country through playing in small towns were sadly well and truly over. Instead Test players found themselves in a never-ending cycle of observing cities through a hotel window or standing at an airport carousel. If this was Monday, it must be London. If it is Tuesday, it must be Johannesburg. What were once exotic countries to players now became nothing more than destinations. And in the end all football grounds and hotel rooms looked the same.

Being a Wallaby had lost its spontaneity. Rugby was now big business, and touring became grim and hard nosed. For many players their prime motivation appeared to be to make as much money as possible in the shortest possible time before injury or poor form put them out of the team. Trouble, brewed by frustrated and often idle minds, was inevitable. It became a trial for those in charge to keep teams buoyant.

As a succession of Australian coaches including Deans discovered, with the pressure came inexplicable switches in form. In 2008 the Wallabies suffered Australia's biggest loss when the Springboks swept through them in Johannesburg to win by forty-five points. This loss occurred a week after the Durban Test where the Wallabies won on South African soil for the first time in eight years.

The madcap rollercoaster ride continued through to the 2009 end-of-season tour when Deans replaced Stirling Mortlock as captain with Rocky Elsom, and Berrick Barnes became vice-captain ahead of Matt Giteau. Mortlock was surprised to lose the captaincy, while the often-pampered Giteau was clearly miffed that a younger player had been chosen as the backs leader. The Barnes promotion did nothing to improve Deans' tenuous relationship with Giteau, the Wallabies' chief playmaker, nor did the changes end the erratic performances.

While the Wallabies picked up their act against England and Ireland, they suffered probably their most embarrassing loss since the Tonga debacle in 1973 when they went down to a lightweight Scotland at Murrayfield. Even the Scots, who witnessed Giteau miss several easy kicks at goal, were in a state of shock after winning their first Test against Australia in twenty-seven years and seventeen internationals.

The debacle at Murrayfield again showed that the Wallabies were unable to take control when pressure was applied. Players who had been given many chances to prove themselves again stumbled. They clearly failed to understand what Deans was trying to get them to do. And again, with a lack of good back-up there were no clear alternatives.

•

At least two years out from the World Cup, the Wallabies' team management knows exactly where their weak links are. There is a desperate shortage of quality second-rowers and wingers, and where they'll come from isn't exactly clear. The team also continues to be embroiled in off-field controversies with Quade Cooper and Kurtley Beale, two of Australia's most promising attacking players, facing burglary and assault charges following the end-of-season tour.

Nevertheless, Australian rugby is renowned for regenerating itself in stressful times. It has dragged itself out of the mire before and will continue to do so again. And despite all the problems the team's core philosophy has remained the same over the years. It is an outfit that thrives on laughter and genuine goodwill.

Weird situations remain part of the Australian team culture, such as Adam Ashley-Cooper's wacky initiation to Test football. In 2005 Ashley-Cooper, then a little-known ACT Brumbies utility player, was summoned to Perth at the last minute for the Springboks Test. Minutes before kick off, believing he would not be required, he headed to one of the Subiaco Oval canteens to buy a pie and a beer. At the same time Elton Flatley suddenly took ill, and Ashley-Cooper was called to the dressing room. Ashley-Cooper spent the next seventy-eight minutes on the bench before replacing Clyde Rathbone. He ran on, dropped the ball and became the eight-hundredth Wallaby—and the first to make his Test debut without a number on his back.

•

Those who will be at the heart of the 2011 World Cup squad bear many similarities to that ruddy mob who headed off to England in 1908 on the adventure of their lives to begin the Wallabies crusade. As Paddy Moran put it one hundred years earlier, today's Wallabies still have their rude virtues and glaring faults. And while their bravado and their testosterone can play havoc with their public image, just about every Wallaby is a genuinely fine character. Some adapt and blossom under the enormous public scrutiny. Others don't and sadly struggle with the mundane post-football life.

As for Moran's observation that the Wallabies were 'quick to resent anything unfair', this is still true today both on and off the field. They know their rights and will push hard for them as numerous administrators and coaches have discovered. But it is 'virility' that continues to hold the Wallabies together. Although often lampooned, it has allowed them to overcome enormous hurdles and to achieve at the highest level.

Virility is why you never, ever underestimate the Wallabies, as the 2011 World Cup could easily prove.

WALLABY TOPS

Top ten Wallabies of the past thirty years

1. John Eales
2. Mark Ella
3. David Campese
4. Tim Horan
5. Stephen Larkham
6. George Smith
7. Chris Latham
8. Nick Farr-Jones
9. Michael Lynagh
10. Toutai Kefu

Top five Wallabies coaches

1. Bob Dwyer
2. David Brockhoff

3. Alan Jones
4. Rod Macqueen
5. Des Connor

Top five Australian captains

1. Nick Farr-Jones
2. John Eales
3. Trevor Allan
4. Andrew Slack
5. John Thornett

Best fifty Wallabies of all time

1. John Eales
2. Mark Ella
3. David Campese
4. Ken Catchpole
5. Trevor Allan
6. Tim Horan
7. Stephen Larkham
8. Col Windon
9. George Smith
10. Dick Thornett
11. Mark Loane
12. Ray Price
13. Chris Latham
14. Nick Farr-Jones
15. Jon White
16. Tom Richards
17. Michael Lynagh
18. Toutai Kefu

19. Dally Messenger
20. Rob Heming
21. Cyril Towers
22. Phil Kearns
23. Phil Hawthorne
24. Matt Burke
25. Matt Giteau
26. Ewen McKenzie
27. John Thornett
28. Greg Davis
29. Des Connor
30. John Hipwell
31. Tom Lawton Senior
32. Brendan Moon
33. Willie Ofahengaue
34. Johnnie Wallace
35. George Gregan
36. Ben Tune
37. Joe Roff
38. Russell Fairfax
39. Jack Ford
40. Roger Gould
41. Paul McLean
42. Tony Shaw
43. Stirling Mortlock
44. Geoff Shaw
45. Michael O'Connor
46. Peter Johnson
47. Simon Poidevin
48. Alec Ross
49. Jason Little
50. Will Genia

Best Australian XV

Fullback
Chris Latham
Wingers
Brendan Moon
David Campese
Centres
Tim Horan
Trevor Allan (vice-captain)
Five-eighth
Mark Ella
Halfback
Ken Catchpole
Back row
Mark Loane
Col Windon
George Smith
Second row
John Eales (captain)
Dick Thornett
Front row
Ewen McKenzie
Phil Kearns
Jon White
Reserves: Peter Johnson, John Thornett, Ray Price, Tom Richards, Nick Farr-Jones, Stephen Larkham, Dally Messenger
Coach: Bob Dwyer
Selectors: Bob Dwyer, Bob Templeton, Joe French
Team manager: Joe French

BIBLIOGRAPHY

Blucher, Michael, *Perfect Union*, Macmillan, 1995

Burke, Matthew, *Matthew Burke: A Rugby Life*, Macmillan, 2005

Cameron, Don, *Rugby Triumphant*, Hodder and Stoughton, 1981

Campese, David, *On a Wing and a Prayer*, Macdonald Queen Anne Press, 1991

Dwyer, Bob, *Full Time: A Coach's Memoir*, Macmillan, 2004

Ebury, Sue, *Weary: The Life of Sir Edward Dunlop*, Penguin Books, 1994

Finnane, Steve, *The Game they Play in Heaven—Australian Rugby from the Inside*, McGraw-Hill, 1979

FitzSimons, Peter, *John Eales: The Biography*, ABC Books, 2001

——*Nick Farr-Jones: The Authorised Biography*, Random House, 1993

——*Rugby Stories*, Allen & Unwin, 1993

Gregan, George, *George Gregan Halfback Half Forward*, Pan Macmillan, 2008

Growden, Greg, *Gold, Mud and Guts: The Incredible Tom Richards, Footballer, War Hero, Olympian*, ABC Books, 2001

——*The Snowy Baker Story*, Random House, 2003

——*With the Wallabies*, ABC Books, 1995

Harris, Bret and Mark Ella, *Ella: The Definitive Biography*, Random House, 2007

Hickie, Dr Thomas V., *A Sense of Union, A History of the Sydney University Football Club*, Playright Publishing, 1998

Howell, Max, *Born to Lead: Wallaby Test Captains*, Celebrity Books, 2005

Howell, Max and Lingyu Xie, *Wallaby Greats*, Rugby Publishing Limited, 1996

Howell, Max, Lingyu Xie and Peter Horton, *Bledisloe Magic*, Rugby Publishing Limited, 1995

——*Stan the Man*, Celebrity Books, 1997

Jenkins, Peter, *The Top 100 Wallabies*, Random House, 2004

Jenkins, Peter and Matthew Alvarez, *Wallaby Gold*, Random House, 1999

Johnson, Peter, *A Rugby Memoir*, self-published, 2000

Larkham, Stephen, *Stephen Larkham's World Cup Diary*, Penguin Books, 2004

Masters, Chris, *Jonestown: The Power and the Myth of Alan Jones*, Allen & Unwin, 2006

McGregor, Malcolm, *Paul McLean*, University of Queensland Press, 1985

Meares, Peter and Maxwell Howell, *Wallaby Legends*, Lothian Books, 2005

Moran, Herbert M., *In My Fashion*, Peter Davies, 1946

——*Viewless Winds*, Peter Davies, 1939

O'Neill, John, *It's Only a Game: A Life in Sport*, Random House, 2007

Pollard, Jack, *Australian Rugby Union: The Game and the Players*, Angus & Robertson, 1984

Sayle, Jeff, Chris Handy and John Lambie, *Well I'll Be Ruggered*, Ironbark Press, 1993

Shehadie, Sir Nicholas, *A Life Worth Living*, Simon and Schuster, 2003

Slack, Andrew, *Noddy: The Authorised Biography of Michael Lynagh*, William Heinemann Australia, 1995

Zavos, Spiro, *The Gold and the Black*, Allen & Unwin, 1995

——*The Golden Wallabies*, Penguin Books, 2000

Zavos, Spiro and Gordon Bray, *Two Mighty Tribes*, Penguin Books, 2003

[illegible]
[illegible] *Moral* [illegible] [illegible]
[illegible]
[illegible] Random House, 2005
[illegible] *Colour* [illegible] 1999
Jenkins, [illegible] Random House, 2004
Jenkins, Peter [illegible] *Vatican* [illegible] 1999
[illegible] Published, 2000
[illegible] Stephen, [illegible] World [illegible] Press, [illegible] 2004
[illegible]
[illegible]
[illegible] University of Queensland Press, [illegible]
[illegible]
[illegible] Peter [illegible]
[illegible] Random House, [illegible]
[illegible] 1964
[illegible] Press, 1993
[illegible] Nicholas, [illegible] Simon and [illegible]
[illegible]
[illegible]
[illegible] 1993
[illegible]